THE BEST OF AMERICAN

BEER & FOOD

PAIRING & COOKING WITH CRAFT BEER

BY LUCY SAUNDERS

"Beer & Cheese - fermented friends."
Cheers, Lucy Saunders

brewers publications

A Division of the
Brewers Association
Boulder, Colorado

Brewers Publications
A Division of the Brewers Association
P.O. Box 1679, Boulder, CO 80306-1679
www.beertown.org

Printed in the United States of America
10 9 8 7 6 5 4 3 2 1

ISBN-13: 978-0-937381-91-5
ISBN-10: 0-937381-91-8

Library of Congress Cataloging-in-Publication Data

Saunders, Lucy.
  The Best of American beer and food : pairing & cooking with craft beer / by
Lucy Saunders.
     p. cm.
  ISBN 978-0-937381-91-5
1. Cookery (Beer) 2. Cookery, American. 3. Beer--United States. I. Title.

TX726.3.S275 2007
641.6'23--dc22

                              2007025540

Publisher: Ray Daniels
Copy Editor: Daria Labinsky
Index: Daria Labinsky
Production & Design Management: Stephanie Johnson
Cover and Interior Design: Julie Lawrason
Photography: Souders Studios, Rick Souders, www.SoudersStudios.com
Digital Retouching: Square Pixels, John Wood
Food Styling: Stephen Shern
Cover Beer Photo © Don Mason/Corbis
Illustrations © 2007 Art Parts and Unlisted Images, Inc.
Recipes pictured on cover (clockwise from top left): Porcini Pork Medallions
(pg. 139), Waterzooi (pg. 179), Flourless Chocolate Cake with Molten Ganache
(pg. 191)

Table of Contents

Acknowledgements

Thanks to the many recipe contributors, brewers, and chefs who supported this project. In alphabetical order, they are: Diane Alexander, Fal Allen, Stephen Beaumont, Angie and Larry Bell, Larry Bennett, Nathan Berg, Eddie Blyden, Jim Bradley, Fred Bueltmann, Sebbie Buhler, David Burke, Sam Calagione, Veronica Callaghan, Deb and Dan Carey, John Cochran, Mike Cooper, Will Deason, Tim Donnelly, Charles Edson, Rose Ann Finkel, Jeff Foresman, Jason Fox, Dave French, Adam Glickman, John Hall, Greg Hardesty, Greg Higgins, Ben Johnson, Andy Husbands, Jaime Jurado, Greg Koch, Marcel Lavallee, Jason Noble Lee, Shawn Malone, Vince Marsaglia, Rick Martin, Liz Melby, Jeff Mendel, Bill Metzger, Ted Miller, Brian Morin, Ian Morrison, Brett Muellenbach, Art Nermoe, Bruce Paton, Sean Paxton, Francois Pellerin, Larry Perdido, Tom Peters, John Raymond, Justin Scardina, Tim Schafer, Daphne and Richard Scholz, Bart Seaver, Orlando Segura, Adam Siegel, Tony Simmons, Chuck Skypeck, Pete Slosberg, Renata Stanko, Chris Swersey, Rob Tod, Emil Topel, Wendy and Rich Tucciarone, Kathy Tujague, and Darron Welch.

Kerri Allen, Jamaine Batson, Jay Brooks, Lew Bryson, Tom Dalldorf, Sheana Davis, Stan Hieronymus, Jim Javenkoski, Greg Kitsock, Lisa Morrison, and Sean Paxton contributed to the content and helped with interviews and source material. Thank you.

Thanks to the volunteer testers—craft-brewers, students at culinary schools such as Denver's Johnson & Wales, and members of the BeerAdvocate.com and RateBeer.com communities—recipes have been adapted for home kitchens.

Special thanks to Lee Custer, Tyler Hougaboom, Adrienne Lee, Julie McDonald, Gerri McBride, Joel and Missy McCollick, Chris Myers, Jason Paltanavich, Sean Paxton, Emily Romain, John Stueland, and Jenni and Matt Van Wyk.

My gratitude goes to the staff of Brewers Publications, especially Ray Daniels, Julie Lawrason, Stephanie Johnson, Bob Pease, and copy editor Daria Labinsky. Thanks to Souders Studios and staff for their wonderful food photography.

With love and gratitude to family and friends, especially Tom for all his patience, proofreading, taste-testing, and much more; Bill and Sally, Margery, Kris, Maia, Tony, Amy, Julia, Katerina, Brit, Annabelle, Ginna, Bob, Gretchen, Wes, Lisa, Piper, Lily, Mark, Kate, Sarah, Jeff, Ryan, Sona and Gary, Nicholas and Andrew, Roger and Gaylon, Marietta, Peter and Jack; and the Budd, Carter, Miller, Piper, Saunders, Theis, and Woodruff families.

Indulging in simple pleasures is one of the keys to happiness. Great beer, moderately enjoyed, is among the greatest of these. Well-matched food, of course, only magnifies the experience. One completes the other, and both complete your life. I expect you've had a taste of this already.

Beer and food are natural partners, as we shall soon see. The diversity of beer, which makes it suited to so many foods, can also be daunting at first. There is no single rule, no "white with fish, red with meat" crutch as there is with wine, so becoming a food and beer matchmaker requires a certain intimacy with both. It's a challenging pursuit, but the rewards are delicious, and the journey itself can be a lot of fun. Be assured that there are no wrong turns that can put you in a scary or dangerous place. Think of this book as a sort of illustrated road map, containing as it does the collective wisdom of the best and brightest of America's craft beer movement.

Foreword
By Randy Mosher

One thing I know for sure about brewers is that they like to eat. They *really* like to eat. Almost to a man (and woman), these are people who gave up perfectly good jobs in a quest to create something flavorful, bold, and soul-stirring. Craft-brewers know their beer doesn't exist in a vacuum. It's part of a new gastronomy, one that mixes fresh, flavor-packed ingredients, global culinary traditions, and lovingly made beers with a playful, unpretentious approach. When you have someone with the passion and experience of Lucy Saunders cherry-pick the best of this creativity and fine-tune the recipes, then, well, you've really got something. Try even half the dishes in here and you'll be a different, happier, person, much beloved by those who share your table.

A Little Beer and Food History

In the beginning beer was food—as the Germans say, "liquid bread." The story starts about 10,000 years ago in the part of the Middle East now called Kurdistan, with the gradual cultivation of wild cereal grasses. Those Neolithic people discovered that sprouting and drying (malting) stabilized and made barley more palatable. It's a small step from sweet soup to thick beer, and at some point it became more beverage than meal.

Culinary choices were once severely limited by available ingredients and technology. Cuisines tended to evolve slowly and in harmonious form. The beer, bread, and onions of ancient Egypt sounds like a tasty snack today, but it was substantial enough to raise the mighty pyramids up from the plains of Giza. The alewives and brewing brothers of the Dark Ages brewed beer seasoned with the same exotic spices used in the food of the day. Pork, pretzels, and *dunkel* came to reign in Bavaria. Britain's sometimes dreary foodways sparkled with such gems as stout and oysters.

In present-day Britain, changing attitudes and a willingness to incorporate bits and pieces of its once vast empire have led to a blossoming good beer and food movement, manifest by the "gastropub" movement, now in full swing. Lucy was there early on, working as a line cook at the White Horse in Parson's Green, a first-rate beer and food destination.

Across the channel in tiny Belgium, beer gastronomy blossomed into a high art. The fantastic beers, succulent dishes, and most of all a point of view that places beer absolutely central to the dining experience make Belgium the world capital of beer cuisine. Lucy took a tall drink of this knowledge when she interned some years ago at the famous In't Spinnekopke, a *cuisine de la bière* restaurant in Brussels.

Historically in America, our attitude toward food has been more about fuel that artistry. Food you eat while you drive is not cuisine. Since the mid-nineteenth century, the industrialization of food, combined with our longing to create a homogeneous culture from the great melting pot, led to a pretty low common denominator for food and drink. Writer Henry Miller once said, "You can travel fifty thousand miles in America without once tasting a piece of good bread," but that comment could have applied equally to cheese, beer, coffee, and much more.

While there's still plenty of gastroindustrial monoculture here, things are changing. America's craft beer scene is a hotbed of creativity, turning out delicious, memorable beers by the tun-load. America, according to experts such as Michael Jackson, is now the best place in the world to drink good beer. And there's more. Bread, cheese, and coffee in their artisanal forms are increasingly available, too. After more than a hundred years of the pendulum swinging the other way, people are finally giving beer and food their due. Better choices are popping up almost everywhere.

The first person I saw really taking beer and food seriously was Charles Finkel, founder of Merchant Du Vin and Pike Brewing, and a true *bon vivant* in every sense. He hosted innumerable beer and food evenings as a way to get his beers on restaurant menus and into customers' mouths. Back in the early 1990s he hosted an annual homebrew gathering, and I was lucky enough to be invited. Food was always a priority. Memories of singing scallops in *weissbier* and truffles spiked with imperial stout and rolled in powdered black malt are still sloshing around in my mind.

Michael Jackson was a voice for beer gastronomy early on, and he must have felt a bit like he was tilting at windmills, but eventually the rest of us started to get it.

As a measure of progress, consider my own Chicago Beer Society's Brewpub Shootout. First held in 1999, the event is a competitive tasting of beer and food from Chicagoland breweries and brewpubs. The first couple of years coughed up a scruffy assemblage of brats, chili, and brownies. Not bad with beer, but not exactly raising the gastronomic bar. Then, one bold brewpub showed up with a table full of fresh flowers and a hot pan to sauté duck breast right at the table. It won by a mile. After that, everybody got the picture, and since then we have feasted on treats such as bison, lobster, scallops, venison, whole hog, and Gulf shrimp in ever more sophisticated dishes and pairings. It's no wonder the event sells out in a week!

Be Bold. Be Brave.

Beer has a rightful place at the table. But all too often in the world of fine food, wine swaggers into the dining room like it owns the joint, while beer is left to skitter in the shadows from crumb to crumb. Don't let this happen. Sure, wine has had 10,000 years to market itself as the drink of royalty, but people who are willing to come to their own conclusions about what is good know that beer gives up nothing to wine. How is it that wine, the beverage that claims primacy at the table, can completely write off soup and salad courses, spicy cuisine and most vegetables, is weak-kneed in the presence of cheese, and can only feebly whisper "port" when the subject of chocolate comes up? Clearly, there are cracks in the castle walls. Time to storm the gates.

Beer *rocks* as a food companion. With its vast range of strength, color, bitterness, sweetness, and aromatic delights to work with, it is a rare food that fails to find a beery partner. Salads? How about a hoppy *pils* or a lighter India pale ale to go with those bitter greens? Spicy food? Malty lagers and crisp bitters do the trick. The unpairable asparagus? Maybe a nice *maibock*, or better, a spicy *saison*. Say cheese? We just did a tasting in Chicago with twenty-four different pairings, not a dog among them. And dessert? Well there's a whole chapter later in the book. Don't forget to wipe your drool off the pages.

Brooklyn Brewery Brewmaster Garrett Oliver's uproarious beer-wine smackdowns are an inspiration to us all. In these New York City beer vs. wine taste-offs, the beers are chosen by Oliver and the wine by an accomplished sommelier. Both are matched with a range of tricky dishes. It's almost always at least a draw, if not an outright win for the beer.

Armed with this book, you too can go forth and amaze people. There are plenty of specifics later on, but matching up beer and food is really about using common sense and paying attention. I've never met anyone who could remain unmoved by a taste of IPA with a bite of creamy blue cheese or a sip of imperial stout as a chaser to flourless chocolate cake. These are transformative experiences for people.

The good beer movement is very hands on, so get busy. You can play a part in getting people to abandon their habitual behavior and shock them—with dazzling beer and food—into thinking about eating and drinking in a whole new way. Doesn't that just sound like the most deliciously subversive kind of fun?

I hope you're hungry by now. I know I am.

The Best of American Beer & Food captures the tastes and creative energy of craft-brewers and chefs who enjoy pairing beer and food, and cooking with beer, through conversations and favorite recipes shared with you.

Why celebrate craft beer at the table? It's part of a national trend to drink better-quality beverages with meals. Handcrafted artisan ales made with ingredients such as fruits, herbs, spices, even cocoa nibs and jasmine, raise the bar for better-tasting beer.

Certainly, the rise in craft-brewing goes hand-in-hand with rising interest in many artisanal food products over the last decade. Small-batch roasted coffees, handmade ice creams, specialty cheeses, boutique

About This Book

distillations such as American rum and malt whiskey, even locally grown produce such as fresh herbs, have become almost standards for consumers.

Small businesses account for more than half of the jobs created in the Americas, and many consumers take pride in supporting local bakeries, local chefs, and increasingly, their local brewers, too. A 2006 survey by the Brewers Association showed that the average American lives within ten miles of a craft-brewery.

As Portsmouth Brewery founder Peter Egelston said, "We've seen dramatic changes in the way people relate to their food, and entire communities form around the interest in handcrafted foods and sustainable agriculture."

"There's a growing awareness of (artisan) products with integrity behind them," Egelston said, "and really a deep-seated preference on the part of many consumers for food—and beer—that's handmade and flavorful. I think mainstream brewers underestimate that preference. Craft-brewing is not just another fad."

"And chefs are hungry for information about craft beer," Egelston added. "Our Smuttynose brewer, David Yarrington, spoke to a group of student chefs who had formed a beer club, and there's a very high appreciation for the flavors and sophistication of craft beer."

When chefs present craft beer selections with as much care as they do wines, people feel more confident in trying the new styles. It's a matter of building social confidence, because there are centuries of tradition bolstering acceptance of wine and food pairings. "So many times, someone will say, 'I don't like beer,' and then when they taste something like a *maibock*, they are surprised," Egelston said.

You'll read similar stories throughout the first half of this book, which hones in on the creativity and innovation of twenty-first century American brewers. Also, you'll find profiles of key chefs who enjoy craft beer, as well as food producers and entrepreneurs who support the brewing community by region.

At no time in history have so many styles of beer been available for tasting, pairing, and enjoyment with food. With so many choices, where do you start?

1

First, relax, because craft beer is immensely versatile with food. From family favorites such as beef stroganoff or pizza, to ethnic specialties with Asian, Mexican, Latin American, and Indian spices, there's a craft beer style to match. In fact, the motto of my website, www.beercook.com, is that *beer is food*.

Because beer is food, it is capable of being enjoyed on several levels simultaneously, including the texture of carbonation, the aromatics as each tiny bubble in the crown of foam bursts, and the flavors perceived on the tongue and palate. Jim Koch of Boston Beer Company has even designed a special glass to funnel beer flavors to the drinker's palate.

Yet I always hesitate a bit when asked to pair a beer style to a foodstuff, such as chicken or fish. Is the chicken rubbed with curry powder, or braised with morel mushrooms and leeks? Is the fish grilled on cedar planks, or stewed in a creamy *waterzooi*? Preparation, seasonings, heat, and so many other factors influence possible pairings.

Most food and beverage professionals are taught about the three "C"s—*cut, complement, and contrast*— in creating any pairing. Stephen Beaumont, author and beer consultant, counsels that the hoppiness in beer parallels the acidity in wine. Randy Mosher, author and homebrewer, prefers to think in terms of resonance between two flavors that add up to a greater whole. And Garrett Oliver, author and brewmaster of Brooklyn Brewery, discusses flavor "hooks" that emerge in the sequential order of sniffing, sipping, and swallowing a taste of beer.

I think about balancing what's on the plate, the food's seasonings and preparation, factoring in the preferences of the drinker's palate and what's in the pint, especially the complexity of the beer. Yes, complexity: Some beers offer layers of flavors and nuances that defy the notion of what most people think of as "beer." The level of hoppiness, fermentation flavors, alcohol, body, and aging of the beer lead to multidimensional tastes. Some complex ales deserve the simplest of foods, but balanced in intensity, as in a bottle-conditioned barley wine that offsets a buttery aged cheddar but overwhelms a lighter Swiss cheese.

Building a bridge between key ingredients and beer characteristics is another way to enhance a pairing. Offer a nut brown ale with a roasted pork loin that has been sprinkled with toasted and chopped pecans, and the harmony will emerge almost effortlessly. Got a hoppy pale ale? Mince fresh rosemary or grated lemon zest into your dish to enhance the hops aromatics.

Tangy flavors from spontaneous fermentation are found in sour ales, such as the Flanders red style. Many brewers are rediscovering the flavors from barrel aging and blending beers, both common practices in Belgium. Brewmaster Ron Jeffries of Michigan's Jolly Pumpkin Artisan Ales adds that "wood aging is capable of imparting unrivalled complexity" and points out that unfiltered beers will change flavors with aging in the bottle.

Caramelization in cooking almost always enhances the malt flavors in a beer pairing, so think about cooking techniques to emphasize malt-dominant ales and lagers. For example, some Belgian-style ales have fruity fermentation esters of pear, so to emphasize those notes, caramelize a few diced pears in melted butter over high heat in a sauté pan, and sprinkle the warm, golden pears over a salad to bring out the sweetness in the ale.

Spicy and salty foods often taste better paired with sweeter, less hoppy ales and lagers. Thai curry is outstanding with malty bocks and amber ales. A favorite snack, popcorn dusted with salty Parmesan cheese, tastes wonderful with a mild brown ale. Yet Beaumont thinks that very hoppy India pale ales are best with chiles and spicy foods, because the hops can match the heat of the food.

Sometimes "fighting fire with fire" does work best, as in a pairing of *chiles rellenos* with Rogue's Chipotle Ale. On its own, the ale was intense, but paired with the cheese-stuffed pasilla chiles, the ale turned quenching and refreshing. The sum was greater than the two parts and immensely pleasing.

But even the best-made matches can be derailed by mood, setting, and weather. A perfectly grilled steak with shiitake mushrooms in brandy would have tasted fine with a stout. However, the temperature was above 88 °F, and the party was on the patio, and it was just too humid to drink something so roasty, so I chose an unfiltered cream ale instead.

When making a menu, it's unnecessary to have every dish prepared with beer, or pair a dish with the same beer used in cooking. "Menus can be constructed with more thought to a progression of flavor and intensity," said Tim Suprise, president of Arcadia Brewing Company of Battle Creek, Michigan. "And it doesn't have to be a huge feast—you can demonstrate the range of beer flavors with just three courses, small plates like *tapas,* or even a casual tasting."

With so many factors influencing taste, I offer "suggested pairings" in terms of beer styles, designed to fit my subjective notion of what tastes best. Choices may differ based on what's available to you, so I hope that exploration will help you find the beer affinity to fit your palate.

Please don't dismiss Pilseners as being unworthy of being served at the table with lighter or simpler fare, as many craft-brewers are restoring the brightness and luster to a style that suffered commercial debasement in the last century. A bready yet crisp Pilsener tastes outstanding with a freshly grilled burger—it's simple and very good.

That said, some of the recipes included in this book are far from simple and could only be termed ambitious. These time-consuming recipes show that craft beer can pair with complex foods just as well as with burgers, sausages, and pizza. The many chefs who shared their favorite recipes have the advantage of kitchen staff to help with prep, so when possible, I've streamlined methods to make them simpler.

Recipes are clustered in the second half of the book for ease of use, with more than eighty recipes divided into seven chapters. Special sections on beer with chocolate and specialty cheeses enhance your understanding of beer flavors and nuances. Food pairings and recipes are adapted from brewers, chefs, cheesemakers, artisan food producers, and restaurateurs, with credit for their contributions in the headnotes.

To learn more about the individual contributors and get additional recipes, interviews, and profiles, visit bestofamericanbeerandfood.com.

On behalf of the hundreds of people who have contributed to this book, I hope you will find inspiration, recipes, and yet another reason to bring North American craft beer to the table tonight.

Cheers,
Lucy Saunders

4

Even if you're a bit intimidated by cooking, there's an easy way to bring out the best flavors in American craft beer: Just add cheese to taste.

Virtually all cheeses will pair well with at least one of the more than seventy-five styles of beer, as befits the brew known as "liquid bread." "Beer has low acidity, but the bitterness from hops contrasts nicely with fatty foods such as cheese, and the carbonation refreshes the palate," says Randy Mosher, Chicago-based homebrewer, author, and beer consultant.

Craft Beer and Cheese:
A Perfect Pairing

Cheese is a fermented food that originated as a way to preserve milk. Texas cheesemaker and author Paula Lambert calls it "concentrated milk," but I would add "concentrated flavors." Depending on the milk source (cow, goat, and sheep are most common), whether pasture-grazed or grain-fed, and the cheesemaker's choices in enzymes, salt, fermentation, and aging, cheese flavors range from delicate, sweet, and creamy, to intensely meaty, piquant, and acidic.

Cheese is similar to beer in so many ways. Both are fermented and aged and can be artisanal, handcrafted, or mass-produced. The bacteria and natural molds that help develop flavor in cheese can be compared to yeasts and their esters and flavors. Just like beer, proper aging and handling can enhance or destroy flavors, depending upon temperature, exposure to light and oxidation, and packaging.

As is true of the brewing of beer, the making of cheese centuries ago was a domestic skill that became an artisan's work. Cheesemaking turned into a mass industry in the nineteenth century, and now the mass market is returning to artisan styles across North America. Jeanne Carpenter of the blog Cheese Underground estimates that in 2007, more than half of the cheeses produced in Wisconsin were artisanal or specialty styles. And according to Ricki Carroll, owner of the New England Cheesemaking Supply Company (www.cheesemaking.com) and author, "The art of cheesemaking continues to flourish in homes, though it's not as widely practiced as homebrewing."

American artisanal cheesemakers are embracing the craft-brew movement for inspiration and even a few key ingredients. At a recent conference of the American Cheese Society, a panel of craft-brewers offered advice on how to tap the market for artisanal tastes. Cheesemakers are making vibrantly flavored and aged cheeses that match the intensity of even the most extreme ales. Some cheesemakers are even adding beer to the process.

One example is the Chocolate Stout Cheddar cheese from Rogue Creamery of Central Point, Oregon, which has won numerous awards at the Fancy Food

5

Shows and American Cheese Society competitions. For the Rogue Chocolate Stout Cheddar, the curds are hand-rolled with Rogue Ales Chocolate Stout and organic chocolate syrup from Dagoba of Ashland, Oregon, both for color and to help bind together the ale-soaked curds, giving it a chocolate-veined or marbleized appearance. Jack Joyce, owner of Newport-based Rogue Ales, notes the combination of the two Rogue companies' products works so well, there's even a Soba Cheddar made with the Morimoto Soba Ale.

Cheesemaker and homebrewer Jim Wallace of Shelburne Falls, Massachusetts, teaches artisanal cheese methods at New England Cheesemaking Supply Company. He likes to use his homebrewed *Pils*, redolent of Saaz hops, for a rind wash on homemade Gruyère cheese as it ages. "It adds a lot of wonderful aromatics," Wallace said.

Rind washing is one of the easiest ways to add flavor to a cheese. A hard cheese may be bandaged in gauze strips and bathed in a rind wash such as *Brevibacterium linens*, spritzed with spirits such as brandy or apple Calvados, daubed with a double IPA, or even soaked in olive oil and herbs. Naturally, the longer the cheese ages, the more intense the flavor and aromatics from the rind wash.

Cheesemaker Willi Lehner of Bleu Mont Dairy, Blue Mounds, Wisconsin, even uses the rinds of old cheeses ground into a rind wash to add exotic flora to the mix. "I added the ground rind of an imported Swiss Gruyère to the rind wash for a new batch of cave-aged cheeses," Lehner said, and that makes the cheese aromatics more robust.

Rinds can also be flavored with rubs such as minced herbs, smoked salt, ground black pepper, grape leaves, or even ashes. One of my favorites is a

TIPS FOR A BETTER BEER- AND CHEESE-TASTING PARTY

Buy cheese the day of the tasting, or the day before, for the freshest product, says Neville McNaughton, a cheese judge and tasting consultant (www.cheezsorce.com). If the cheese is fresh or bloomy, like a Brie, store in its original packaging. Unwrap aged or hard cheeses sold in plastic wrap, as most plastic-wrapped cheeses turn moist and absorb some of the plasticky smell. Prepare any leftover cheese for storage to prevent the tendency for the cut surface to become oxidized and develop tallowy off-flavors. To store properly, wipe the cheese dry, and then wipe it with a thin layer of canola oil on the cut surface and the exterior (in this order). Cheese should be wrapped in parchment to allow it to breathe, placed in a resealable container, and stored as close to the bottom of the fridge as possible (such as the vegetable drawer).

Allow 1 to 2 ounces of cheese per person, per tasting. Use a cheese shaver or cheese wire to cut thin slivers or tiny cubes that will come to room temperature quickly. Cut just before serving, or cover with parchment or tent with plastic wrap to prevent the cheeses from drying out.

hops-crusted white cheddar, made with dried hop cones pressed into the rind of the cheese for an aromatic finish that definitely melds with the taste of an American India pale ale.

So, are these all completely original innovations? Not according to Julia Rogers, partner in the Toronto-based firm Cheese Culture. "Even the most unusual craft cheeses usually have a European counterpart that's equally obscure, but typically hundreds if not thousands of years older," she said. "For example, Back Forty's Bonnechere (made in the Lanark Highlands of Ontario) is a scorched-rind, raw sheep milk cheese that I thought was unique in the world. Nope! Maker James Keith was inspired by a rare Pyrenees example. This is not to suggest a lack of originality. Simply, cheesemaking is so ancient that if something creative can be done, it's probably already been tried before."

Yet the fastest-growing category in the American Cheese Society's annual awards competition is the "American Originals" category, according to cheese retailer Steve Ehlers of Larry's Brown Deer Market in Brown Deer, Wisconsin. "I think there's a definite analogy between craft-brewers and artisan cheese-makers, both coming out of the background of centuries of tradition and now gaining the confidence to create all these original interpretations of those old styles," he said.

But it's best to consider the analogies between craft beer and cheese through actual tasting. Sheana Davis, proprietor of Epicurean Connection, an agricultural marketing firm in Sonoma, California, consults with retailers about craft beers and pairing events. "One of my favorite events was the 'Dusty Beers and Crusty Cheese'

Allow 2 to 4 ounces of beer per person, per tasting. That's enough to sample the beer before and after tasting the cheese, and if tasting six styles of beer, stay within responsible limits for consumption. Offer sparkling and still water to cleanse the palate between tastings.

Choose accompaniments to enjoy with cheese, as a mixture of foods will make the sampling turn into a feast.
- Fresh fruits, such as berries, sliced apples, or pears
- Dried fruits, such as apricots, cherries, or raisins
- Preserves/confits/chutneys, such as rose petal jelly, mild chutney, or even grilled or pan-caramelized peaches
- Nuts, such as toasted almonds, hazelnuts, pecans, or walnuts
- Bread, such as French bread, nut bread, dark rye, seeded breads, or assorted crackers
- Cured meat, such as American country ham, prosciutto, or salami

If you're putting together a spread for a crowd, consider setting up tasting stations, clustering the beers that you think will pair well with the cheeses on small tables, with the accompaniments best suited to those styles.

tasting," Davis said. "I worked with Lagunitas Brewery to pair their aged beers with aged cheeses, and it was amazing how well the flavors worked together."

And the flavors are naturally so complementary: The toasted malt taste of beer echoes the breads that are natural partners to cheese, and the tangy flavors of fermented, rind-washed, and aged cheeses find balance with hop aromas and flavors. Whether the beer's carbonation is bold and energetic or as creamy and smooth as the cheese, it will offer a textural component to the tasting.

Davis recommends that consumers understand their comfort zones for personal tastes and start with choices in that range. "If you're a fan of lighter Pilsener lagers, then you may not want to start with the three-year-old, stinky, rind-washed cheese and instead try the mellow jack cheese that's fresher and lighter on the palate," she said. Knowing your preferences will let you choose the best beer and cheese pairings at the outset—but then be willing to expand beyond those preferences.

At the "Dusty and Crusty" tasting, Davis said, "We broke through a few boundaries just by serving aged beers with flavor nuances that were more like sherry or port or even distilled spirits." With the aged Lagunitas Brown Shugga barley wine, Davis paired the full-bodied, washed-rind, aged brick from Widmer's Cheese Cellars of Theresa, Wisconsin. "The two-year-old aged brick stood up to the barley wine, and the intensity of the flavors really surprised a lot of the tasters," Davis said.

Planning Your Tasting

When faced with a pairing, which do you taste first, the beer or the cheese? My preference is to taste the beers separately first, and assemble a few choices that I think may go well with the cheeses. After all, if you don't like the beer at the start, it may ruin the cheese pairing for you, too.

The butterfat in cheese coats the palate, so I like to start with a sniff to catch the aromatics of both the cheese and the beer. Then take a sip of the chosen beer, then taste the cheese, followed by a sip of beer. Examine how the flavors of the cheese change when tasted with the beer, and vice versa. Whatever makes the pairing hum appreciatively on your palate, "Mmmm," is what works for you.

Putting together a tasting at home is easy. Start with just three or four cheeses and brews, Davis suggested. "It's not an overwhelming number to taste, and it's important to make it accessible and affordable," she said.

That said, Davis is known within industry circles for her ability to set out an amazing spread featuring many styles of cheeses and beer, plus samples of local specialty foods. For example, she has drizzled sage honey over fresh *chèvre* and served aged cheeses with Meyer lemon and olive tapenade. At a tasting at the EcoTrust in Portland, Oregon, Davis assembled accoutrements such as dried fruits, toasted almonds, whole-grain and sourdough breads baked with seeds and nuts, fig-balsamic syrup, and even flower jams.

"I use a rose petal jelly to pair with cheeses and ales fermented with wild yeasts such as *brettanomyces* to offset the sour flavors with some floral notes," Davis said. "Accompaniments can help bring out the elements that you want to emphasize in a pairing," such as nutty flavors from a brown ale served with toasted hazelnuts on the side. Davis cautions that some cheeses are so acidic that the taste will flatten the beer—and a few accompaniments can help boost flavor on the palate.

That's a tactic used by Taste, a specialty cheese retailer in San Diego, which offers frequent beer and cheese tastings organized with Tom Nickel, proprietor of O'Briens Pub, also in San Diego. "My wife and I saw they were organizing cheese classes, and thought, 'Let's bring in some beer.'"

"When you've got more than a hundred domestic cheeses in the store, you need to think about organizing the search for the best possible pairing," said Mary Palmer, partner with her husband, George, at Taste. *Terroir*, or the taste of the region that epitomizes the flavors found in wine, seemed like a traditional starting point. "We have a lovely raw milk aged *chèvre* called Sunlight, made by the Haystack Mountain Goat Dairy of Longmont, Colorado. We experimented in pairing this cheese, which is very challenging and quite acidic, with both wine and beer. The best pairing in wine was with a very tannic red, but in terms of beer, the best was a light, straw-colored, and hoppy *Kölsch*-style ale from Ballast Point Brewing Company, called Yellowtail Ale, which surprised us all. Truly it was the lightest of the six pairings but really delicious with the toasty malt taste of the ale."

Of the classes at Taste, Tom Nickel said, "We start with about twenty-five beers and cheeses, thinking in terms of balance and milk sources, and winnow it down to six pairings. We try to set it up so that people taste the more robust cheeses toward the end." Sometimes, the base flavors offer clues as to what beer styles will work. The nutty flavors of a cave-aged Gruyère wound up tasting a bit sharp at the outset, with a creamy and mellow finish. "The Anderson Valley Brother David's Double offers dark fruit flavors and a malty finish that works really well with the Gruyère," Nickel said.

Nickel emphasizes picking beer styles with sufficient intensity to match the cheese style. Tomme Arthur, brewer of Lost Abbey beers, paired the Avant Garde French-style farmstead ale with a cumin-spiced Gouda from Winchester Farms, near Temecula, California. "It's a soft Gouda, but firm enough to slice, and absolutely redolent with cumin," Nickel said, "so it's got a lot more tang than a typical Gouda. The farmstead ale style has lots of malt character plus hops to balance the cheese."

"We've found that cheese pairs so much more easily with beer, in part because of the consistency," said Mary Palmer of Taste. "The refreshing texture of carbonation and citrus hops flavors really lend themselves well to pairings. In fact, our tastings are so popular that we turn people away from every class."

To make a tasting more educational, think about focusing on a trio of milks or a trio of cheese styles, such as a vertical tasting of cheddars aged one, two, and three years. Or you can select beers and cheeses from within a certain area to find any regional affinities.

At home, a guided tasting can cluster around a specific style of cheese—such as a vertical tasting of double-crème, ranging in age and milk source—or a particular region. It's also fun to offer more than one style of beer for each cheese, so that each taster can find a complement or a contrast.

Here are some tasting notes to get you started:

Very soft, fresh cheeses, such as mascarpone and ricotta, are more like cream than cheese, being raw, concentrated with rennet or by lactic fermentation, and so soft as to be served with a spoon. With such mild, milky flavors, the cheeses go best with softly carbonated wheat ales, Pilseners, and lightly hopped amber ales with more bready notes.

Baby Swiss is a semisoft Emmental–style cheese. It is an elegant, mild cheese with a sweet nutty finish, typically made with cow's milk. Try it with an unfiltered farmhouse ale, cask-conditioned to keep the fruity esters that bring out the nutty flavors in the cheese.

A semisoft, full-flavored, double-crème, rind-washed cheese is reminiscent of classic Camemberts, oozing with earthy, almost barnyard flavors. Try it with a *maibock*, which is strongly malty, gold-amber, and spritzy, with a mild sweetness. The finish has some buttery notes and light syrup sweetness. The peppery notes from the higher alcohol content offset the rind flora in the cheese. Try a ripe, bloomy-rind Brie with a continental Pilsener style, which is bready and toasty.

Most soft aged *chèvre* (goat's milk) or sheep's milk cheeses are very buttery, yet acidic and tangy in taste. They pair well with the spicy aromatics of a *hefeweiss* or American wheat ale. Sometimes, the astringency and saltiness of an aged *chèvre* demand higher-gravity ales, such as a strong golden ale.

A semisoft pressed cheese such as Gouda showcases the flavor of the enzymes used as well as the springy texture of the pressed and aged cheese. Some Goudas are flavored by cold-smoking or adding spices such as toasted cumin or fenugreek. Goudas are delicious with bocks and Vienna or Oktoberfest lagers, and the smoked varieties are wonderful with *dunkelweizens* and porters.

11

A peppery jalapeño jack cheese has a creamy texture with wonderful, intense chile aromas. The hot peppers dominate the flavor at first, but the finish is creamy. Try it with a black wheat ale, full of roasted malts, wheat, dark chocolate aroma, and spicy esters from yeast. The flavor is roasty, with some hops spiciness. The finish is tangy and gently carbonated, and will complement the heat of the peppers.

Asiago (aged at least six months) is an Italian-style table and grating cheese, exuding a creamy, mild palate with just a touch of piquancy and nutty finish. Pair it with a dark amber lager with medium hops aroma, for a quenching note that will stand up to it. Romano cheese also pairs well with amber lagers.

Aged cheddar made from cow's milk and natural enzymes delivers a more robust aged character in the front of the palate, with an aftertaste that is almost meaty and rich in autolyzed protein flavors. A sweet stout, with rich hops and chocolate malt flavors, will complement the full flavors of the cheddar, as could a strong dark porter. Aged cheddar from goat's milk will pair nicely with a hoppy India pale ale.

Grating cheeses such as Parmesan are very crumbly and dry in texture, with a mellow, nutty aftertaste that melds well with *doppelbocks* or *dubbel* ales.

Inoculated cheeses such as blue, Gorgonzola, and Stilton deserve very toasty ales such as stouts, imperial stouts, brown ales, and even barley wines to pair with the strong aromatics and oily buttery texture. Factor in the age of the cheeses, too. Sometimes, a young blue cheese will have such a fresh milky base that a strong Belgian-style golden ale will better counterbalance the creamy sweetness.

Use these recommendations as starting points for your own taste explorations. Columnist Steven Frank of *Mid-Atlantic Brewing News* said, "I was surprised at how challenging it is to predict matches of particular beers and cheeses without first having tasted them. I suggest purchasing some different cheeses and experimenting yourself with several of your favorite beer styles. You can make it as simple or as complex as you want. The real secret is to enjoy yourself while doing it."

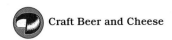

RECIPES

Farmstead Wisconsin Gruyère Fritters

Adapted from a recipe by chef Govind Armstrong of Los Angeles' Table 8 Restaurant, these fritters must be served while gooey and warm, so plan accordingly.

    2 cups canola oil
    8 ounces grated Wisconsin Gruyère
    ¼ cup all-purpose flour
    ¼ teaspoon freshly grated nutmeg
    1 teaspoon salt
    ¼ teaspoon cayenne pepper, or to taste
    2 eggs
    ⅓ cup farmstead or *saison*-style ale
    2 tablespoons minced chives
      Romaine lettuce cups

1. Pour oil in a 9-inch-deep skillet, to a depth of at least 1 inch, and place over medium-low heat. Heat oil slowly while preparing the fritter batter.
2. Place Gruyère into medium mixing bowl. Stir together flour, nutmeg, salt, and pepper in a measuring cup, and add to cheese. Toss the cheese to coat evenly with flour mixture. Whisk together the eggs, ale, and chives in a large bowl, and then pour into cheese mixture. Stir to blend.
3. When oil temperature reaches 360°F, begin adding the fritters. As you add the fritters, the temperature of the oil will drop to about 350°F, which is ideal. Don't crowd the pan, or the fritters won't cook evenly, and you'll wind up with greasy lumps of cheesy dough. A deep 9-inch skillet can hold 4 small fritters with room for a pair of tongs to turn them.
4. Use tablespoons to shape fritter dough into mounds. Fry in batches of 4 fritters. Cook until golden, then turn and fry another 30 seconds. Remove and drain on paper towels. Before adding the next batch of fritters, filter out browned bits with a mesh sieve or slotted spoon to prevent oil from turning bitter. Let oil reheat to proper temperature and then fry again.
5. When fritters are cool enough to handle but still warm, serve in Romaine lettuce cups.

Makes 12 fritters
(Recipe courtesy of Wisconsin Milk Marketing Board)
Suggested pairing: Strong golden ale or *saison*-style ale

14

Twice-Baked Lady Apples with Wisconsin Brie, Raisins, and Dates

Chef Mindy Segal of Chicago's Hot Chocolate is famed for "CheeseBeer-Chocolate," featuring an artisan beer, cheese, and chocolate dégustation every Sunday night.

    6 lady apples or small apples, about 3 inches in diameter
    1 cup apple cider
    ½ cup light brown sugar
    ½ cup golden raisins
    ¼ cup brandy
    4 ounces Wisconsin Brie cheese, diced
    1 cup chopped, pitted dates, divided
      Kosher salt and pepper

Vinaigrette
    2 shallots, minced
    ½ cup sherry vinegar
    1 teaspoon grainy mustard
    ½ cup olive oil
    3 heads Belgian endive, julienned

1. Heat oven to 350°F. Cut a small slice from top of each apple and scoop out core. Place in baking pan. Spoon cider and brown sugar over apples. Bake 45 to 55 minutes or until tender.
2. Meanwhile, soak raisins in brandy. When apples are tender, combine drained raisins, cheese, and ½ cup dates in small bowl. Fill centers of apples with cheese mixture. Sprinkle with salt and pepper. Bake 10 minutes or until cheese is melted.
3. In a small saucepan, cook remaining ½ cup dates with ½ cup water until dates are soft. In blender or food processor, combine the cooked dates, shallots, sherry vinegar, and mustard. Blend until smooth. While blender is running, slowly pour in oil. Blend until thick and smooth. Season with salt and pepper to taste.
4. Serve each apple with some of the endive. Drizzle vinaigrette over the endive.

Makes 12 servings
(Recipe courtesy of Wisconsin Milk Marketing Board)
Suggested pairing: *Maibock* **or strong golden ale**

Blue Cheese Crisps

Try making these adaptations of classic cheese straws with Maytag Blue cheese and serve with a glass of Anchor Steam.

    8 ounces crumbled blue cheese, at room temperature
    ½ cup salted butter, softened
1 ⅓ cups all-purpose flour
    3 tablespoons poppy seeds
    ¼ teaspoon cayenne

1. Place softened cheese and butter in a medium mixing bowl; beat on MEDIUM with an electric mixer until fluffy. Stir in flour, poppy seeds, and cayenne, scraping sides of bowl. Divide dough in half, and place each half on a long sheet of plastic wrap. Roll dough into logs about 8 inches long and wrap well. Chill until firm, about 3 hours.
2. Preheat oven to 350°F. Line 2 baking sheets with parchment paper. Remove dough from refrigerator and unwrap. Slice into ¼-inch-thick slices, and place on parchment paper. Bake 8 to 11 minutes, or until golden brown. Remove from oven and slide parchment paper onto countertop. Serve warm.

Makes 5 dozen crisps
Suggested pairing: California common

Q&A with Canadian beer writer Robert Hughey, consultant to Toronto's Bar Volo on pairings and tasting events

Q: What is the best way to approach a beer and cheese tasting?

A: What happens in the mouth when cheese meets beer reveals as much about the cheese as it does about the beer being tasted. Sometimes you hit a brilliant combination on the first go-round and without much effort. And sometimes it requires some educated guesses and some serious tasting to hit just the right flavor notes in the mouth. Having said that, everyone's palate is different, and it changes day to day depending on individual consumption. Fatty foods, cigarette smoking, and spicy foods deaden the palate. People have different thresholds to different tastes, from salty to buttery to bitter, which impact any recommended cheese and beer pairings. It may be perfect for me but not necessarily for everyone else at the tasting, which is fine. After all, any exercise in finding matches, perfect or otherwise, is really about finding what works for the individual.

Some of the main cheese flavor components are saltiness, nuttiness, butteriness, creaminess, etc., depending on the style of cheese.

Then I think of one or two beers that might cozy up to the cheese and accentuate certain flavors, depending on the cheese. I also check out the contrasting side of things. Then I taste the cheese again, then one of the beers, write more notes, and then have a bit of water and/or plain bread. Then on to the next one, cheese, beer, water, and so on, writing down initial and secondary responses to each, while building a profile of each beer and cheese combination. What do I like about each cheese and beer pairing? Is there an unusual flavor that maybe I hadn't expected, which would cause you to drop a given pairing? Then I rank what I have tasted, and then drop half of the beers, and then re-taste, thereby narrowing toward what should be the best match.

Q: Do you think there are specific styles of cheeses that go best with craft beer styles?

A: Craft beers by their nature offer such a variety of flavors that you instantly have a head start to finding something in a beer to pair up with a given cheese flavor.

I'd always taste the cheese first, get inside its essential flavors, and then think about the presented beer match. I usually already know or have a very good idea of the essence of many beers, either from the stated beer style and, therefore, expected flavor profiles, or from personal tasting experience. I'd also make a few tasting notes, especially of first impressions of the cheese and then when the cheese meets beer.

Q: What advice would you give to a consumer who wants to set up a beer- and cheese-tasting party at home?

A: Unless you know all of your guests are really big into hoppy brews, I'd leave the boldest India pale ale and double IPA pairings out for the first time. When it comes to a mixed group of people, the maltier beers seem to have more of what the majority would think of as a good match.

It's really quite a subjective thing when trying to find a beer to match a cheese, but with a little practice it becomes much easier. Here are a few examples to get started:

One of my favorite pairings is the Midnight Moon year-old Gouda-style goat cheese from Arcata, California, with Rose, a strong ale brewed by Hair of the Dog Brewing Company of Portland, Oregon. The cheese has a dense paste with a fragrance of nuts and sweetened condensed milk. It's a bit salty-sweet and reminiscent of *fleur de sel* caramels; the full-flavored paste has a smooth finish suggesting pecans. Rose, 9.4 percent alcohol by volume, is brewed with hibiscus flowers, beets, and pink peppercorns, which results in bright, fruity,

17

floral aromas. It is low in hops and hop bitterness with a sweetness that is present but not overbearing.

The sweetish beet flavor at the core of the Rose beer strikingly enhances the persistent caramel flavor of the Midnight Moon, while mollifying its tangy edge of saltiness.

And hoppy ales do go well with tangy, raw-milk cheeses, such as the Jensen Cheddar from Ontario, paired with Southern Tier India Pale Ale, a 7 percent abv IPA brewed by the Southern Tier Brewery of Lakewood, New York. Southern Tier IPA features very floral hops in the nose and a pronounced but balanced hop bitterness throughout.

The fruitiness and persistent hop bitterness of the Southern Tier IPA enthusiastically embrace the sharp bite of the Jensen Cheddar in a wonderful palate-tingling sensation. The result is nutty and buttery and very complementary to the cheese.

TO LEARN MORE ABOUT ARTISAN CHEESES, VISIT THE FOLLOWING WEB RESOURCES:

United States:
American Cheese Society, www.cheesesociety.org
Epicurean Connection, www.epicureanconnection.com
Wisconsin Milk Marketing Board, www.wisdairy.com

Canada:
The Ontario Cheese Society, www.ontariocheese.org
Quebec Cheeses, www.societedesfromages.com
Canada Cheeses, www.cheeseculture.ca

Blogs:
www.cheesediaries.com
www.cheeseunderground.com
www.pnwcheeseproject.com

If chocolate is your favorite flavor, you are part of a happy majority. More than half of Americans name chocolate as their favorite dessert flavor. And if you adore the taste of craft beer, there's a magical match in chocolate, whether sweet or savory.

Chocolate:
Another Fermented Favorite

Stephen Beaumont, Toronto-based author and editor of worldofbeer.com, is one of the champions of pairing "the elegant social elixir known as beer" with chocolate. The range of complementary flavors is huge: toasty, spicy, roasted, even chocolaty and bitter flavors in beer that are echoed in the chocolate. Judging from the sheer number of chocolate and craft beer tastings held at festivals, restaurants, and cafes, the desire to explore these complementary flavors is growing.

Best of all, many styles of craft beer make the flavors of chocolate expand on the palate. The combination of malt and carbonation create a textural pairing on the palate. Often, wine can't stand up to the richness and bittersweet flavors of chocolate, while craft beer extends and lifts the flavors of chocolate.

Chef Bruce Paton of the Cathedral Hill Hotel in San Francisco organizes entire feasts around the tastes of chocolate, both sweet and savory. Paton has paired barley wine, Belgian-style ales, even fruit ales with chocolate. But one of the executive chef's best recipes at a beer dinner was the Stone Smoked Porter presented with a trio of dark- , milk- , and white-chocolate flans.

At the Tria Fermentation School in Philadelphia, owner Jon Myerow and author Chris O'Brien teamed up to offer "Beer Is Divine," a tasting of "sacred" ales and chocolate.

Theobroma cacao, the botanical name for the cacao plant, translates as "food of the gods," so chocolate was the natural choice for a divine pairing with craft beer. "We served the Dogfish Head Pangaea, which has lots of ginger, with a spicy chocolate made with cinnamon and a hint of pepper," O'Brien said. "Chocolate is a transcendent food, as recognized by the Nahuatl Indians who presented it in a hot drink with ground chiles and other spices during religious ceremonies."

And chocolate offers a uniquely delicious "sensory synergy" when paired with selected styles of craft beer according to Jim Javenkoski, the Chicago-based culinary attaché of Unibroue, who holds both B.S. and Ph.D. degrees in food science. At a recent beer and chocolate tasting, a whiff of Unibroue's Trois Pistoles (a strong dark ale at 9% ABV) triggered a tingle in my forehead after eating a bit of chocolate truffle.

Javenkoski explained, "Trigeminal sensations experienced in the nose and mouth are important to our perception of flavor. Sensations include heat (from

19

spices), cooling (from menthol), pungency (from mustard or onions), astringency (from tea or wines) and carbonation (from beer). When we eat or drink something, our perception of flavor is a combination of aromas, fundamental tastes (sweet, sour, salty, bitter, and umami), and trigeminal sensations. Think of it as an equation: flavor = tastes + aromas + trigeminal sensations."

"Since beer (and refermented ales, in particular) is bubbly, it stimulates part of the trigeminal nerve and enhances our perception of flavor - of the beer and the food we consume with it," Javenkoski said. "I contend this is the primary reason why wine is a lesser 'culinary beverage' than beer, especially refermented ales. Wine offers at most two trigeminal sensations: astringency (from tannins in the grape skins) and heat (from the volatilization of alcohol on the palate). In comparison, beer offers the consumer at least three trigeminal sensations: astringency (from polyphenolic compounds in the hops), heat (from the alcohol and spices added to certain beer styles) and most importantly, carbonation (produced during fermentation and refermentation). which amplifies our perception of many flavors, thereby enhancing the eating experience.

"This effect is evident especially when pairing beers with rich foods like chocolates with a high percentage of cacao, which offer complex flavors that are more perceptible when not masked by lots of sugar or milk."

And where do those rich flavors of chocolate begin? With fermentation, of course. Chocolate and dark ales make such wonderful partners because both are fermented foods, and the flavors of dark roasted barley meld with the aromatics of roasted cocoa and the buttery notes of the finished chocolate. To discover how chocolate is made, I visited the Original Hawaiian Chocolate Factory in Kona, Hawaii, the first growers and producers of all-American chocolate.

I think of Pam and Bob Cooper as artisans of American chocolate. Their small factory is set in a grove of cocoa trees, housed in a series of sheds and a bungalow-style factory and gift shop. Peacocks strode by while Bob Cooper showed us how the pods of cocoa beans grow directly from the trunks and branches of the 10- to 12-foot trees. As they grow over five months, the pods ripen from green to yellow to maroon or cherry red. The ripe pods are then handpicked and sliced open. Inside each pod are beans covered with white mucilage that looks and tastes nothing like chocolate.

After extraction, the cocoa beans ferment in slatted wooden boxes. The beans are then spread out and slowly dried on wire racks in the bright sun for almost a month.

Once sorted and roasted, cocoa beans are put through Cooper's handmade "flinger," which removes the shells, leaving behind the pure chocolate "nibs." The nibs are ground into a viscous paste called "chocolate liquor" in a conch/refiner, retrofitted according to Cooper's own design. The conch is a large, heated, stainless-steel stockpot with a built-in paddle for slow, smooth mixing of ingredients without aeration.

At this point cocoa butter, sugar, vanilla powder, and/or milk powders are added, depending on whether dark or milk chocolate is being made. Cocoa butter is almost flavorless, but it does melt at body temperature, which gives finished chocolate the desirable "melt in your mouth" texture. After a second conching of up to twelve hours, a small amount of lecithin is added for emulsion and to prevent "blooming," or the whitish coating that appears on chocolate as it partially melts and re-crystallizes.

But the biggest flavor compatibilities stem from the chemistry of roasting. According to Javenkoski, "Kilning of barley (or wheat) to produce malt for dark ales, and fermenting cacao nibs to produce cocoa, produce color and flavor compounds that are similar. When those compounds are presented to our senses in the form of beer and chocolate, our brain integrates the sensations, determines that they are similar and therefore pleasantly complementary." So that's what caused all those "ooohhs" and "aaahs" as Javenkoski poured samples of Unibroue's refermented ales to accompany bittersweet ganache. The creamy carbonation lifts the chocolate flavor, and the peppery notes of alcohol add to the complexity.

Unibroue has partnered with Vosges, Scharffen Berger, Chocolate Pleasures, and other companies at special events. But on the other side of Canada, Spinnakers Brewpub of Victoria, British Columbia, produces its own chocolate pairings in-house, as a flight on the pairings menu, available year 'round.

Pastry Chef Crystal Duck said that Spinnakers began the pairings after noticing that drinkers were purchasing chocolates from the pub store and taking the sweets upstairs to the bar. "Now, when the brewer makes a new style, he brings me samples," she said. "We'll taste the beer together and pick out the complementary flavors. For example, with the Scottish Ale, we served a whiskey-spiked chocolate sprinkled with chopped butter toffee, to bring out the caramel sweetness of ale."

As varietal chocolates become more widely available, subtle fruit flavors such as black currant, pineapple, banana, and passionfruit may be tasted. Dried and puréed fruits often appear in chocolate desserts as well. As a result, a malty-fruity combination in beer often pairs well with chocolate—even ales such as *hefeweiss*, with its spicy notes of nutmeg and fruity fermentation esters of banana.

Duck's creativity in picking out flavors extends to white chocolate, which is pure cocoa butter sweetened and flavored with vanilla. Spinnakers' Hefeweizen ale has fruity flavors accentuated when tasting with a confection of white chocolate with fresh basil and lemon. Even an India pale ale can pair wonderfully with a ganache of creamy white chocolate, wasabi, and ginger. "I chose something sweet with a bit of spice to complement the naturally spicy hops notes of the IPA," Duck said.

21

Beer and brewing ingredients such as barley malt can flavor recipes prepared with chocolate, too. "With our Titanic Stout we pair a chocolate truffle sprinkled with finely ground chocolate malt barley that we use to make the beer," Duck added.

Stout and chocolate make a terrific base for cake, brownies, mousse, and even ice cream. When I bake with chocolate, I always try to add beer to the batter. Hundreds of bakers have tried the addition of stout to chocolate bundt cake mix, always raving about the moist and tender texture that results from substituting stout for water.

And in the realm of frozen delights, Gramercy Tavern's pastry chef, Michelle Antonishek, has prepared a special stout ice cream with the Black Chocolate Stout from Brooklyn Brewery. Ice creams made with chocolate and stout, porter, or even dark lagers such as Shiner Bock can be found at pubs and restaurants at beer dinners and events.

But it is a bit trickier to make confections and candies with beer. That's because the acidity of beer's hops and sheer volume of water both change the texture of chocolate ganache (most chocolate candies are filled with creamy centers called ganache). Pastry chefs always keep water away from melted chocolate, because even a drop of water will make the liquid turn grainy and "seize up" into a stiff and unappealing mass.

So, how can you add the taste of beer to a chocolate confection? New York City Pastry Chef Eric Girerd is an accomplished chocolatier; whose love of making unusual chocolates borders on wizardry. His line, which sells for close to fifty dollars per pound, consists of ganache centers flavored with spices, herbs, tisanes, and even wasabi. At the request of Daphne and Richard Scholz of BierKraft in Brooklyn, New York, Girerd developed a line of beautiful chocolates, sold exclusively at BierKraft and flavored with brews such as Abita Brewing's TurboDog and Purple Haze.

"I taste the beers and try to find one where the acidity is balanced, so that it will not overpower the taste of the chocolate," Girerd said. Then he blends the beer with melted butter and warmed heavy cream to make an emulsion, and uses that emulsion to flavor the ganache. "The high butterfat makes it possible to add the beer-buttercream without making the chocolate seize," he said. Once blended, the ganache is chilled for several days to ripen and grow firm. The refrigerated air slowly removes excess moisture from the ganache, which makes a perfectly smooth filling for confections.

Girerd is working to make his own proprietary blend of chocolate beans to use in making fine bittersweet chocolate. "It is so difficult to find wonderful tasting, pure chocolate," he lamented. "Just a few very large companies dominate the world market for chocolate, so it is harder and harder for the small artisanal chocolatier." (Such a lament should sound awfully familiar to craftbrewers. ...)

Another fabulous flavor match is made with macadamia nuts and strong dark ale. In Portland, Maine, Bibo's Madd Apple Café serves a rich Chocolate Macadamia Stout Paté that the chefs call "Fudge with an Attitude." It's a mind-bending blend of ground macadamia nuts with a stout-infused ganache, served in small scoops atop a swirl of puréed raspberry and mango.

Nor is the combination of craft beer and chocolate limited to sweets. Savory blends of chocolate and spice work well with beer in sauces such as Mexican mole. Try ales such Rogue's Chipotle Ale or Furthermore's Knot Stock Ale, made with black peppercorns, to add both beer flavor and heat.

"There are several variations on moles that work well for savory pairings with beer, such as a cocoa and spice-rubbed roasted pork loin with a cinnamon chocolate mole," said John Raymond, executive chef of Roots Restaurant in Milwaukee. Raymond uses whole cinnamon sticks to prepare the sauce, simmered in stock with chiles and other spices. "With lengthy simmering, the cinnamon bark will become tender, and when ground into the sauce adds both flavor and texture," he said. With this pork dish, Raymond would serve a strong amber ale, not too dark, "because the taste of the cocoa provides plenty of roasted flavors, and I'd want the peppery alcohol flavor to match the chiles."

So, go ahead and explore the dark side of good taste through chocolate and beer pairings. Here are several recipes that feature the food of the gods, chocolate, in its many guises.

Beercook Barley Wine Bonbons

Ganache
    1 can (14 ounces) condensed milk
    ⅔ cup barley wine, at room temperature
    12 ounces bittersweet chocolate, very finely chopped, divided
    4 tablespoons unsalted butter

Covering
    Melted white couverture or dark chocolate couverture* (about 1 pound)
    Chopped macadamia nuts (or other nuts)
    Ground dried coconut
    Powdered cocoa
        (Scharffen Berger is the darkest cocoa powder I've found)

1. Mix condensed milk and barley wine. You should have 2 cups of liquid. Pour into a heavy saucepan and heat just to a simmer. Chop 8 ounces chocolate very fine and place in a heavy, nonreactive bowl. Set aside remaining 4 ounces chopped chocolate for later use. When the barley wine mixture just bubbles and is hot, pour steaming blend into the 8 ounces chopped chocolate and stir slowly with a spatula, until the chocolate melts. Set aside.

2. Melt unsalted butter in the same saucepan, and when it is almost bubbling, remove from heat and stir in the remaining 4 ounces of chopped chocolate. Stir until chocolate melts and then slowly stir the melted butter mixture into the barley wine base. Stir slowly, so air pockets and bubbles do not form. When smooth and glossy, pour the ganache into a 9-by-9-by-2-inch glass pan, and let cool. When cooled, cover and chill 1 to 2 days.

3. Form centers by cutting ganache into squares, and place on parchment-lined pan. To make bonbons, choose an assortment of coverings. Roll or dip each piece of ganache in the desired covering, and place on a parchment-lined baking sheet. Chill uncovered for 6 hours, then pack into candy cups and place in a sealed container. Keeps refrigerated for up to 3 weeks.

Makes about 3 dozen bonbons
Suggested pairing: Coffee stout

* Couverture chocolate is chocolate mixed with extra cocoa butter to melt evenly, used to coat candy centers. You may find it in a baker's supply store or online at www.KingArthurFlour.com.

Barley Wine Banana Split

½ cup barley wine
¼ cup dark brown sugar
1 cup chopped almonds
3 tablespoons butter
4 small ripe bananas
  Assorted ice creams
  Chocolate sauce, or melted ganache (see recipe above)

1. Place barley wine, brown sugar, almonds, and butter in a small saucepan over low heat. Simmer until sugar melts, stirring well. Remove from heat. Peel and slice bananas and place in serving dishes. Divide warm barley wine mixture evenly over bananas. Top the bananas with scoops of your favorite ice cream, and chocolate sauce or the melted barley wine ganache. Serve immediately.

Makes 4 servings
Suggested pairing: Barley wine or strong golden ale

Chocolate Stout Sorbet

¾ cup unsweetened cocoa powder
¼ cup powdered sugar
2 cups water

  1 cup granulated sugar
10 ounces chopped bittersweet chocolate
  8 ounces stout, at room temperature
 ½ teaspoon vanilla extract

1. Sift cocoa powder with powdered sugar into a medium bowl, and set aside. In a 2-quart saucepan, whisk together water and granulated sugar, and bring to a boil over high heat, whisking often. When simmering, add cocoa powder mixture by the tablespoon, whisking after each addition. Reduce heat to low, and simmer uncovered for 25 minutes, until thick and syrupy, whisking occasionally. Remove from heat and let cool for 5 minutes.
2. Slowly add chopped chocolate to hot syrup in the saucepan, whisking after each addition. Stir with a spatula, scraping the sides of the saucepan, until mixture is smooth. Strain through a fine mesh sieve into a medium bowl, and cool to lukewarm. Whisk in the lukewarm stout and vanilla extract. Cover bowl and chill for at least 3 hours. Freeze the sorbet in an ice cream maker according to manufacturer's directions.

Makes 4 servings
Suggested pairing: Cherry ale or vanilla porter

Dark Lager Mole

You can use a traditional Mexican dark lager such as Negro Modelo, or swap a peppery craft beer such as Rogue's Chipotle Ale or Furthermore Brewing Company's Knot Stock Ale to make this sauce. Pepitas, dried pumpkin seeds without salt, are sold in the bulk foods sections of most natural food stores or by mail order. Toast the tortillas in a toaster oven or 300°F oven while preparing the chiles.

  6 dried Anaheim chiles
  6 dried mulato chiles
  3 cups hot chicken stock
  4 chiles en adobo, with 2 tablespoons sauce
 ¼ cup sesame seeds
 ¾ cup pepitas (dried unsalted pumpkin seeds)
  1 tablespoon red pepper flakes
  1 tablespoon freshly ground black pepper
  1 teaspoon cumin seed
  1 teaspoon coriander seed
  2 cinnamon sticks, crushed
  2 tablespoons canola oil
  1 cup chopped yellow onion

1 cup peeled and chopped tomatillos (or substitute chopped tomatoes)
    3 tablespoons minced garlic
    1 tablespoon dried Mexican oregano
    3 small corn tortillas, toasted until brown
    6 ounces chopped Mexican chocolate (Ibarra brand is widely available)
    8 ounces dark lager or pepper ale, decanted and whisked to remove
        carbonation
        Salt
    1 wedge fresh lime
4 to 5 cups shredded cooked chicken or pulled pork
8 to 10 fresh corn tortillas

1. Place dried chiles in a large iron skillet or heavy frying pan over medium heat and toast lightly, about 1 minute. Bring chicken stock to a simmer in large saucepan over medium heat. When chiles are toasted, scrape into the hot stock and set skillet aside. Simmer chiles over low heat until tender. Add chiles en adobo with 2 tablespoons adobo sauce and remove from heat. Let cool to lukewarm.

2. In the reserved skillet, place sesame seeds, pepitas, red pepper flakes, black pepper, cumin, coriander, and cinnamon, and toast over medium heat until sesame seeds turn golden. Add 1 cup chile-chicken broth and simmer until cinnamon sticks are tender. Place lukewarm chiles, 1 cup adobo-broth cooking liquid, and toasted spice-seed mixture in a blender. Reserve remaining adobo-broth mixture. Cover blender and pulse on HIGH until chiles, cinnamon, and seeds are ground to a paste. Reserve mixture in blender.

3. Place canola oil in the large skillet used to toast the spices over medium-high heat. Add onion, tomatillos or tomatoes, and garlic, and sauté 5 minutes, stirring often. When onions are soft, add oregano. While onions cook, crush the toasted tortillas to make crumbs. Stir the crumbs and chopped chocolate into the onion mixture. Cook until chocolate melts. Scrape the onion-tortilla mixture into the blender and reserve skillet.

4. Add the flat dark lager or pepper ale to the blender, with $1/3$ cup adobo-broth mixture. Cover, and hold blender lid in place with a towel. Pulse on HIGH until mixture is pasty and smooth. Add more broth as needed to reach desired consistency. Return sauce to skillet, and heat. Add salt and juice from lime wedge. Stir well and heat. Add 4 cups shredded cooked chicken or pulled pork, and serve with fresh corn tortillas.

Makes 4 ¹/₂ cups sauce
Suggested pairing: Mexican dark lager or bock

Across the Northeast, from Northern Virginia to Canada, you may find hearty food and beer that dates back centuries ... and traditional recipes that reverberate still today.

At Fourquet Fourchette of Chambly, Québec, you may order a pot pie of braised caribou or *Amerindienne* deer sausage studded with dried wild blueberries and a strong Unibroue ale, to fit the historic-themed menu devised by Chef François Pellerin to highlight *bières et cuisine de la Neuve France.*

At Gadsby's Tavern in Alexandria, Virginia—a favorite watering hole of George Washington, lovingly preserved—you can still order eighteenth-century fare like cider-braised duckling or venison pie and wash it down with a Samuel Adams Boston Lager (named after a Revolutionary War-era maltster and rabble-rouser).

The Atlantic:
History by the Pint and Plate

The City Tavern in Philadelphia, a 1976 re-creation of an Eighteenth-century public house, features three colonial-style beers brewed by nearby Yards Brewing Company: George Washington Tavern Porter (made with molasses), Thomas Jefferson Tavern Ale (brewed with honey), and Poor Richard's Tavern Spruce.

The craft beer revolution didn't hit the East Coast with full force until the 1990s, but beer cuisine has blossomed since then. One of the epicenters of American beer culture is the Brickskeller in Washington, D.C. The comfortable subterranean bar, which opened on October 7, 1957, (three days after the Soviets launched Sputnik), offers more than a thousand beers (mostly bottled), earning it a mention in the *Guinness Book of World Records.*

In 2003 owners Dave and Diane Alexander opened a second restaurant, RFD Washington, "to do what the Brickskeller didn't do ... draft beer and *cuisine á la bière,*" Dave Alexander said. RFD stands for "regional food and drink," and its motto is "from brewer's vat to chef's pan." One of the mainstays is a recipe that Dave credits to his wife, Diane, a graduate of the Culinary Institute of America: Chicken with Artichokes and Mushrooms stewed in Anchor Steam. "When figs are in season, dice them up and add to the sauce; it's just fantastic," he said.

RFD offers beer-accented dessert fare, including ice cream sodas made with fruit beers. Dave Alexander has also experimented with chocolate beer floats. He has found that the roasty flavors of American dry stouts like Rogue Shakespeare Stout and Stoudt's Fat Dog Stout work fine when incorporated into homemade ice cream, but if you're pouring the beer over ice cream, you need a sweeter stout.

Dave Alexander is a leader in the cause of beer education. He assists the National Geographic Society in staging an annual beer seminar and hosts numerous Smithsonian Institution events, ranging from a Philosophy on Tap mini-course to a lecture on monastic brewing by British beer author Roger

27

Protz. The Brickskeller has also been holding its own series of beer tastings and dinners since 1985.

Jim Koch, president of the Boston Beer Company, recalled, "When we held our first beer dinner in 1986, someone mocked it in the media, as if beer had undue aspirations to be served at a fine dining event. But now virtually everyone can appreciate the strengths of craft beer because of the enormous variety of flavors, tastes, and styles."

"Though we've been doing this for twenty-three years now, we don't want to keep offering the same recipes and recommendations," Koch said. "The most interesting chefs now tend to draw on inspiration from tropical cuisines (that) are spicier, bigger, heartier, and expansive. Even pasta can be given a topping of Thai mussels instead of a traditional Bolognese and will go well with our lager."

"The new generation of chefs have grown up with craft beer," Koch said, "so they understand the flavors and appreciate the complexity, because when they were emerging as chefs, the craft beer movement was beginning. Craft-brewing represents one of the culinary discoveries of their era, and there's a much greater level of sophistication."

Other early adopters of the educational beer tasting are the Culinary Institute of America's American Bounty Restaurant and St. Andrews Café, in Hyde Park, New York, offering beer dinners for student chefs and the public since the mid-1990s.

"Beer has always been a complement to food, but with the rise in smaller producers comes more experimentation and focus on variety in style, age, process, and ingredients," said American Bounty Chef Anita Olivarez Eisenhauer. "Just as with wine, flavor, body, temperature, type, and environment all stamp their signature. The subjective experience in all dining is the most memorable, and that's why cooking, winemaking, and brewing are all arts."

Eisenhauer approaches pairings as endless possibilities. "Because of the fermentation and 'fizz,' one could easily see why spicy and strongly flavored foods may be perfect," she said. "There are smoky, fruity, and very malty beers, and with such a large variety, the choices are wide." At a beer dinner with Ommegang Brewery of Cooperstown, New York, she paired the Hennepin farmhouse ale with grilled shrimp basted with savory anchovy butter and roasted cauliflower. Dessert was tender tempura-battered apple slices with dipping sauces paired with Ommegang's Three Philosophers for contrast.

At another event, Eisenhauer paired the Southampton Saison from Southampton Publick House, Southampton, New York, with braised monkfish—a traditional Belgian dish given an American twist with peppery chipotle chile butter and glazed almonds, atop wilted spinach with smoked onion-apple cider vinaigrette.

At the Brewer's Art, a Belgian-style brewpub in Baltimore, owner Volker Stewart features beer cuisine from haute entrées to *frites*. Stewart tries to have his seasonal beers match his seasonal menus. In warm weather, he recommends the smoked trout salad paired with his Saison de Mysteres, flavored with lemon balm and heather. For heartier winter fare, Stewart serves a pork tenderloin brined in his Resurrection Ale (an abbey-style brown). Soaking the pork in a mixture of beer, salt, and spices "makes for a very tender piece of meat," Stewart said.

The Belgian influence is also felt at Monk's Cafe in Philadelphia, where you can order *pommes frites* with a bourbon mayonnaise dip, as well as mussels prepared eight different ways. The fries are cut from locally grown Bintje potatoes, a flavorful yellow potato that's less mealy and holds up to frying. That fits into the philosophy of Chef Adam Glickman, who said that almost 80 percent of the food they buy is from local farmers.

"Almost every item on the menu is made with beer," added co-owner Tom Peters. As an example, he cited the pan-seared pheasant roasted with Dogfish Head Craft Brewery's Raison d'Etre, an ale brewed with raisins and dark Belgian candi sugar. "I like hoppier beers for pairing with spiced foods; darker, richer, sweeter beers go well with meats," Peters said.

Monk's holds monthly beer dinners, some quite unique, such as a 2001 all-*lambic* dinner thrown in Michael Jackson's honor. "We work backwards, start with the beers, and then decide on the food," Peters said. "Pairings are more natural that way." He believes that Glickman's best meal ever was a January 2007 feast showcasing the beers of the Russian River Brewing Company in Santa Rosa, California. Every course was accompanied by grilled fruit, from spicy Thai shrimp and grilled watermelon paired with Russian River Temptation, to a pork tenderloin sandwich with grilled pineapple served alongside the immensely hoppy Russian River Blind Pig.

"As you cook with beer, sample it regularly," Peters advised. "It makes you more relaxed and lets the imagination open up."

Cities such as New York, Philadelphia, and Baltimore were the first ports of call for millions of immigrants, who have had a tremendous influence on the area's cuisine and brewing. In 1683, Franz Pastorius founded Germantown, Pennsylvania, the first permanent German settlement in the New World. A descendent of Franz, Tom Pastorius, now runs the Penn Brewery in Pittsburgh. There, a bilingual menu offers *bierkäse* (sharp cheddar and cream cheeses flavored with Penn Pilsner), *sauerbraten*, and *wienerschnitzel*, among more standard American dishes.

While it has long since expanded its original German beer lineup to include Belgian and English styles, Stoudt's Brewing Company in Adamstown, Pennsylvania. still features a "Best of the Wursts" buffet at its tri-annual Great Eastern Invitational Microbrewery Festival. Carol Stoudt oversees the brewery, and husband Ed operates a bakery called Eddie's Breads, incorporating beer into several of his recipes (the multigrain bread contains Scarlet Lady Ale, an extra-special bitter, while the Harvest Dark is made with Fat Dog Stout).

The hoagie, the unofficial state sandwich of Pennsylvania, is said to derive its name from Hog Island in the Delaware River, where Italian workers munched on elongated sandwiches filled with antipasto. You can enjoy a craft beer and a hoagie, as well as more exotic fare ranging from Mexican to Indian to Laotian, at the Philadelphia area's many BYOs. BYO means "bring your own." These restaurants have either elected not to apply for a liquor license or are in dry townships where liquor sales aren't allowed, so they let their customers bring in their own alcoholic beverages. George Hummel, who runs the home-brew supply shop Home Sweet Homebrew with his wife, Nancy, notes that the area's amateur brewers like to meet at BYOs to try their homebrew against various cuisines.

In 1905 an Italian immigrant named Gennaro Lombardi opened the country's first pizzeria in New York City. It wasn't until the mid-twentieth century that pizzas became popular frozen foodstuffs. Today, the trend is away from pre-fab pizza and toward fresh, hearth-baked breads with imaginative toppings.

American Flatbread has three locations in the state of Vermont, but only the Burlington branch brews its own beer. Brewer Paul Sayler worked at the bakery in Wakefield (American Flatbread's original location) and became thoroughly acquainted with the food—fresh pizza made in wood-fired clay ovens—before installing a brewhouse in 2005. In addition to his half-dozen house beers, the pizzeria carries a selection of more than sixty draft and bottled brands.

"It gets harvested and we put it right on the flatbread," said Matt Wilson, who helps in both the kitchen and brewery. "We support local farmers as much as possible. Our salad contains local greens and carrots, and local raspberries go into the vinaigrette. We use all local mozzarella cheese." Many of the ingredients, such as the vegetables used in the sauce, are organic as well. "Our maple-fennel sausage pizza is awesome," Wilson said, especially alongside the house-brewed Villiers ESB.

In Washington, D.C.'s upscale Georgetown neighborhood, Pizza Paradiso offers seventeen draft selections and more than eighty bottled beers. Its gourmet pizzas range from the basic (tomato and mozzarella) to exotic toppings like capers, mussels, eggplant, and *bottarga* (cured fish roe). "Pizza and beer go together in general," said Chef Ruth Gresser. "They're very similar—you need grain and yeast to make the dough."

Pizza Paradiso holds beer dinners once a month. These events are intimate affairs, limited to thirty-five guests and taking place in a cozy downstairs bar called Birreria Paradiso. Gresser and manager Greg Jasgur describe them as "very communal, with a lot of interaction between customers."

Beer puts people at ease in a way that wine can't, they believe. "I don't think it's true, but with wine, there is an idea that you have to know something about wine in order to appreciate it," Gresser said. Added Jasgur, "With wine sellers, I'm always a little intimidated I'm going to say something wrong."

Gresser isn't afraid to go against the common wisdom when devising pairings. "Imperial stout with a salad is something that intuitively doesn't seem to make sense," she said. "But we have a balsamic dressing with a very strong vinegar component. Maybe they would go together well."

It took a while to get the formula right for the beer dinners, she said. "The first one we did, we offered fifteen beers and four courses to fifty people. It was just too overwhelming for some people, and hard to service. Just think of the logistics of washing seven hundred and fifty glasses!"

The Spanish custom of *tapas*—an assortment of hot and cold appetizers served as small tastes in place of a single entrée—is currently in vogue in American restaurants. Rustico in Alexandria, Virginia, a neighborhood bar and lounge with a beer list of about two hundred and fifty (the second-biggest selection in the Washington, D.C. area, after the Brickskeller), is the latest to offer small plates.

Rustico's "Mosaics" menu features tasting portions of delicacies paired alongside six-ounce pours of appropriate beers. Three of these dishes equals one light meal. Customers can mix and match from several categories, enjoying, for instance, grilled North Atlantic yellowfin tuna with Brooklyn Lager; a beef shank pot pie with a Stone Smoked Porter; and a soup of Grafton cheddar paired with Wolaver's Brown Ale.

Executive Chef Frank Morales has a boundless enthusiasm for beer cuisine. "I'm a Connecticut Yankee discovering foods of the region and taking indigenous ingredients like country ham to pair with beer," he said. It's a way to build off the fundamentals, he explained. "Sausage plates are the traditional beer pairing in Northern Europe, so we offer traditional country ham, which is the closest thing we Americans have to prosciutto."

Rustico has two hundred and eighty beers by the bottle and thirty on tap, "so I just keep tasting," Morales said. "And I'm getting cherry notes, caramel notes, big hops nose, unfiltered fermentation flavors, so I make decisions about when to go with the flavors or offer a contrast. There are so many more things I can do with beer than I can with wine, I feel that we haven't even skimmed the surface of cooking and craft beer."

What does the future hold for beer cuisine in the Northeast? Many breweries in this region are imitating their West Coast counterparts and brewing very hoppy India pale ales and double IPAs. Cooking with these beers can be a challenge. In reducing them, you risk concentrating the bitterness to the point where it becomes abrasive. "You'd have to shave your tongue after you eat!" joked Tom Peters of Monk's Cafe.

John McDevitt, owner/chef of High Street Grill in Mount Holly, New Jersey, recommends adding honey or brown sugar or fruit to soften the bitterness from

31

hoppy brews added to a recipe. Ron Walker, chef at the Blue Mermaid Island Grill in Portsmouth, New Hampshire, added, "A good hoppy beer is excellent with a jerk marinade or anything spicy. And being a Caribbean restaurant, we're all about the heat!"

Brooklyn Brewery Brewmaster Garrett Oliver thinks that super-hoppy beers might find their place alongside very spicy Asian cuisines, such as Thai curries. "What else would you drink with these foods?" he said. "Sweet tea, maybe. But they're too fierce for most beers and wines."

Brewers are beginning to think about the culinary possibilities of their beers as early as the formulation stage. Sam Calagione, president of Dogfish Head Craft Brewery in Milton, Delaware, has designed brews to be ideal partners for foods. "We brewed our Raison D'Etre to pair perfectly with grilled steak, and our World Wide Stout (the world's strongest dark beer at 18 percent alcohol by volume) has all the depth, complexity, and age-ability of a fine port and is designed to be the perfect partner for chocolate desserts," Calagione said.

Garrett Oliver echoed Calagione's thoughts. "When we were formulating our Smoked Weissbier, one of the first things that entered our minds was how well this would go with braised pork belly," he said.

Rob Tod, president of Allagash Brewing Company in Portland, Maine, urges brewers not to jump to premature conclusions. "When we formulate a beer, we have a good idea of what we want the outcome to be, but there's always an element of surprise ... flavors you haven't anticipated," he said. "You need to drink the final result. That's when ideas come to mind."

Tod—who specializes in Belgian styles and has experimented with wild fermentations and wood-aged beers—actively promotes beer cuisine. He hosts about twenty beer dinners a year, from Maine to California, and posts suggested food pairings on the Allagash website. (The versatile Allagash Grand Cru, for instance, goes well with curried or spiced entrées such as lobster or shrimp *diavolo*, as well as desserts like bread pudding and carrot cake.) Allagash also sponsors an annual cooking contest with the Institute for Culinary Education in New York City, awarding a $1,000 scholarship to the winner.

Tod's reputation has spread throughout the country. Shawn Malone, general manager for Tuscarora Mill in Leesburg, Virginia (which has been holding beer dinners for the last fourteen years), paired seared Tasmanian salmon with wild mushrooms with Allagash Victoria Ale. For dessert, he served a fruited Hawaiian chocolate cake layered with a filling of ripe bananas and sweetened coconut to pair with Curieaux, a rich, Belgian-style ale full of fruity flavors.

Another brewery Malone praises is Victory Brewing Company in Downingtown, Pennsylvania. Among his favorite recipes is a reduction of Victory Doppelbock with rosemary, black pepper, and caramelized onions, which he said makes "a dynamite sauce" slathered over filet mignon.

Look also for brewpubs and beer bars to shake up the formulaic beer dinner, making these meals more novel and interesting. There is, for instance, no rule that says you have to wait until 6 p.m. to enjoy fine food and beer. "People here don't have much to do on a Saturday afternoon," said John McDevitt of the High Street Grill, which holds four-course beer luncheons on a monthly basis. He employs a variety of themes, focusing on a particular brewery, a region, or, just for fun, style-centric tastings, such as solely serving wheat beers.

The Royal Mile, a Scottish-themed pub in Wheaton, Maryland, held a sumptuous beer breakfast on the Saturday before St. Patrick's Day 2007. As owner/chef Ian Morrison recalled, the nine-course meal began with a "beer mimosa" (equal parts orange juice and Unibroue's spiced cherry ale Quelque Chose), paired with a melon salad. Subsequent dishes included caviar *blinis* leavened with yeast from Oxford Hefeweizen from the Clipper City Brewing Company in Baltimore, paired with the same ale to bridge the flavors.

The Royal Mile offers sixty bottled and draft beers, and Morrison is always happy to suggest food pairings. He believes the relationship between beer and food should be symbiotic. "I use them to bring out the flavors in each other," he said, and that's the goal he sets for his quarterly beer dinners.

Beer dinners are also being organized around specialized themes. Restaurant Nora in Washington, D.C., hosted a 100 percent organic beer dinner featuring Wolaver's ales. For the past six years, the Nodding Head Restaurant and Brewery in Philadelphia has held an annual vegan vegetarian beer dinner. Managing partner Curt Decker turns the kitchen over to Eric Tucker, head chef at Millennium in San Francisco and author of several vegetarian cookbooks. "He puts in more than a dozen hours of prep work," Decker said. "There's a lot of slicing and dicing involved." The four-course vegan meal attracts more than one hundred diners, many of them repeat attendees.

Yet carnivores throng to a barbecue and beer event at Redbones in Somerville, Massachusetts. Rather than offering many beers for a few hours, the restaurant taps more than fifty outstanding Northwest craft beers for six weeks in the late autumn. Elysian Brewing, Full Sail, Siletz, Pelican Pub, and New Old Lompoc are among past participants.

Harpoon Brewery even hosts a barbecue festival on the grounds of its packaging brewery in Windsor, Vermont. By the shores of the Connecticut River, teams of cooks compete in the Harpoon Championships of New England Barbecue, a certified event that now draws more than fifty teams from across the region.

Wood smokers are part of each kitchen in the Iron Hill Brewery's five brewpubs in Delaware and Pennsylvania. Slow-smoked pork and chicken are featured in entrées and sandwiches, even quesadillas. An herbal blend of dried thyme and oregano elevates the pepper-salt spice rub for the ribs, and the housemade barbecue sauce is sweetened with the brewpub's root beer. "Iron Hill is one of my favorite places, because they consistently do a good job with both the beer and food," said Lew Bryson, a Pennsylvania-based beer writer and author of several regional brewery and pub travel guides.

Barbecued and grilled foods are festival specialties of Chef Marc Kadish, owner of the Sunset Grill & Tap in Allston, Massachusetts. He caters many of the Beer Advocate festivals, such as the American Beer Fest held in June. Ale-infused sausages with red onions and beer mustard sauce, lager-steamed mussels in a broth with roasted garlic and sweet corn, and Brontosaurus BBQ Ribs—enormous beef ribs braised in beer until falling off the bone—are samples of Kadish's ambitious and delicious fest foods.

Beyond barbecue, there are other specialties yet to be explored, such as a gluten-free beer dinner. An estimated 2- to 3 million Americans suffer from celiac disease, meaning they can't digest glutens, a class of proteins found in barley, wheat, and rye. A few gluten-free beers available in the Northeast include a honey beer from Ramapo Valley Brewing Company in Hillburn, New York, and the Pilsener-like Dragon's Gold from Bard's Tale Beer Company in Lee's Summit, Missouri.

Brasserie Beck in Washington, D.C., a Flemish-style bistro, stocks eighty to a hundred bottled beers, almost all of them Belgian. But beer specialist Bill Catron makes an exception for New Grist, a sorghum-based brew from the Lakefront Brewery in Milwaukee. This eccentric, almost Belgian-like beer falls

MONDIAL DE LA BIÈRE

One of the best beer festivals in North America for craft beer and specialty foods is Mondial de la Bière, held at the Windsor Station in Montreal, Quebec, Canada. Festival president Jeannine Marois and organizer Marie-Josée Lefebvre assemble a truly remarkable assortment of seminars, tastings, and food vendors to complement the hundreds of craft and specialty brews served over the five-day festival. A brewing competition drew judges from around the globe, from Bill Metzger of the *Brewing News* in Amherst, New York, to Dick Cantwell of Elysian Brewing in Seattle.

At the 2007 event, a pavilion exhibit for cheeses made in Quebec showcased the many flavors and styles of specialty cheeses, with guided tastings offered each day. Belgian-style grilled sandwiches, spicy bison kebabs, and gourmet chocolates filled with crushed malt ganache offered a departure from the standard pub grub of burgers, sausages, and *pommes frites* (although even the french fries were presented with freshly prepared dipping sauces).

But the taste epiphany of the event was sampling a mousse-like meat paté with an effervescent golden ale. Where else can you sample hundreds of craft beers from around the globe, with accompanying canapés such as *paté en croûte* or shrimp terrine?

The highlight of the festival was a special feast prepared by restaurateur and chef Tim Schafer of North Carolina, working with Chef Alain Pignard and the sous chefs of the Fairmont Queen Elizabeth. Catered in a historic hotel

somewhere between a *hefeweizen* and a *lambic* in flavor. Catron suggests pairing it with grilled fillet of skate or a savory salad entrée.

Increasingly, beer is challenging wine on wine's own turf. "Beer has at least as much diversity, complexity and food synergy as wine," argues Dogfish Head's Sam Calagione. "We have done over a hundred beer dinners in the last two years to prove this point." They include a series of "he said beer, she said wine" dinners that Calagione has collaborated on with Philadelphia sommelier Marnie Old, in which diners are asked for their opinion on which beverage better accentuated the meal.

Kevin Garry, assistant beverage director of New York City's Gramercy Tavern, is expanding its beer pairings and tasting menus to build on the quality of American brewers' offerings. "Craft beer is so much more accessible and goes with our tavern foods such as grilled steaks," he said. Across the board, he attributes much of the growth in craft beer and food to Garrett Oliver of Brooklyn Brewery, "who has helped us enormously with our beer lists and staff tastings."

Gramercy Tavern expanded its beer list to feature cellared and vintage ales, along with more seasonal releases, "because in the winter, people want warming beers such as strong old ales, stouts, and smoked porters, and in the summer, we move into the lighter Pilseners, American pale ales, and more refreshing styles," Garry said. "Sixpoint Craft Ales of Brooklyn has some idiosyncratic brews such

renovated into a luxurious space, about two hundred guests dined on a meal that brought *cuisine de la bière* to new heights.

American Tony Forder of *Ale Street News*, Canadian Mario D'Eer of *BièreMAG*, and French writer Jean-Claude Colin assembled the pairings for the feast, which included samplings from the United States as well as Canada. A crisp endive salad found its match in the tangy, tart notes of Boréale Cuivrée, a strong golden ale from Brasseurs du Nord. Pan-seared scallops with porcini mushroom crusts tasted lush against the sparkling St. Sylvestre Trois Monts.

Perhaps the crowd favorite was the pairing of Dogfish Raison d'Etre with the beef short ribs, caramelized into "meat candy," as author Randy Mosher dubbed the dish. But Tom Dalldorf, publisher of *Celebrator Beer News*, was most impressed with the Beer a Misu dessert, the lightest confection of ale, ladyfinger cakes, and mascarpone cheese, swirled with a caramel ale sauce and served with the espresso-like McAuslan St.-Ambroise Noire.

Beyond the feast, the festival celebrates gastronomy and good beer over five days of seminars and guided tastings and talks, delivered in both French and English. "It's an inspiration to festival organizers everywhere," said Julie Johnson Bradford, editor of *All About Beer* magazine. – L.S.

as the Bengali Tiger English IPA, with apricot notes that go perfectly with salads and grilled vegetables."

Beer and food emporium BierKraft in Brooklyn, New York, collaborates with Sixpoint and Michigan brewer Arcadia Brewing Company in a novel retailing arrangement: growlers to go from the grocery store. Owners Richard and Daphne Scholz adapted a cooler space to dispense beer from kegs at the retailer, and every Saturday, a line forms with customers waiting to fill up their growlers and also purchase specialty cheeses, artisan breads, and other edibles.

"Unlike wine, there really aren't too many foods that you can't match up with beer," said Chris Leonard, brewmaster for the General Lafayette Inn and Brewery in Lafayette Hill, Pennsylvania. "Asparagus is impossible to pair with wine, but it goes so well with some Belgian-style beers that you can't tell where one begins and the other ends."

— *with interviews by Greg Kitsock*

From beer-bread bruschetta to strawberry-stout sauce, top chefs in the Mountain West are bringing craft beer into their kitchens, at the same time that the biggest beer festival in North America is now putting chef demonstrations on stage with craft beer.

Chefs and brewers take to the center stage at the Great American Beer Festival, as culinary interest mirrors the momentum of the industry. The incredible array of food-friendly flavors is driving the growth of beer dinners, with the bonus that craft beer is still vastly more affordable than many wines.

"We offer 10 minutes of pleasure," says Peter Bouckaert, brewer at New Belgium Brewing Company of Fort Collins, Colorado. Interpret that in the context that the first taste of a beer is the most intense, and as the pint is sipped, the palate becomes more accustomed to the

The Mountain West:

New Peaks for Craft Beer and Food

flavor. So the impact of a beer and food pairing is sensed immediately, and other nuances of flavor take hold as the meal proceeds. "I think of a chef as an artist using an artist's inspiration," Bouckaert said, "and the beauty lies in how the beer flavors are developed with the food." At a New Belgium beer dinner in Seattle, a chef prepared a sauce with Fat Tire Ale seasoned with nutmeg. "Nutmeg is a strong spice, and at first I was worried that it would overpower the beer, but the ale has caramel flavors and hoppiness, so it surprised me how well the flavors tasted together," Bouckaert said.

Another ale that pairs very well with intensely flavored cuisines such as Thai or Indian foods is Juju Ginger Ale from Left Hand Brewing Company of Longmont, Colorado. President Eric Wallace says the brewery has been making it with organic ginger root since 1994. It also paired wonderfully with a bitter greens salad, topped with fresh *chèvre* cheese, warmed and drizzled with honey and lemon. Left Hand Brewing Company was featured in a beer dinner at the Kitchen restaurant in Boulder, Colorado. Ray Decker, the Kitchen's general manager, said, "One of the best pairings was so simple—a housemade buttery potato gnocchi topped with herbs and orange zest gremolata, paired with the St. Vrain Ale, which had the savory *triple* fermentation flavors to make it meld together." That's high praise coming from Decker, who has overseen the expansion of the Kitchen's beer list into a formidable selection of nearly fifty craft brews.

In the same way that a brewer will choose ingredients and methods to bring out flavors, chefs strive for multiple dimensions of flavors. Sometimes that can be accomplished with beer as an ingredient. At the Altitude Chophouse and Brewery in Laramie, Wyoming, Chef Sean Seaton uses craft

37

beer as often as possible. Envision a glossy strawberry-stout sauce atop a grilled beef tenderloin, or a hearty soup made with pale ale and cheddar, or even barbecued pork in which the pork itself is braised in amber beer and water until tender.

The strawberry-stout sauce is simple: Reduce a good stout down by about half, add diced fresh strawberries, a splash of vegetable broth stock, fresh minced thyme, balsamic vinegar, and a little salt and pepper, and then cook until thickened and syrupy. While the sauce is simple to make, the flavors are incredibly complex and marry perfectly with grilled beef tenderloin. "The stout sauce goes really well with roasted beef," Seaton noted, "and the strawberries are just sweet enough to counter the bitterness created by reducing a heavy beer like stout."

Seaton thinks that beer is more complex to cook with than wine, especially if you don't know the characteristics of certain styles, but he doesn't see that as any reason to avoid cooking with it at home. He advises home cooks to keep it simple, and to keep it relative. "Try to match flavors in the food with flavors found within the beer you choose," he said. "For instance, I like to make a pumpkin sauce with our seasonal pumpkin ale, and I like to serve that sauce under a piece of graham cracker-encrusted salmon. The pumpkin ale already has a lot of spices in it, like clove and coriander, and when reduced and concentrated, those spices go really well with the sweetness of the graham crackers and the oily richness of the salmon. It's a natural match."

Bill Heckler, chef at Gordon Biersch Brewery in Tempe, Arizona, combines craft beer and food frequently. Speaking of combining beer styles and cuisine, he said, "The obvious starting point is to match the beer styles of a country to examples of its regional cuisine, such as an Oktoberfest lager with grilled sausages." At Gordon Biersch, beer is often used in the core menu items as well as in seasonal items and daily specials, and even if beer is not included as an ingredient in a dish, it is always used as the inspiration for the menu items. "Our food is designed to go with the beer," Heckler said. "We try to develop our food flavors to keep up with the beer. You'll find beer in everything from our carrot cake to the barbecue sauce to the beer batter. It's a main component in our house vinaigrette, and it finds its way into several other items."

Yet Heckler also believes that beer is a more complex beverage than many wines, with components such as bitterness, carbonation, and sour and sweet notes. "When cooking with beer, the characteristics change," he said. "When you use it fresh and uncooked, you know what to expect, because it'll taste as it does in the bottle, but when you cook it, the flavors evolve. As it cooks, both the bitterness and malty sweetness in the beer concentrate and become stronger, but the hops tend to concentrate quicker than the sweet malts, so you need to be careful. Brief simmering is essentially fool-proof, but a reduction can change the flavors completely."

38

Heckler thinks that beer brings a lot to the table as a companion beverage and doesn't hesitate to state that. "Honestly, the last thing I want to see is a bunch of rules being made up about beer and food that will make people feel intimidated to try an IPA with a date and caramel tart," he said. For newcomers to beer and food pairings, he recommends starters and snacks, such as toasted pecans tossed in barbecue-chile seasonings, served with Havarti and a good Märzen or Pilsener.

Mike Shetler, co-owner of Rosemary's Restaurant in Las Vegas, offers a lengthy beer list and often suggests beer pairings with spicy and well-seasoned foods. There's a difference, he said. "Creole food isn't necessarily spicy, but it is certainly seasoned and lends itself wonderfully to beer pairings. A duck and andouille gumbo with a dark roux is perfect with an amber or brown ale. Wheat beers, hoppy ales, and crisp, dry Pilseners complement spicy Asian foods and barbecue nicely."

In designing a beer dinner at Rosemary's, Shetler starts with a cold first course for both pairing and logistical reasons. "We like to balance the menus between seafood and meat, so we will generally start with a few appetizers with seafood, such as a wheat ale with salmon tartare and crème fraiche, then fowl or white meat, red meat for the entrée course, and finish with a sweet course."

As for cooking with beer, Shetler believes in bridging the flavors with culinary preparations when it makes sense. "We use beer most heavily in braising and sauces, but will use it in everything from ice cream to a syrup garnish," Shetler said. "The one thing we don't do is throw beer into a recipe just to put the beer's name on the dish. It has to enhance the flavor in some way, and not all beers do that when you cook with them." Nor do all beers need to be paired with food in order to be appreciated.

"Yet beer is still a secondary beverage in fine dining in Las Vegas," Shetler said. "My biggest frustration is to go to Asian restaurants that offer great food and boring beer lists. But Vegas has come a long way in five years, and I foresee that the beer culture will continue to expand."

Young chefs such as Robin Baron, who heads the kitchen of Udi's Bread Café in Stapleton, Colorado, grew up in the region where the microbrewery movement began and so have an appreciation for craft beer. Baron even bakes an artisan bread made with Oskar Blues Old Chub Scotch Ale and has teamed up for cooking demonstrations at the Great American Beer Festival with Oskar's Marty Jones. "I enjoy the flavors of craft beer and also like the fact that it's not pretentious," Baron said. "For a long time, chefs overlooked bread, as something just tossed in a basket, and thought of beer as something to guzzle. Now there's an appreciation growing in America for foods that are locally produced and handmade, including fresh artisan breads and craft beer."

At the Front Door in Boise, Idaho, hearty Mediterranean cuisine, including pizza, is often featured with craft beer. At a beer dinner with Full Sail brewer

39

John Harris, the chef prepared grilled dorado with a white bean purée seasoned with fresh thyme and garlic, paired with the Full Sail Pale Ale. Next came a toasted *panzanella* salad with kalamata olives and grilled *haloumi* cheese—a Greek-style cheese so hard and bready that it can be sliced and flame-broiled—with the Full Sail Amber, also full of toasty and bready notes, followed by Greek-seasoned roasted leg of lamb, sliced very thin. The dessert of Top Sail Imperial Porter made into a float with homemade vanilla bean ice cream was a refreshing finale. "Full Sail does really well at the Front Door," said general manager Shane Randel. "But we offer more than eighty brands from brewers across the West, and the selection is growing. Three years ago, we changed our format to focus on all craft beer, and our sales have tripled." He attributed the fast growth to pent-up demand. "We get people thanking us for bringing better beer to the table," he said.

Tim Husband, executive chef of Rendezvous Catering Company in Jackson Hole, Wyoming, finds creative and delicious ways to use craft beer. Due to the desire to support local enterprises, Husband favors fresh beer from Snake River Brewing Company. A braised pork belly is made with Snake River's porter mixed with a bit of veal stock, herbs, and garlic. "The porter brings a depth of flavor that is highly desirable with this cut," he said. "The beer brings richness with it that goes well with the robust flavor of the meat."

All of the catering company's housemade barbecue sauces include beer, most often pale ale or a lighter lager. "We add the beer with the onions and spices at the beginning," Husband said, "and as the beer reduces with the sauce, it intensifies the flavor." Advice for the home cook comes in the form of simplicity. "If you see a recipe that calls for stock, whether it is chicken, beef or fish, try substituting half of the stock with beer.

Jennifer Talley, brewer at Squatters Pub in Salt Lake City, understands the dynamics of bringing together food and beer flavors. Star anise is a hugely aromatic component of Asian five-spice powder, often used in spice rub blends for Asian barbecue such as *char siu*. Star anise has hints of licorice and harmonizes with the many Asian-inspired dishes served on the Squatters menu. Talley used a filtered infusion of crushed star anise to make the aromatic Second Revelation *dubbel*-style ale, which, when fermented with Belgian ale yeast, yielded plenty of spicy notes, despite the limitations of Utah's cap of 4 percent alcohol by volume.

"A beer doesn't have to be hugely hoppy or extremely high in alcohol to be flavorful and enjoyable," Talley said. "In fact, some of the medium-bodied, lower-gravity ales work better with food, because you can have several choices over several hours of dining."

Eric Dunlap, chef at Red Rock Brewpub in Salt Lake City, uses beer to batter fish, to add depth to soups, to deglaze pan sauces, and to add pleasant mystery to various ice creams. He contends that beer always imparts a unique taste to any food you cook it with, and reaches for it whenever he wants to add a sweet, malty accent, or a bitter note to the dish he's preparing. Although Dunlap enjoys traditional pub grub, he also likes vegetables with beer. A green salad goes wonderfully with a fresh glass of American wheat ale on a warm summer day; the citrus-like finish in the beer plays off of a bold vinaigrette wonderfully, and can tie the two together on your palate.

When asked to offer advice to the home cook, Dunlap cautioned, "Beer has at least a hundred and twenty-two named and identifiable flavors, so you'd do well to learn some of them and then translate that to your dish." And most importantly, Dunlap also likes to mix it up. Simply put, "Most countries have at least one beer style that they are famous for, so pick a beer and then research the food. After you've familiarized yourself with some of the more common matches, you can easily branch out."

Greg Neville, proprietor of Salt Lake City's Pine Restaurant, partners with Uinta Brewery for its annual beer dinners. "At the Pine, we offered an optional wine pairing as well and found we had so many more people attend," Neville said. "It was a wonderful sharing event for couples, as one person would get beer and one would get wine and taste the pairings back and forth. In fact, the hard part was finding the wine that could stand up to the beer pairing."

Beer was the focus in terms of creating the menu. "We really felt that made it more cohesive when looking for the right match and the right flavors," Neville said. "We prepared sea scallops with a rub of chili flakes, pan-seared the scallops in browned butter, and deglazed the pan with the IPA to add the citrusy hops flavors. For dessert, we made the Uinta Kings Peak Porter dark ale into a barley syrup with a few peppercorns, cloves, orange zest, and cinnamon stick, finished with a bit of honey and reduced until very thick, and served on top of vanilla bean gelato."

Desserts often can stand up to the strongest beer flavors. At the Big Beers, Belgians, & Barley Wine Festival in Vail, Colorado, Chef Kelly Liken used warming spices such as cinnamon and nutmeg in a pumpkin crème brûlée, served with pecan-crusted vanilla ice cream and a deep brown caramel sauce. By letting the sugar in the caramel sauce darken to toasty gold, it heightened the bittersweet caramel flavors in the Great Divide Brewing Company's Oak Aged Yeti Imperial Stout.

Chocolate can also meld very well as a dessert or when used in a savory dish, as is typical of Southwestern cuisine. At an Avery Brewing Company beer dinner at Zolo in Denver, a chocolate empanada topped with almond cheese and finished with a ground chili and cocoa mole sauce brought out the malt character of Ellie's Brown Ale. And dark sugars such as panela, sorghum, or molasses can add depth to a pan-glaze sauce made with stout, to pair with grilled game or meats such as bison.

Wild game is more popular in the Mountain West, with pheasant, elk, and venison served more often than in other regions of North America. Even rabbit was featured in a menu from Four Peaks Brewing Company in Tempe, Arizona, but presented as roasted meat, boned and chopped and shaped into spicy rabbit cakes topped with a *hefeweizen* and rabbit reduction, served with pickled green beans, tri-colored peppers, sundried cherries, spicy salsa fresca, and citrus sections, tossed in citrus vinaigrette and paired with the brewery's Hefeweizen.

Southwestern preparations such as mole and masa infuse the menu of the Chama River Brewing Company of Albuquerque. "We rotate through monthly special dinners, focusing on beer, wine, tequila, or Scotch whiskies, just to mix it up," said general manager Robert Griego. "Ted Rice, our brewer, will keep it fresh by experimenting with seasonal releases or special beers, and set those aside so that even the regular customers will be interested. He'll do a tasting with our chef, Stephen Shook, to come up with the menus, and their palates are pretty harmonious."

Indigenous foodstuffs wind up in both the Chama River pub and special event menus, from chorizo-stuffed pork chops to an Anaheim green chile and ale fondue. And sometimes the beer and the food share ingredients: At a Halloween dinner, caramelized pork ribs with butternut squash purée paired with Sleepy Hollow Ale made with another famous squash, pumpkin. "People have always heard about wine dinners and are still learning to accept the concept of a beer-tasting dinner, but the learning can be fun with craft beer," Griego said.

As a beverage, Altitude's Seaton contends that craft beer brings life itself to the table. "A perfectly poured glass of fresh beer is beautiful, so, whether by tasting, seeing, or smelling, the beer is there for you to enjoy," he said.

— with interviews by Jamaine Batson

42

Slowly and surely, the South is rising in its appreciation for craft beer, as most states lift restrictions in brewing regulations to permit some of the most flavorful beer styles.

The Free the Hops movement in Alabama holds events and tastings to change the state's restrictions on beer alcohol content. South Carolina lifted restrictions on the alcohol content of beer in 2007. And North Carolina's Pop the Cap advocacy group organized the passage of House Bill 392 in 2005, which lifted the 6 percent alcohol by volume restriction on beer brewed and sold in the state. Now, the real work begins.

"Our mission is to elevate craft beer culture in North Carolina through beer tastings, events, outreach, and seminars for chefs and restaurateurs," said Sean Wilson, president of the group. He has got plenty of company across the South.

The South:
Craft Beer and Food Trends

"As craft-brewers, we are driving trends for customer appreciation of beer that's different—a beer with flavor," said Chuck Skypeck, head brewer of Boscos in Memphis. Although the Memphis "restaurant for beer lovers" still caters to a middle-aged clientele, the demographics are changing. Over the twelve years that Boscos has operated in Nashville, the trend is toward reaching young adults who haven't been exposed to craft beer before.

"And that's in keeping with demographic changes in the South," Skypeck said. "More people, and especially younger consumers, are moving to cities like Atlanta and Nashville and Charlotte, and as those consumers learn about craft beer, they want to find the right foods for pairings. Craft beer deserves to be on the same footing as wine as a companion to food, and this generation is more open and receptive."

Yet there are substantial differences in flavors and tastes. Boscos opened a location in Little Rock, Arkansas, where imported beers have been strong sellers. "Newcastle Brown is a huge import favorite in Little Rock, so we keep our brown ale on tap because people can more easily relate to the name and flavors, while in Memphis, we have more customers asking for the hoppier pale ales," Skypeck said.

Skypeck notes that the selection of foods ranges from elaborate and spicy (such as the guajillo sauce with grilled pork) to mild and casual (portobello mushroom sandwich) and several vegetarian options (such as a creamy spinach-and-cheese-stuffed pasta). "Our servers offer beer pairings in terms of flavors, so that the grilled pork would be presented with beer with a malty flavor to complement all the grilled and caramel flavors, like the Isle of Skye Scottish ale," Skypeck said. "We want to keep it easy for everyone."

43

Nationally, the consumer who enjoys craft beer tends to be someone with higher levels of education and income. "As more people move around the South, there's lots of change in the brewpub industry to match," Skypeck said. "We can offer wonderful food and draw in people from a culinary base."

Award-winning breweries such as Abita Brewing Company of Abita Springs, Louisiana, draw on outside culinary talent to help promote pairings with craft beer at the table. At Juban's of Baton Rouge, Louisiana, sous chefs Jason Juban and Evan Lieber matched tastings of seared Creole jerk ahi tuna paired with Abita Amber, grilled India pale ale-marinated lamb chops, and seafood kabobs with pineapple-infused reduction of Abita Restoration Ale, the first ale brewed after Hurricanes Katrina and Rita, sales of which help fund the Louisiana Disaster Recovery Foundation.

Saint Arnold Brewing Company of Houston celebrates beer with food through special ales in the Divine Reserve series, with flavors that chefs find inspirational. At Houston's Bistro Toulouse, Saint Arnold owner and brewer Brock Wagner paired his outstanding ales and lagers with pan-seared steak topped with Elissa IPA Béarnaise, Brown Ale orzo salad with Red Trinity in cucumber ribbons, and for dessert, a winter Stout Ginger Cake with hazelnut chocolate crème anglaise.

"Consumers are drawn to both better foods and local producers, and both of these trends benefit craft-brewers," Wagner said. "There is also an interest in more and more esoteric foods, and as the craft-brewing industry matures, you see more breweries pushing the envelope with new beers and beer styles."

Bars such as the Flying Saucer Draught Emporiums also promote craft beer and food in a decidedly casual way that fits with tasting and sampling. With eleven locations across the South and Southwest, the Flying Saucer is among the first to feature brews from startup craft-brewers such as Yazoo Brewing Company of Nashville and Duck-Rabbit Craft Brewery of Farmville, North Carolina, as well as flagship brews such as Shiner Bock.

One of the culinary transplants to the South is "The Brewchef" Tim Schafer, now operating his fine dining destination in a beautiful historic home at Lake Norman, Sherrills Ford, North Carolina. Formerly based in New Jersey, Schafer sees several changes influencing craft beer and cuisine. "Beer culture is growing and maturing," Schafer said. "When the beer law changed in North Carolina to permit strong beers, we expanded our list to more than sixty brands. Our beer dinners here sell out even faster than they did in New Jersey."

Wilson of Pop the Cap agrees that beer dinners are growing in numbers. "We organized a series of beer dinners to showcase the brews that won medals at the Great American Beer Festival," he said. "The five GABF dinners were remarkably different in style, with no overlap at all, but the best turnout we had was in Chapel Hill and Charlotte, where the chefs were eager to taste the beers and discover the nuances and herbs to complement each."

"Beer is the ultimate democratic beverage, so we have to make beer appreciation accessible," Wilson said. Beer dinners and festivals are good ways to approach the goals of tasting and education. It is Wilson's dream to have a North Carolina "East meets West" barbecue festival to showcase both the Eastern, tangy, vinegar-pepper basted whole hog, and the Western or Lexington style, adding some brown sugar, molasses, and ketchup to the baste, as well as special sides such as red coleslaw. "With barbecue and breweries from across the state, we can mix it up and celebrate our diversity," Wilson said.

How exactly does barbecued food taste paired with craft beer? Of course, it depends on the style, but there are a few common elements. First, there are the aromatics. Smoke can overwhelm many wines, but hops and a whiff of caramel malt and roasted notes in craft beer melds with the smell of smoke. Citrus hops notes accent the aromas of seared foods and spices such as roasted garlic and chiles. And last, carbonation helps cut through the grease and spices.

If the brew is wood-aged, then hints of the wood smoke can accent the barrel-aged aromatics of the beer. Rustico in Alexandria, Virginia, takes wood barrels used in aging the Jefferson's Reserve Bourbon Barrel Stout from the Bluegrass Brewing Company and dismantles the barrels. The wood is then used to plank-cook salmon, served with tender grits and ginger-Vidalia onion glaze.

"Wood smoke is a must for true barbecue in Louisiana," says David Blossman, president of Abita Brewing Company, with hickory and pecan being the prevalent woods. "Next, you've got to have a spice rub, such as the Paul Prudhomme line or Tony Chachere's. And dark roasted malts in brews such as our Turbodog go well with grilled strip steaks and roasted red peppers."

Barbecue is big in Texas, but relatively few barbecue restaurants serve an extensive list of craft brews. By far the biggest regional brew is the Spoetzl Brewery's Shiner Bock. The brewery offers recipes and assistance to chefs interested in creating beer dinners, or as Gambrinus brewing executive Jaime Jurado calls it, "beer-enhanced cuisine." The Moonshine Patio Bar & Grill in Austin, Texas, features homestyle cooking and Texas favorites such as flat-iron steaks and "corn dog" shrimp. Moonshine Chef Larry Perdido is a fan of Texas beer, offering not only Shiner Bock and its seasonal releases, but also beers from Saint Arnold Brewery, Real Ale Brewing Company, and Lone Star.

The concept of pairing fresh local beer with regional culinary specialties that also highlight local purveyors is one that captivates many chefs, according to Pop the Cap's Wilson. "By focusing on seasonal beers and seasonal foods, brewpubs have upgraded their menus. We now have pubs with wood-burning barbecue, sampling artisanal cheeses, and focusing on Carolinian food favorites given an updated twist," he said.

Giving Southern ingredients a new spin is one way to sell the concept of craft beer with food. Tim Schafer takes shrimp and grits to another level with his preparation. "I make the stone-ground grits with smoked Gouda, chopped bacon, and searing hot spicy shrimp, and pair it with the high-gravity Unibroue Maudite, which is one of my favorite food beers," he said.

Terrapin Beer Company founder John Cochran recalls a pairing he sampled at a Savannah, Georgia, bed-and-breakfast, the Foley Inn. "We had spicy shrimp and grits, but when I had a taste of our Terrapin Rye Pale Ale with the dish, I was blown away," he said. "It was the most perfect pairing of beer and food I have ever had the honor of enjoying. I could not stop raving about it for months."

Athens, Georgia, where Terrapin began its beer marketing, is a thriving university town. David Sturgis, executive chef of Farm 255 in Athens, says the restaurant seeks to reconnect food to its roots and people to their food. "We serve local, seasonal, and sustainable food for supper nightly," Sturgis said. "In addition to the Farm we manage Full Moon Farms, a seven-acre organic/biodynamic farm in Athens."

Sturgis has yet another mission. "I am trying to create a 'gastropub' by tying the craft beer and wine served with the food," he said. "We are adding more taps and more bottled beer to try to feature more regional brews, because people are interested in what's local." And what's local helps sustain the environment, because beer travels less of a distance, and that saves on energy.

Trends in food and beer that interest Sturgis include seafood paired with craft brews. "Mussels steamed with *saison*-style ale, pale ales with oysters, a hoppy IPA with seafood curry, all these flavors harmonize," Sturgis said. "I try to select beer styles to go with the spices and preparations."

Another Athens restaurant on the map for fine food is the 5&10, where Chef Hugh Acheson has prepared beer dinners regularly for patrons. Acheson occasionally features the beers of a single brewer in an evening. For a dinner with Sweetwater Brewing of Atlanta, Acheson prepared a lobster and citrus chowder to pair with the India pale ale, soft local grits with stewed sweet onions, braised pork belly, and wilted bitter greens to taste with the Sweet Georgia Brown ale, and a rich coconut tapioca pudding with caramelized banana, fennel roasted grapes, and a coconut sorbet, to echo the sweet and spicy aromatics of the Festive Ale. Yet Acheson, named by *Food & Wine* as a top chef, presents far more wine dinners overall.

Thanks in part to its focus on craft beer, the Muss and Turners gourmet deli in Smyrna, Georgia, has experienced tremendous growth. "The operation started as a deli by day, but very chef-driven," said manager Ric Brown, and it grew into a full-service restaurant as well. Muss and Turners is described as an "upscale eatery with value-priced beer and wine." Its customers could be business people in suits, or, as Brown says, "the guy in flip-flops eating *foie gras*." It's one of the few places in town with a beer list as long as the wine list.

Muss and Turners features casual pairings, such as the Tuscan Raider sandwich of grilled chicken, prosciutto, mozzarella, and fresh chopped oregano with a pale ale. "Because of all those flavors, a sandwich requires more finesse than a regular entrée," Brown said. "The pale ale has to be on the hoppier end of the scale, because the fresh oregano needs to be brought out."

Even with extensive staff training and outreach, Brown still thinks that craft beer appreciation has "a ways to go." After centuries of wine and cuisine pairings, Brown said, "Consumers are willing to try craft beer, but the expectation is still for wine with fine dining." To change the mindset, choose beers of suitable complexity, Brown advised. "If your entrée is really wonderful, with three or four different layers of flavors, like a remoulade sauce on top of roast salmon with steamed vegetables, that really calls for a beer with several dimensions of flavor. The beer might start fruity, taste malty in the middle, and finish with some peppery, roasted notes."

On the casual end of the spectrum, Brown enjoys a grilled burger made with coarse-ground, grass-fed beef, dusted with a little bit of chipotle and poblano and topped with aged cheddar cheese, served with a Scottish-style ale. "The grill and pepper bring out the smokiness in the ale style," Brown said.

Carmen Capello, chef and owner of Global Culinary, a catering consultancy in Atlanta, says his interest in craft beer has grown as the range of flavors and styles continues to expand. "Craft beer brings something new and unexpected to menus, because people are surprised by the complexity of these beers," Capello said. "I think people are starting to see that certain styles of beer are as complex as certain wines, and in many instances, it actually pairs better with some foods than does wine."

For example, Capello cited pairings such as cream ale served with sea urchin and poached quail eggs, over a wild raspberry sauce and Japanese black salt, a combination where the sweet and salty and fruity flavors would annihilate most wines. A crisp Pilsener pairs well with seared otoro tuna, edamame purée, and candied apricots, in Capello's book.

"And I've even made ice cream with beer," he said. "I feel it's important to use the beer in one or two courses in a beer dinner to show the versatility of the flavors. Most of all, be practical about using proper stemware, serving the beer at the proper temperature so that it gets to the consumer the way the brewmaster intended it to."

Capello sees the demand for craft beers growing, because of flavor complexity combined with its casual appeal. "With proper beer education and awareness of what beer can truly be, it will be a growing trend for the future," he said.

Gary Essex, brewer at McGuire's Irish Pub of Destin, Florida, agrees. "Education of the public to all things beer is a top priority by the local brewers," he said. "Speaking from our experience of having just hosted our first beer dinner in 2007, the demographics of the attendees was very wide."

One of the best aspects of beer is its casual appeal. "As beer has always done throughout its history, it brings a variety of people together," Essex said. "We had young people brought up in households with their parents enjoying craft

47

and imported beer, homebrewers, and beer aficionados, as well as wine lovers. We have noticed that people who enjoy good beer also enjoy finer foods and are open-minded and willing to try offerings from the world of wine. However, there's a bit more reluctance from the wine drinkers to cross over to accepting beer as a companion to fine dining."

McGuire's has always offered monthly wine dinners, and Essex credits the higher profile of craft beer for prompting culinary interest. "We have five house-brewed beers on tap with a seasonal rotation tap and will only do beer dinners when we have a sufficient number of special small-batch or barrel-aged brews," he said.

The Dunedin Brewery in Dunedin, Florida, experiments with a wide range of beer styles, including fruited ales such as the Apricot Wheat, fermented with real fruit. It's one of the pub's most refreshing drafts, and draws the tourist trade as well as locals.

The Tampa Bay Brewing Company of the Ybor City area of Tampa, Florida, features an extensive menu with Cuban-influenced cuisine, such as a roast pork loin rubbed with garlic, cumin, and oregano, served with saffron rice, black beans, and fried plantains. A trophy case attests to numerous awards won by Tampa Bay over the years. Randy Mosher, Chicago-based author and homebrewing consultant, has hosted beer dinners with Tampa Bay Brewing Company as well.

Orlando Brewing Company brewer Ed Canty released a Doble Imperial IPA to commemorate the life of his friend, John Doble of Tampa Bay Brewing. "Tampa Bay Brewing is really inspirational," Canty said. "The pub was one of the first in the state to promote craft beer and food pairings, and was even featured on the Food Network by Al Roker in his series on best brewpubs."

Travis Hixon, brewer at the Blackstone Brewery and Restaurant in Nashville, says that tastings with staff and the chef are key to making better beer. "We work to educate the chef on the different flavors and nuances," Hixon said. "That's because the flavors of our beer help sell a significant amount of food. Many customers choose to have lunch or dinner at our place because they want a great beer with their meal."

Hixon also believes that lighter, simpler styles such as *helles* or Pilsener can be just as sublime in a pairing as an aged Belgian-style ale. "A hoppy pale ale with spicy Mexican on a sunny day in the backyard, or some brown ale or porter with some homemade pulled pork barbecue is pretty special, too," Hixon said. "It is not only the food and the beer, but also the atmosphere and environment that makes a good pairing all come together."

Craft beer has the potential to become as common as wine when paired with food, but Hixon cautions "elitist thinking and snobbery could come with that. … Beer is still the everyman's everyday beverage, and it should remain approachable. But if you can mutually improve both your dining experience and your beer drinking experience through pairing, why wouldn't you?"

Andy Klubock has been promoting craft beer and food together at his Summits Wayside Taverns in Cumming and Snellville, Georgia, for more than a decade. "I love food. I love beer. I love cooking. It seemed obvious to me to find a way to combine my passion for the three in a way that is interesting," he said.

"Our perception is that beer is more accessible and more affordable than fine wine, and as beer styles have evolved over the last twenty years there are so many more choices out there, so when dining out why not share a gourmet bottle of craft beer over dinner instead of a bottle of wine? The barrier to entry is much lower in terms of cost, and the opportunity to try something different is there."

Klubock's personal preference is to pair more malty and robust ales with wild game and beef. "However, a nice tart *lambic* paired with chocolate or fruit is hard to beat!" he said. "I also try to present traditional pairings; for example, a crisp, Czech Pilsener served with a fresh roasted chicken is a perfect match." The rise of specialty grocery stores has also increased the pressure to carry more diverse beer selections. When a home cook can buy a terrific smoked porter to pair with barbecue, there is naturally the expectation to enjoy wider selections when dining out. "There's definitely room for more craft beer at the table," Klubock said.

- with interviews by Kerri Allen

Across the Midwest, craft-brewers produce casks and kegs of luscious lagers, barrel-fermented sour ales to rival any from Flanders, black wheat beers, amber ales from light to auburn, fruited ales, bocks, doppelbocks, and even a dark triple bock that tastes more like malted cognac than a beer. What better way to celebrate the bounty of craft beer in the Midwest than to create a meal to match?

The Midwest:
A Banquet for Beer

Chef Rick Martin of the Free State Brewing Company in Lawrence, Kansas, gets inspiration from the brews of head brewer Steve Bradt to develop beer banquets, held annually for more than a decade. Five-course feasts with some dishes prepared with brewing ingredients, such as a molasses malt reduction made with wort, draw customers from several states. "There's a waiting list to get in," Bradt said.

Martin is careful to create flavor progressions, building on ingredients and seasonings from course to course. The following example should explode any lingering misconceptions about bland Midwest beer cuisine: Martin paired a complex and spicy Belgian-style *dubbel* ale with roasted Berkshire pork tenderloin rubbed with a spice dust of ancho chiles and powdered porcini mushrooms, served with a Mexican cocoa demi glace, organic orange coulis, wilted winter greens, and celery root custard.

"Often the pairings that may be pushing the edge turn out to be the customer's favorites," Bradt said. "And we have been surprised by how adventurous our customers are. For the longest time, we didn't think we could sell a dark beer in the summer, and now we pour our barrel-aged Owd Max Imperial Stout."

Adventurous palates can be found across the region. In Wisconsin, Chef Leah Caplan, owner of the Washington Hotel on Washington Island, off the coast of Door County, celebrated the launch of a new beer with origins on the island with a special beer dinner. "I bake with flour made from organic wheat grown here," Caplan explained, "and when we had a bumper crop, I told the grower to talk to a brewer." Caplan contacted Kirby Nelson, brewer at Capital Brewery of Madison, Wisconsin, and the extra organic wheat wound up in the mash for the Island Wheat Ale.

"I made a saffron and whitefish chowder to pair with the ale," Caplan recalled, so the creamy soup would contrast with the effervescent beer. Artisan cheeses and a duck confit salad with wild rice all complemented the chosen brews. Nelson still raves about the dinner, which culminated in caramelized apples with a spice cake, topped with tangy buttermilk ice cream and paired

51

with a pint of Capital's Autumnal Fire. "The beer has a bit of a spicy edge to it, too," for a perfect finish, Nelson said.

And that's just the beginning for craft beer at the table. More chefs in the Midwest are embracing beer flavors, from celebrity chefs such as Paul Kahan of Blackbird, and Mindy Segal of Hot Chocolate, both of Chicago, to upscale tavern chefs, such as Matthew Hinman, of the Happy Gnome in St. Paul, Minnesota.

For a special dinner for Michigan's Bell's Brewery, Hinman made appetizers of seared sea scallops over microgreens, with a foam sauce made of the Winter White Ale and puréed apples. Grilled venison tenderloin presented with corn polenta, shallots, and currants met its match with Third Coast Old Ale, and for dessert, a molten chocolate cake oozed bittersweet cocoa flavors paired with Cherry Stout crème anglaise. Although Happy Gnome is well known for its burgers and fries, it's obvious that Hinman believes craft beer makes an exceptional pairing for all kinds of foods, not just pub grub.

The Old-Fashioned in Madison brings back Wisconsin roadhouse specials, from crispy fried smelt, to sausage and cheese platters, and even crispy beer-battered cheese curds given a mod-tavern twist with a dipping sauce made with smoked paprika. New Glarus Brewing Company's roster of specialty brews are included on the lengthy beer list, as are brews from Lake Louie, Sand Creek Brewing Company, South Shore Brewing, and many other small Wisconsin breweries that only distribute in-state.

At Kuma's Corner in Chicago, burgers are reincarnated with names of metal bands, such as Metallica and Iron Maiden, with toppings such smoked Gouda and caramelized onions or spicy cherry peppers with avocado. "It's a place with attitude, relaxed and playful but focused on great food, and the kitchen can pull it off," said Fred Bueltmann, vice president of New Holland Brewing Company of Holland, Michigan. "Even corner bar and tavern owners are more serious about good food with beer."

GREEN IS THE BREWER'S KITCHEN GARDEN

Great Lakes Brewing Company is at the forefront of breweries that are re-examining all their practices through the lens of sustainability. The company also supports the entire sustainability community in northern Ohio by hosting events and sponsoring the annual Burning River Fest to draw attention to water quality issues affecting the Cuyahoga River and Lake Erie.

The company also has supported the development of a local market for alternative fuels. Its "Fatty Wagon" shuttle van for Cleveland Indians games runs on straight vegetable oil. The company converted a large semi-truck to run on vegetable oil and bio-diesel, so now its beer deliveries emit a faint odor of french fries.

Flavor rules for Bueltmann, who is an avid home chef. "It's important to make a meal with a variety of flavors that build from course to course," he said. "You wouldn't serve tomato soup with pasta marinara and a salad of sliced tomatoes." Bueltmann recommends starting with lighter flavors and progressing to stronger flavors, with stronger brews to match.

Another home cook is Larry Bell, president of Bell's Brewery in Kalamazoo, Michigan, who personally catered a beer dinner in Canton, Michigan, for a fund-raiser for the Coach Carr Breast Cancer Research Foundation. Larry and Angie Bell prepared a five-course dinner for a dozen people, starting with appetizers, a roasted onion and garlic soup laced with Bell's Special Amber Ale, salad tossed with a citrus-ale dressing, and wild mushrooms with braised beef.

Surprising to some guests, the appetizer, a smoked fish dip, was paired with one of Bell's most potent brews, the Sparkling Ale. Although it is a light golden hue, the ale is very strong, at 8.2 percent alcohol by volume. The peppery nose from the alcohol cut through the smoky, rich fish flavors and made an elegant contrast.

But craft beer on draft, and the conviviality of dining out, draws most people to experiment with pairings at pubs and restaurants. Though the term "gastropub" isn't widely used in the Midwest, the concept of fine food and excellent beer applies in taverns, cafes, and bistros.

Boulevard Brewing Company of Kansas City, Missouri, works with chefs at local cafes to put together tastings and beer dinners. At one event at Yia Yia's in Wichita, Kansas, the five-course menu presented by Chef Brent McCollar featured grilled flat iron steak, dusted with green peppercorns and a demi glace sauce with crumbled Maytag Blue cheese. Paired with the Boulevard IPA, the peppercorn sauce and caramelized meat found matches in the hops and malt of the ale.

Cooper's, a neighborhood "eatery" in Chicago, is owned by Craig Fass, a chef with a background in fine dining, and Mandy Franklin, who urge patrons to

And sometimes, going green involves food. A local baker produces the cracked barley beer bread and pretzels found on the menu using spent grains. Killbuck Farms uses spent grains, mixed with sawdust and paper, as a substrate for growing organic shiitake and oyster mushrooms used in entrées. Local farmers who raise livestock on a diet of brewery grains then sell their meats and poultry to the pub kitchen. A community garden that produces vegetables for the Great Lakes Brewpub was the site for a passive solar greenhouse project. To reduce the waste of discarding "low-fill beers" (bottles of beer that cannot go to retail because they are not filled to the maximum level), GLBC chefs use the beer in salad dressings, sauces, and the Stilton Cheddar Cheese Soup. Local vendor Mitchell's Ice Cream uses low-fill bottles of the Edmund Fitzgerald Porter in a chocolate chunk ice cream, also sold at the pub. All told, it's a tasty way to save energy.

"come for the food and stay for the beer." It's all good food, handmade throughout, such as the brined pulled pork sandwich made from a pig roast that's smothered in spice rub, brined, smoked for hours, and braised until meltingly tender. Cooper's offers more than one hundred beers, up from thirty-five brands when first opened, and hold special beer tasting dinners, such as a dinner with Unibroue of Chambly, Quebec.

Farther north in Chicago is the Hopleaf, Michael and Louise Roper's family business that pays homage to Belgian cuisine and brewing. The bar gets its name from a collection of beer signs imported from Malta. However, its decade-old reputation as a beer-lovers' destination comes from the stellar selection of more than two hundred brews.

Four years ago, the bar expanded into the back of the building, carving out a dining room. In a tiny kitchen about 20-by-10 feet, the chefs at the Hopleaf produce a small but exquisite selection of beer-friendly food, such as grilled Nueske's brand ham on toasted pumpernickel with Gruyère cheese and apple-tarragon coleslaw, and five entrée choices, such as a fabulous pan-roasted pork chop marinated in farmhouse ale with golden Yukon potatoes and vegetables. A tiny cheese board offers a selection of three small slices of artisanal cheeses, plus sliced berries and breads. But it also has classic bar food, such as beer-batter smelt, with a side of pickled red onions and saffron aioli.

What makes the Hopleaf achieve true bistro status is not only the beer or the service but also the kitchen garden just outside the dining room. After buying the building, the Ropers began work on establishing a kitchen garden in the porous soil of lakefront Chicago. The organic kitchen garden produces heirloom tomatoes, herbs, greens for salads, and more. So, when the menu promises "vine-ripe tomato slices" on a sandwich, you can be sure that they will be (at least in August or September). It's part of the trend toward using local produce that Slow Food helped to promote.

Slow Food convivia throughout the Midwest include craft beer in their events, from barbecue cookouts to tastings of artisan cheeses. At the Milwaukee Public Market, a group of Slow Food devotees gathered together artisan cheese-makers and craft-brewers for a casual tasting event. Neville McNaughton, a cheese judge based in St. Louis, reveled in the tasting of artisan brews, especially a blonde *doppelbock* he had never sampled before.

Chef Justin Scardina of La Rana Bistro in Decorah, Iowa, specializes in seasonal cooking with organic ingredients, and features many craft brews on the menu. Scardina also volunteers for local charity dinners, including as a guest chef for the Upper Midwest Organic Farming Conference, a group that helps educate farmers about switching to organic methods. "It's amazing how much cleaner the flavors are with most organic produce," Scardina said. "And craft beer makes a great match with vegetables." La Rana's owners, Mark and Joanie Smeby, believe in clean food to the point that there's not even a fryer in the kitchen.

Although some independent brewers find that independent restaurants such as La Rana are most receptive to their creations, there are a handful of successful brewpub chains. The Midwestern chain Granite City Food & Brewery, headquartered in St. Cloud, Minnesota, offers just four core styles: India pale ale, *maibock*, amber lager, and stout. However, as the chain expands across the region, the menu is designed to appeal to all ages—and to the Midwest's sweet tooth. For example, the *maibock* is more of a sweet bock style, medium-bodied and mild enough not to overwhelm pan-seared crabcakes with cheddar cheese.

Rock Bottom is highly successful in the Midwest, where just over one-third of its units are located. The motto "serious about our food, crazy about our beer" holds true for many of the locations, where brewers support the craft-brewing community by donating beer and event space for festivals, homebrew clubs, and more. (Note: the author worked as a consultant for the launch of the Milwaukee unit).

But one of the Midwest's very best beer destinations is in Toronto, where Brian Morin, executive chef of the beerbistro, creates outstanding beer and food pairings. Augmented by a wine list and complete bar, the beerbistro is a haven for beer lovers who enjoy fine dining.

Three sous chefs, working under the direction of chef Morin, assemble dishes and work the grill. While a few basics such as a club sandwich and burger do appear on the menu, the execution of these dishes is anything but basic. For example, the burger is bathed in brown ale, which adds a hint of malty sweetness to the grilled meat.

The extensive beer menu offers details on each beer, including style, alcohol by volume, and tasting notes. As often as humanly possible, beers are served in the brewery's correct glassware and at the correct temperature, thanks both to a specially commissioned draft system and a good cellar manager.

Morin also loves to bake with beer. One of the amazing appetizers is grilled beer flatbread with several dips: best bitter hummus, curried squash, and ale-infused herbed tomatoes. Note that three of the four items in this appetizer use beer as an ingredient. That ratio spans the entire menu, including appetizers, soups, salads, pizzas, mussels, sandwiches, and entrées.

About 70 percent of the dishes use beer in some phase of preparation, but my favorites are the beer-cured smoked salmon and the brown ale-brined pork bellies that are smoked to make the bistro's own bacon. Even the bacon for the club sandwiches is made in-house, adding Morin's culinary creativity to the most basic dishes. Smoked sausage for the pizza is made from ground lamb marinated in McAuslan's award-winning St. Ambroise Oatmeal Stout with rosemary and pepper, a classic combination. Sour cream used to garnish a luscious lobster quesadilla is made with a sour starter cultivated from Cantillon Gueuze. Author and beer consultant Stephen Beaumont's favorites on the menu are the cherrywood-smoked baby back ribs, braised in six liters of Éphémère Pomme and finished with spicy barbecue sauce until completely juicy and tender.

So, why doesn't craft beer get the respect it deserves at tables around the Midwest? Perhaps it's here, in lager land, where so many people associate beer with frat-boy quaff, that restaurateurs take refuge in fine wine. Some gourmets flat-out refuse to even try to taste craft beers.

Andy Ayers of Riddle's Penultimate Café in St. Louis has been presenting beer dinners for more than twenty years. His take is that craft-brewers can find a place at the table at independent restaurants, where chefs and owners aren't tied to corporate or centralized purchasing. Stan Hieronymus, editor of www.appellationbeer.com agrees, saying, "Where there's a vital community of independent restaurants, you're more likely to find smaller brewers represented."

Fred Bueltmann of the New Holland Brewing Company believes that as chefs and restaurateurs develop pairings that work within their menus, more people will choose craft beer. "A server should have a spectrum of beer knowledge that lets them offer a specific pairing to make the craft beer flavors come alive,"

OVERJOYED BY OVERNIGHTS

Small hotels and inns across the Midwest are tapping new customers with combinations of beer dinners and overnight stays. The American Club of Kohler, Wisconsin, offers a series of beer dinners on Tuesday nights, with special packages to stay overnight after sampling. Given the rich menus and lavish sampling at most beer dinners, staying overnight is a wise choice.

At a beer dinner for the Rogue Brewery, Chef Brett Muellenbach prepared a five-course meal that began with beef carpaccio paired with Dead Guy Ale, a salad with a coronet of toasted rye bread paired with the Half-a-Weizen, pan-seared walleye, roasted chicken with American Ale, and a finale of Rogue 10,000 and a velvety soft chocolate cake, prepared by Pastry Chef Richard Palm. It was a sumptuous meal, and knowing that the comforts of a down-filled duvet awaited made the evening all the more enjoyable.

It's a formula in use at the Iron Horse Inn in Glendale, Ohio, where strong holiday ales and winter warmers are served alongside wild game entrées in a special January feast. Chef Jackson Rouse served wintry specialties such as Sierra Nevada Celebration Ale with a tossed salad of arugula and smoked oysters, with a creamy Caesar salad dressing; honey-roasted quail with Berghoff Hazelnut WinterFest Ale; braised venison shanks with browned butter and apples with Avery's Old Jubilation Ale; and more.

The Chalet Landhaus Inn and Restaurant of New Glarus, Wisconsin, prides itself on offering a taste of Swiss hospitality. That extends to special beer dinners, such as the one prepared by Chef Mike Nevil for Deb and Dan Carey

Bueltmann said. "The knowledge base of the typical beer drinker has changed enormously." The willingness of brewers to challenge misconceptions starts with opening bottles for sampling.

Sampling is an important part of presenting the barrel-aged sour ales produced at Jolly Pumpkin Artisan Ales of Dexter, Michigan. Brewer Ron Jeffries finds that tastings with chefs and consumers at festivals "will open their minds to a set of flavors that are both unfamiliar and exciting." Sipping is one of the best ways to try the complex flavors of award-winning ales such as Oro de Calabaza and Bam Bière. Jeffries also makes the Fuego del Otoño ale with Michigan chestnuts, and through the addition of an unusual foodstuff, the ale is tapping more interest among chefs.

A multi-unit tavern in Ohio, the Winking Lizard, bases its success on rewarding sampling and tasting. By treating craft beer like a food item, served with perfectly clean lines and stainless steel dispensing equipment, the Winking Lizard offers drinkers the purest tasting pints. An annual trivia quiz called the World Tour of Beers encourages customers to sample styles side by side, gaining an understanding of the dimensions of each beer style.

of the New Glarus Brewing Company to celebrate the brewhouse expansion. Nevil used beer in several preparations, but one of the favorites was a salad topped with nutty shaved Emmentaler cheese from the Edelweiss Creamery, served with a Raspberry Tart vinaigrette. "I took the Raspberry Tart beer and reduced it with some lemon juice, fresh tarragon, minced sweet onion, and balsamic vinegar, and then blended that reduction into a creamy base," Nevil said. "Brewmaster Dan Carey just loved the flavor."

Some brewers even become innkeepers themselves. Bill and Michelle Tressler of Green Bay's Hinterland Brewery became the proprietors of the Whistling Swan Inn at Fish Creek in Door County, Wisconsin. Urban flavors, surrounded by intimate comfort, best describes the Whistling Swan. The menu, designed by Hinterland Executive Chef Kelly Qualley and Whistling Swan Executive Chef Adam Schierl, explores contemporary American cuisine. Their journey to create bold flavors traverses a diverse selection of locally foraged produce, wild game, and freshwater and ocean fish. "It's been a tremendous adventure," said Bill Tressler of the decision to become an innkeeper.

And Leah Caplan, a chef turned innkeeper at the Washington Hotel on Washington Island, Wisconsin, relishes the relationships she's able to nurture with returning guests, local foragers, farmers, fishermen, and now, the Capital Brewery. She even plans to bring in a guest chef for a beer cooking class each summer. "I'm more of a wine drinker," Caplan admitted, but many of the inn's guests do appreciate beer. At the very least, craft beer can be an equal at the table and in the mini-bars of more hotels and inns.

Also, the Great Lakes Brewing Company of Cleveland supplies the beer for Winking Lizard events and tastings. Great Lakes Brewing Company and the Winking Lizard's other co-promotion is a homebrewers' competition for Northeast Ohio. The grand prize-winning recipe is brewed at Great Lakes and served on draft at Winking Lizard for the month of January. It's a win-win for the local homebrewers and for the Winking Lizard.

Several beer and food tasting events are held at Winking Lizard's eight locations throughout the year, with featured speakers from the brewing industry, including Garrett Oliver of Brooklyn Brewery in 2004 and Jaime Jurado of the Gambrinus Company, then-president of the Master Brewers Association of the Americas, in 2005.

Brewers can make beer dinners even more interactive and informational. Beyond giving away T-shirts or pint glasses, the New Holland Brewing Company puts together a small brochure for special dinners, listing the menu and beer pairings, sections for tasting notes, and a few sample recipes. "The menu has gone from being a throwaway and a cost for the event to becoming something useful, to keep and enjoy," Bueltmann said.

When putting together a beer dinner at home, be sure to taste and sample each recipe ahead of time. Rehearsing the preparation will let you keep track of time, and also fine-tune seasonings. Chef Kim Chase of the Grand Rapids Brewing Company in Grand Rapids, Michigan, taste-tests all pairings for beer dinners with Brewer Jon Svoboda to be sure that the flavors will meld before serving guests. Stephen Beaumont also tests beer pairings at home before serving, and likes to research the breweries so that guests will learn more about the beer's origins and style.

Consider introducing contrasting flavors within a single dish, so that the food can harmonize in several ways. For example, a spinach salad with caramelized pecans and dried sour cherries includes sweet and tangy, mineral and nutty flavors. That way, the salad course would pair well with an amber ale with loads of caramel character, as well as a spritzy *weiss* beer with a big, yeasty aroma.

That's a technique often used by Chef John Raymond of Roots in Milwaukee, Wisconsin. For a beer dinner with the Founders Brewery of Grand Rapids, Michigan, he presented layers of flavor within every dish, but one of the crowd pleasers was the wild honey-macerated raspberries, with sweet and spicy black pepper shortbreads, anise-flavored whipped cream, and candied pine nuts, paired with the raspberry Rubaeus ale. "It was such a surprise to taste the pepper," recalled Dave Engbers of Founders, "but it all came together really well on the palate."

And for the beer, consider setting out small glasses with assorted bottles to sample, as does Greg Hall, brewmaster of Chicago's Goose Island Beer Company, for his guests. He cites the influence of years of informal tastings held at the pub with the Chicago Beer Society, plus the fact that "buying good beer is still an affordable luxury."

In the Pacific Northwest, Portland, Oregon, lays claim to the title of "Beervana," thanks to the presence of more craft-breweries than any other metropolis in the world. Thanks to pubs, taverns, and restaurants interested in promoting craft beer, even the *Seattle Post-Intelligencer* now includes a search option for "notable beer list" in its online index of dining choices.

Pacific Northwest:
Beervana and Beyond

Noteworthy beer lists number in hundreds across the region, from Henry's 12th Street Tavern in Portland to Brouwer's Café in Seattle. But perhaps the best-known destination for craft beer and creative cuisine is Higgins Restaurant in Portland. Owner and chef Greg Higgins paved the path for generations of aspiring beer chefs through the ambitious beer selection and fresh food featuring local ingredients.

Higgins has been on the forefront of movements such as Slow Food and sustainable agriculture. He was ordering organically raised vegetables from small farmers and grass-fed beef from organic ranchers long before most restaurateurs were. The seasonal menus created by the chef feature local berries, hazelnuts, fish, organic cheeses, and more. Higgins loves simple bistro fare and makes his own pickles, plus he brines, cures, and smokes foodstuffs such as pastrami and peppered salmon for sandwiches and deli platters of sheer delectation.

A fellow chef, Alan Sprints, is the owner/brewer of Portland's Hair of the Dog Brewery. Sprints hosted a dinner for beer writer and local legend Fred Eckhardt, preparing a "Fred Feast" with visiting friend and homebrewer-chef Sean Paxton, a meal that both chefs called "an amazing success."

"We made the marinades four days before the party, got up at dawn, and went to the farmer's market on the day of the feast, and spent about six hours cooking together," Sprints recalled. "I got the beef from a rancher who takes my spent grain for feed, and found the morel mushrooms at the farmer's market "

The mushroom soup was served in cappuccino cups, with a marinated mushroom embedded in a foamy mushroom mousse atop each cup. Grilled rabbit loin was marinated in oak-aged Fred ale and chicken stock with spices. Sprints cooked the rabbit over a smoky pecan wood fire and served it with a Belgian-style ale. Beef cheeks were marinated in Hair of the Dog's Adam, rosemary, and plenty of garlic, and braised for about four hours until amazingly tender and rich. "Even my kids liked them," Sprints said.

Though most people won't labor for days cooking feasts like his, Sprints said that creating a menu with beer and food pairings is worth doing at home, where people can be more relaxed. "People are still so surprised about beer and food

59

pairings," he said. "A lot of times people will say they don't like a certain beer, but when it's paired with a food it's a different thing altogether."

"And what's missing from a lot of beer festivals right now are more guided tastings, more education, more outreach to encourage people to experiment," he said. "I did a seminar on beer and cheese pairing at the Spring Beer & Wine Fest (in Portland) and was pleased to see so many people turn out to taste and learn. The tasting was an eye opener for a lot of people who hadn't had beer and cheese together before."

Brewery tours and tastings are so common in Portland that there are several beer blogs devoted to keeping track of the events. A vibrant state brewers' guild also attracts consumer members who call themselves S.N.O.B.s, or Supporters of Native Oregon Beer. A beer dinner benefit for the Oregon Brewers Guild has evolved from simple picnic foods, such as beer brats and grilled chicken, to a full dinner with spice-rubbed smoked salmon, roasted pork loin, artisan breads, local cheeses, several salads, and dessert.

So the interest in offering good beer and food is growing across the region, just as more producers and farmers are reaching more cooks through farmers markets. Support of a local brewery can be part of the same community spirit that supports local growers.

Growers in the Pacific Northwest harvest blackberries, marionberries, raspberries, pears, plums, apples, and cherries. Bartlett pears are one of the region's major crops, as are hops and hazelnuts. Oregon's hazelnut growers account for more than 90 percent of the hazelnuts used in North America.

Hazelnuts were a key ingredient in the feast for the Glen Hay Falconer Foundation, which funds brewing scholarships. Scholarship winner and brewer Jamie Floyd of Ninkasi Brewing in Eugene, Oregon, teamed with Chef Stephen Ficker of the Mallard in Eugene, site of the Sasquatch special dinner in June 2007. Toasted, skinned, and salted hazelnuts were blended with pepper, minced chives, and softened cream cheese to make a stuffing for chicken breasts.

"We browned the chicken for golden color, and then roasted it with the hazelnut and cream cheese filling until completely tender and the cheese melted," Ficker said. Served over a coulis sauce of puréed smoked and roasted red peppers, the nutty and smoky flavors wrapped around the taste of the Ninkasi Believer ale, a strong "double red ale" with resinous hops flavors. And hops were a key ingredient in a special ale brewed for the fest by Walking Man Brewery of Stevenson, Washington, the Sasquatch Legacy Imperial Steam beer, a vastly hoppier version of a California common beer.

Hops inspired another Oregon chef, Patrick Mullen of the Widmer Pub in Portland, to give a standard grilled chop an entirely new spin. "Because of our German traditions, we offer staples such as roast pork and meatballs with sauerkraut and caraway," Mullen said, "but I explore more spicy foods in the specials,

60

because ginger, garlic, and chilies taste wonderful with hops. When I tasted the Northwest Red Ale, the burst of grapefruit in the hops aromas made me think of a citrus and pepper glaze for grilled pork chops." Mullen believes that craft-brewing has brought dining and drinking beer to "a more sophisticated level than before—a lot of changes and experimentation and events to expose people to new flavors."

Malts, whether fresh-cracked or spent grain, inspire the bakers at Portland's BridgePort BrewPub, where an artisan bakery and coffee shop is housed in the same Pearl district building as the pub and brewery. The artisan bakery starts work at four in the morning, due to the time required for slow pre-ferments of the starters, or natural leaveners. There are parallels in craft-brewing, because the process is basically small-batch production, using traditional ingredients and starter cultures to create complex fermented flavors in the finished breads. Sourdough rolls, fresh soft pretzels, and other specialty loaves are featured in sandwiches and appetizers.

One of the region's most innovative brewers is John Maier, head brewer at the Rogue Brewery of Newport, Oregon. With pub breweries from Issaquah, Washington, to San Francisco, Rogue is expanding the boundaries of what can be called beer. Maier uses marionberries, hazelnuts, and other local ingredients to make brews with distinctive regional tastes.

The Rogue pubs are also on the forefront of experimenting with beer cuisine and guided tastings of artisan cheeses and chocolates. Homebrewer Sean Paxton recalls visiting the Newport pub in 1997 and tasting a salmon chowder made with Old Crustacean Barleywine.

"The chowder worked with the beer flavors on so many levels," Paxton said. "Against the thick, creamy base of the chowder, the barley wine tasted richer and elevated the whole dish." Seafood chowder is also often seasoned with a splash of sherry, so the aged and spirituous flavors of a barley wine make a perfect addition—plus the name, Old Crustacean, pays homage to Newport's fishing industry.

"It's easier to make a good pairing if you start by tasting the beer and design the dish to match its flavors," said Darron Welch, head brewer and food enthusiast at the Pelican Pub and Brewery in Pacific City, Oregon. "As the beers are entering maturation, I give chefs a sample and tell them to start thinking about what would go well with the flavors, and even as we're in the process of filtering, I'll give the chefs another sample to think about ways to present the new beer on our menu. It's one of our top priorities, as we're now offering suggestions on the menus. Beyond that, our special events are engineered around pairings.

Executive Sous Chef Piet Vanden Hogen tweaks and updates the Pelican Pub menu to bring more seasonal ingredients, such as a fresh tomatillo gazpacho made with the Pelican Heiferweizen, actually a *witbier* style, in the soup as a

61

base, garnished with fresh cucumber, minced orange, and cilantro. "It's a fantastic base for the *witbier* flavors and brings out all the spice notes in the beer," Welch said. Sometimes, the chef experiments with brewing ingredients, such as preparing sautéed sea scallops dusted with minced parsley and hops.

For a themed brewer's dinner Vanden Hogen prepared a duck prosciutto, seasoned with coriander and dried Willamette hops. The duck breasts cured for a week and then dried—wrapped in cheesecloth, hung, and cold-aged—for several weeks. They then were served sliced into thin ribbons as part of an antipasto platter.

"We served the duck prosciutto with the Riptide Red Ale," Welch said. The salty, meaty flavor of the duck was offset by the sweet caramel character of the ale and a slight bitterness from the Santiam hops, developed for mild, floral aromas.

Seasonal styles of beer, as well as seasonal ingredients, can influence the drinker's tastebuds, too. Welch experimented with several Belgian-style ales at the Pelican, based on the Kiwanda Cream Ale's wort. "I wanted to brew a beer that's got some flavor complexity, and the Saison du Pélican has lots of spicy herbal notes, dry and snappy on the finish," he said. For a Belgian-inspired brewer's dinner, Welch presented the *saison* with an endive and watercress salad, sliced blood oranges, and a sour beer vinaigrette. "The flavors melded together to make the sum more than the parts, so both the beer and the food have more resonance," Welch said.

Methods of preparation make a huge difference, too. It can be misleading to give blanket guidelines on beer and food pairings, such as "serve fish with light golden ales." For example, Welch paired a pan-seared salmon drizzled in *ponzu* sauce with Doryman's Dark Ale, an American brown ale. "I'd recommend something richer and with a bit more bitterness and round caramel flavors to go with the seared browned salmon," Welch said.

Seafood, especially clams, mussels, oysters, and salmon are mainstays of Pacific Northwest chefs. The coasts offer hundreds of varieties of clams and oysters, although the sustainability debate about wild-caught or farmed seafood impacts the local fisheries. Razor clams are among the most popular, served in a creamy chowder base or steamed in ale. Wonderful chowders are also made from fresh or smoked salmon, with corn and sweet Walla Walla onion.

Creamy smoked salmon chowder is featured on the menu of the Collins Pub, which offers tavern fare to fit the sophisticated palate of the downtown Seattle dining scene. "Seattle, like the rest of the Pacific Northwest, has a wonderful beer scene, but craft beer is still a bit unappreciated as a local food product," said owner Seth Howard. "There's some puzzlement with craft beer dinners, despite the success of wine dinners." Howard works with Chef Addam Buzzalini to create pairings for beer dinners and special menus, so they sit down for guided tastings once a month.

"There are no rules in life for must-have beer tastings," said Howard, "but that said, we try to showcase the beer's flavor in cooking," from mussels and clams steamed in ale, to beer sauce glazes for pan-roasted halibut.

At a beer dinner for the New Belgium Brewery, Buzzalini served appetizers with Fat Tire Amber Ale as the welcome beer, followed by Mothership Wit with a light Bibb lettuce salad tossed with roasted beets, *chèvre*, oranges, and *lambic* vinaigrette. Pan-seared halibut was served with New Belgium 1554 Black Ale, progressing to the stronger Abbey ale with roasted pork tenderloin with caramelized spring onions, and in a nice bridge, the dessert brownie was spiked with Abbey ale but served with the sour, blended La Folie.

Dinners like this inspire Aleisha Loring, marketing manager for Lazy Boy Brewing Company of Everett, Washington, to plan more food events. "We're doing more dinners to help people put beer into a different perspective, because there's still this automatic instinct to serve wine with meals," she said. "I just had a party and paired some of the courses with our beers, and the guest feedback was great—they were a little shocked by how much they enjoyed the tasting."

At the Pike Brewery in Seattle's Pike Place Market, Rose Ann and Charles Finkel bring the best of brewing traditions, an extensive pub menu with myriad guest taps and bottled beers, to a tourism destination centered around fresh produce and specialty foods. "We use seafood and crab from the fish vendors to make our Dungeness Crab Dip, we get Beecher's cheeses for our sandwiches from the market, sausages made by Uli, and even our vinegar for our fish and chips is handmade by Spinnakers in Vancouver," said Rose Ann Finkel.

Pike's history includes education programs such as Homebrew U, conducted with guest lecturers such as Randy Mosher, an on-premise museum of breweriana, tastings and dinners for visiting brewers and authors including British beer authority Michael Jackson, food events for local gourmet groups, and even chocolate and beer pairings featuring confectioners such as Fran's, Theo, and Michael Recchiuti. The Finkels are among the most influential founders of beer culture in America, thanks to their love of good food, good beer, and a good life in the community.

Pike Brewery's beers are mostly British styles, such as the spirited Kilt Lifter Scotch Ale and the roasty Pike XXXXX Stout, used as bases in barbecue, chocolate cheesecake, and dessert sauces. Gary Marx, Pike's executive chef, turns out both affordable pub grub and more elaborate dishes, such as a cocoa-spice rubbed prime rib for a Valentine's Day chocolate and beer dinner. The Finkels have nurtured the talents of many brewers in the Pacific Northwest, with a list of former brewers that includes Shawn Loring of Lazy Boy Brewing and Dick Cantwell, now of Elysian Brewing.

Cantwell and his partner, David Buhler, have expanded the menus in all three of their Seattle locations. Elysian Brewing Company offers appetizers designed to whet the appetite for craft brews such as the Avatar Jasmine Pale Ale or Saison Elysée.

"Because we have three unique places, both in general design and kitchen operations, we give our chefs a lot of latitude to run with their culinary desires," Buhler said. "For example, at the Elysian Fields location, appetizers are huge for us, because it's a place to meet people after work, so we have everything from truffle oil fries to ahi poke salads." Other appetizers include steamed Penn Cove mussels with fried chorizo, garlic, shallots, serrano chiles, lime juice, and cilantro; potato croquettes with tomato jam; skewers of chicken satay with dipping sauces; and other spicy appetizers harmonizing with Elysian's brews.

Elysian Tangletown is an eighty-seat bistro that offers brunches, lunches, happy hour noshes with pulled pork quesadillas, and other pub grub specials. Buhler also does a tasting there every Tuesday evening. "For a vertical tasting of ESBs, our chef prepared an ESB-marinated flank steak with drizzled Welsh rarebit sauce on top, which was a playful way to taste the classic British sauce," he said. "The Capitol Hill location is so busy, we rarely do special events, but offer pub grub standards." The Oasis Platter of hummus and *baba ganoush mezze* is comfort food for many Seattle natives, and virtually every pub offers a hummus platter of some sort. Yet yellowfin tuna fritters served over mixed greens with diced green chiles, lime wedges, and roasted jalapeño peppers, topped with chipotle cream dressing, tasted anything but standard, and paired easily with the Ambrosia Maibock.

Buhler and Cantwell also invite visiting brewers to Elysian for tastings, such as an evening with Adam Avery featuring six tastes of Avery Brewing Company's beers with light appetizers to match. "It's more low key and accessible at just twenty dollars, and gives guests the chance to mingle and talk with the brewer," without the formality of a seated dinner, Buhler said.

Hales Ales in Seattle brings English-style ales to the bar with a pub menu that has expanded from simple pizza made with a spent grain crust to include all kinds of baked breads made with grain left over from brewing. For example, bruschetta are made with toasted spent grain crostini, fresh mozzarella, sliced tomatoes, and minced basil. Smoked pork shoulder is pulled and tossed with Hales Stout barbecue sauce served on a spent grain roll. And spent grain rolls are used for all kinds of sandwiches, including pan-fried fish and a salmon burger seasoned with cilantro, ginger, and lime. It's a delicious system to promote sustainability.

Sustainability can be the impetus for creativity in the kitchen. Spinnakers Taproom in Victoria, British Columbia, serves grilled steaks from spent grain-fed, organically raised Highland beef, and salads with housemade malt vinegars and vinaigrettes, paired with its award-winning ales. Spinnakers beer, from wort to finished brew, is used as an ingredient in many dishes, too.

The thickly malty Spinnakers Jamesons Scottish Ale is the foundation for a rich malt vinegar described as "a precious blend of malts, barley, yeast, water, and hops brought to a particular alcohol level to encourage bacteria growth." Aged in French oak barrels, the Scottish Ale Malt Vinegar is full-bodied and tangy with a soft malt finish. The vinegar is used in the pub's Asian hot and sour soup, marinated seafood ceviches, cranberry chutney, mustards, sauces, and marinades. A splash of malt vinegar is always suggested on the pub's wedge-cut fries and beer-battered fish.

Geoff Larson, president of the Alaskan Brewing Company in Juneau, Alaska, loves to cook, and his beer and food pairings have been in demand at events such as the Aspen Food & Wine Fest, American Culinary Federation, and regional food festivals. Frequent potluck dinners for employees yield a trove of recipes, many of them featured on the company's website.

Naturally, Alaskan seafood is often featured in special dishes. Beyond supporting local growers and food vendors, Alaskan Brewing Company has teamed up with the trade association Alaskan Seafood Marketing Institute to do cooking demonstrations at food festivals in Alaska and in Seattle. Recipes and pairing suggestions are offered for every beer Alaskan brews, along with tips for entertaining and menus.

Themed menus include A Day at the Beach with Alaskan Amber-glazed grilled salmon and picnic snacks, Summer Solstice Feast with Cajun-spiced smoked turkey, and a Dessert Party, with recipes for ice cream, sweet potato ESB pie, even an Alaskan Smoked Porter Chocolate Cake.

At the Midnight Sun Brewing Company in Anchorage, Alaska, chef-turned-brewer Ben Johnson experiments with sockeye salmon in a chili laden with pasilla chiles and tomatillos, and enriched with browned pork and chicken broth. "It's hard to find a food combination that goes well with really hoppy IPAs, but this does," Johnson said. "The spiciness of the chiles and the tanginess of the tomatillos really balance the hops in the IPA, and the sockeye brings out the malt flavors."

Mike Cooper, general manager of the Deschutes Brewery pub in Bend, Oregon, approaches beer and food pairings in much the same way that he approaches wine tasting. "The easiest approach is cooking a dish and pairing it with the same beer," Cooper said, "while another approach to bridging is adding a key ingredient that echoes some of the beer's flavors, such as pairing a malty beer with lots of residual sugars with barbecued ribs that have molasses in the sauce." Consistency and texture are important components, such as pairing a creamy bisque soup with a spritzy beer, "or even pairing a *helles* lager with buttery popcorn to cut through the fat."

"But sometimes the best pairings are when there's an element of surprise, and you don't really know why it happened to work so well," he added. Cooper suggests that home cooks learn to identify hops, which are so widely used in

65

Pacific Northwest brews. "Cascade hops go well with citrus, Centennials are more like rosemary, Simcoe is so intensely bitter that a little goes a long way," Cooper explained. "The characteristics of hops are good to know, because you can get grassy, floral, fruity, citrus, hay, herbs, all sorts of flavors."

Cooper enjoys contrasts, as in a banquet that started with a tiny pot pie, its flaky crust stuffed with diced butternut squash and Dungeness crab, served with tossed greens and peppered bacon. The pairing? A mildly sweet Bëndsch Kölsch, which worked because of the atypically hoppy finish. For dessert, a dense chocolate cake with sweet cream and cherry sauce partnered with Jubelale, which was barrel-aged in old Pinot Noir casks, so that fruity flavors of cherry and grape carried the duet.

Chef Jody Denton of Merenda, a plush grill and restaurant in downtown Bend, often collaborates with Deschutes on beer and food pairings for special events. At the Sagebrush Classic at Broken Top, held annually in July, dozens of celebrity chefs travel to Bend from as far away as Honolulu and Chicago, creating dishes to pair with brews such as the Deschutes cask-conditioned Mirror Pond Pale Ale.

Brewer Tonya Cornett of Bend Brewing Company said, "It's amazing to me that people are seeking out really intensely hop-flavored ales, to the point that it almost seems like a competition to see how much hops flavor can be packed into a pint glass. For me, drinkability is a big deal, and sometimes there's a need for something that's milder to match food. Because I'm brewing in a pub setting, and our restaurant sells a lot of food, that's something I have to think about."

Many beer and food pairings from pubs can transition to the home dining room. At the Concordia Ale House in Portland, beer writer Lisa Morrison featured food-friendly beers in a seminar to teach how to pair craft brews with the appetizers, salad, turkey, and even the dessert served for Thanksgiving dinner. The two-hour course took tasters through several styles of beer to go with Thanksgiving fare, so they can decide which artisan brews to serve with their own holiday meals.

"Thanksgiving is such an American meal," Morrison said. "It's a natural holiday to feature the flavors of craft beer." Learn to make craft beer part of the meal, because it's part of the harvest in the Pacific Northwest.

With the modernization of Anchor Brewing Company and the launch of New Albion Brewing Company in the 1970s, California became the birthplace of craft-brewing. Trends that affect craft beer often start in California, from the reforming of laws enabling the growth of craft-brewing to the rise of the pub pizza kitchen and agricultural marketing that places craft-breweries on par with growers, farmers, and wineries.

With more than two hundred and twenty-five craft-breweries and brewpubs in the state, California leads the nation in sheer numbers. Although tiny by comparison, the craft-brew community in Hawaii is robust, thanks to the success of events such as the Kona Brewers Festival.

California and Hawaii:
Pints Across the Pacific

Celebrations of California craft beer range from regional events such as Anderson Valley Brewing Company's Boonville Beer Fest; to musical events, including North Coast Brewing's sponsorship of the Monterey Jazz Festival and Trumer Brauerei's sponsorship of Beerapalooza in San Francisco; to sports, as in Sierra Nevada Brewing Company's cycling team. Even the State Fair celebrates commercial craft-brewing and homebrewing through an awards competition in Sacramento.

Yet culinary appreciation for craft beer is still developing. When Dean Biersch and Dan Gordon of Gordon Biersch Brewing began their brewpub, they were among the first to champion food pairings on the menu. Dan Gordon admitted bias, saying, "I think German-style lagers are the perfect complements to all kinds of foods, because of the rounded flavor profiles that won't overwhelm the more delicate flavors of seafood and other dishes. Beers with extreme levels of bitterness create more compound flavors and are best enjoyed on their own."

That said, Gordon enjoys high-impact flavors, Thai red and green curries, chili spiced pork, and other spicy foods. "Sometimes a Pilsener will be the most refreshing choice," he said, "but when I cook Thai food at home, I add lots of garlic and ginger, and those flavors meld really well with our Blonde Bock."

Entertaining at home is one of the best ways to convert someone to craft beer appreciation, Gordon said. "I like to grill, so sometimes I'll just hand a glass to someone in conversation, standing around the barbecue, and say, 'Try this,'" Gordon said. "It's easier to convince someone to try something new when it's a one-on-one conversation."

The caramelized flavors of grilled foods are natural complements to beer, but pizza is perhaps the top pub food in California and Hawaii. "Remember that gourmet pizza chains, such as California Pizza Kitchen, got their start on the West Coast," said Jay Brooks, a beer writer based in San Rafael, California.

67

"For craft-brewers such as Gina and Vince Marsaglia at the Pizza Port in Carlsbad and Natalie and Vinnie Cilurzo at Russian River Brewing Company, gourmet pizza is still the classic West Coast pub food."

"We started out as just a pizza place," recalled Gina Marsaglia, "but then we started brewing our own beer, and Tomme Arthur joined us, and the whole selection just expanded from there. Now we have festivals, such as the Real Ale Fest, and still we sell a lot of pizza." Marsaglia feels that having craft beer brewed on-premise "adds a lot of interest to the bar, and people stay longer."

The Pizza Port's offerings don't really fit the classic model of the California-style gourmet pizza. California-style pizzas are typically smaller with a cracker-thin crust. The Pizza Port's dough is made with beer and whole-grain flours, and is thicker and a bit breadier, with more flavor. Toppings range from Hawaiian style with pineapple and Canadian bacon (the Lahaina), to seafood (the Solana), to a barbecue bacon cheeseburger pizza topped with spicy meatballs. Yet with all these choices, prices are still well within range of families and students, judging from the many people who come to the pub for pizza and a pint.

"We chose to serve pizza and focaccia for simplicity and price," said Vinnie Cilurzo of Russian River Brewing Company in Santa Rosa. "There are so many toppings we can offer that go well with our beer, such as Blind Pig IPA with pepperoncini, or Compunction, our barrel-aged blonde ale made with pluots paired with a Pizza Verde made with fresh herbs. The pizza concept works for us because it doesn't require a huge amount of kitchen space."

San Francisco is a food mecca, and many pubs and restaurants offer bigger, more ambitious menus with beer lists to tempt sophisticated palates. On the Embarcadero in the Ferry Building, the Slanted Door offers wonderful Vietnamese food and "an elegant beer list," according to *Celebrator* publisher Tom Dalldorf. The pairing of oysters and stout may be ubiquitous, but for Dalldorf, "one of my favorite pairings is at the Hog Island Oyster Bar, where I can get the North Coast Brewing Company's strong golden ale, PranQster, served on draft with fresh oysters."

At San Francisco's 21st Amendment brewery and pub, innovative ales such as Watermelon Wheat from brewer Shaun O'Sullivan pair with creative adaptations of pub cuisine, such as grilled chicken salad topped with diced pears, spiced pecans, and shavings of aged Pecorino cheese. One of the "21A's" first chefs, Eddie Blyden, also helped start the Alembic Bar's small plates menu.

Dave McLean, owner of the Magnolia Pub and Brewery and Alembic Bar in the Haight district of San Francisco, has two chefs who collaborate as friends and homebrewers, Joseph Boness and David Coleman.

"Both chefs share the same kind of passion and interest in pairing beer and food," McLean said. "Boness is the chef at Alembic and has expanded the small plates menu with even more beer-friendly foods, which reflects a personal interest because he's also an avid homebrewer." Grilled ginger-turmeric shiitake mushrooms, sweetbread-stuffed ravioli in hazelnut cream, and stout-braised oxtails are among the flavorful foods served in tasting portions.

"In comparison, Magnolia is a very casual gastropub, with bigger plates of comfort food like fish-and-chips and grilled chicken," McLean said. "Chef Coleman has updated versions of bangers-and-mash, merguez sausage with Israeli couscous, and a curry beet salad. Both the bangers and merguez are made from scratch right here at the pub." In fact, the sausages are made with Magnolia's beer as a secret ingredient.

Gordon Biersch's Dan Gordon says that using beer as a braising liquid "acts as a natural MSG to draw out flavors of the meat." His technique for ribs involves braising in a mix of beer and broth until tender and finishing the meat on the grill for smoky flavors.

Chef Bruce Paton of San Francisco's Cathedral Hill Hotel is one of the nation's top-ranked brew chefs, whose beer dinners often sell out within days. "I can find a beer to match virtually any kind of cuisine," Paton said, "and can use beer in many cooking methods, from classical braises, to soups, stews, ceviches … really, the list is endless." Most brewers rank their beer dinners with Paton among the highlights of their culinary experiences. That's true for Vinnie Cilurzo of Russian River Brewing Company, who claims that "Chef Paton is a genius because he can make a menu that works instantly, with very little taste testing or revision. He just nails a pairing right away, and it works."

Another chef who inspires many brewers is Eric Tucker, of San Francisco's Millennium, a vegetarian restaurant. "Every year, we do a craft beer and chile dinner," Tucker said, with guest breweries such as Nodding Head of Philadelphia and Russian River. "I like to pair chiles with big beers that are very malty, that have some residual sugar and depth to pair with spicy foods, and all the fermentation flavors that work so well with hot food. Sometimes, a really hoppy beer will fight on the palate, so I choose the less-hopped beers for pairing."

One of Tucker's favorite pairings was a roasted pimento roulade with herbed white chocolate "cheese," actually a base of cocoa butter blended with savory spices instead of sweet. "Cocoa butter is a fat with a thick consistency like a semisoft cheese, so I blended it with smoked paprika and roasted garlic to pair with an *altbier*," he said.

Some brewers use fruits and herbs extensively as ingredients in their brews. Pasadena's Craftsman Brewing Company offers flavorful brews featuring spices, whole Valencia oranges, and mountain sage, made by owner and brewer Mark Jilg.

"After decades of living in the San Gabriel foothills, the overwhelming odor of sage baking in the late summer sun seemed perfect for making a really evocative ale with a local ingredient," Jilg said. However, he added, the strong Belgian ale called Triple White Sage "isn't a beer that I'd pair with food; it's fairly assertive and stands alone, though an eight-ounce serving before a meal makes an excellent aperitif."

Jilg's favorite food-brewing experiment is the Cabernale made with late harvest Cabernet Sauvignon grapes, for an ale that's totally designed around the Thanksgiving menu. "Typically, there are lots of rich gravies and sauces, and delicate poultry, so there needs to be something that bridges both a beer and a wine," he said. "The ale winds up with this somewhat drying effect of the grapes and a bit of fruit, so it goes really well with Thanksgiving foods."

Orange Grove Ale uses whole Valencia oranges with aromatics from the peel and bittering compounds from the pith. "Think about the beer palate, and it's always balancing malt sweetness against hops bitterness, but I decided to do a bitter beer that didn't rely on hops alone for its palate," he said.

In San Diego many brewers bring creativity to their cooking, but few on the scale of the Stone World Bistro & Gardens in Escondido. Far from a typical pub, the menu features no fish-and-chips, pizza, or the like. Instead, there are spicy and flavorful preparations using local and organic ingredients. Selections include housemade kimchee to go with a smoked pork, smoked porter, and sweet potato soup; pan-seared tilapia on a bed of quinoa; spicy tempeh burgers on herbed focaccia bread; and many other inventive dishes.

"We want to give people food that's absolutely fresh, handmade, and of the highest quality to match our beers," said owner Greg Koch. "We don't even serve soft drinks that are made with high-fructose corn syrup." The lengthy menu includes notes on sources, preparations, and suggested pairings for virtually every item. "People want that information," Koch said, "and we train our servers to understand beer and food pairings."

For so many brewers, the missing link in beer appreciation is education of the drinker and diner. At Father's Office in Santa Monica, beer tasting and education begins with the chef-owner, Sang Yoon. He calls himself a "beer sommelier" and

THE BEAUTY OF BEER: BIERGARTENS OF THE PACIFIC

On the Pacific Coast, craft-brewers have hundred of choices to tempt chefs and diners, from cafes, taverns, brewpubs, and restaurants, to theme parks.

That's right, theme parks. One incarnation of the Karl Strauss Brewing Company can be found at Disney's California Adventure in Anaheim. However, the biergarten operation misses the menu that makes the chain so successful in Southern California. Master brewer Karl Strauss of Milwaukee was proud of the brewpubs that bore his name and left a legacy to enjoy good beer and food in settings that reflect the natural beauty of the Pacific.

Perhaps the loveliest Karl Strauss biergarten is tucked behind an otherwise unremarkable office park in Sorrento Mesa, California. There, three outdoor decks with seating wrap around pathways, koi ponds, lush palms, and a has trained many others, including Christina Perrozzi, who now conducts beer tasting classes geared to young women.

Beer schools are popular events at dozens of taverns, from O'Brien's Pub in San Diego to the 21st Amendment in San Francisco. A recent trend that helps educate customers' palates for hops varietals is the "wet hop" or hop harvest brew, using freshly harvested hops to make ales (and sometimes lagers) of surprisingly herbaceous character.

Fresh hop harvest ales have been made by homebrewers for years, but small breweries in England started limited production of these seasonal ales in the early 1990s. Within a decade, thanks to pioneering brewers such as Ken Grossman and Steve Dresler of Sierra Nevada Brewing Company, John Maier of Rogue Brewery of Newport, Oregon, and Bert Grant of Grant's Brewing Company of Yakima, Washington, fresh hop or hop harvest ales could be found more easily.

Just like farmers of other crops, such as cherries and potatoes, there are harvest festivals to celebrate hops with new brews. The Fresh Hop Ale Festival in Yakima is located in the epicenter of the hops farming region. Toronado in San Francisco features a wet hop harvest ale festival in late fall, but one of the largest festivals is held at O'Brien's Pub in San Diego, where Tom Nickel gathers dozens of ales and brewers to celebrate the freshest hops.

Some brewers prefer to hone in on a single varietal, such as Fuggles, Centennial, Simcoe, or Cascade, while others prefer to make fresh hop ales with several varietals for greater complexity. For example, Brian Hunt, brewer at Moonlight Brewing Company, presented GreenBud, a blended fresh hop ale made with homegrown Chinook and Cascade hops at an October 2006 festival organized by Victor and Cynthia Kralj of the Bistro in Hayward, California. Although the Bistro's top awards went to Lagunitas Brewing Company for its

Chinese pagoda, designed so that diners can enjoy flowers, bird songs, and the subtle colors of Asian carp in the water. The dining room features huge glass windows that can be opened to bring the fresh air and sounds of the biergarten into the brewery's restaurant.

Most impressive are the gardens behind the Stone World Bistro & Gardens, where immense boulders and dry stone creeks wind through native plants, grasses, bamboo, and trees, creating paths and secluded spots for conversation. A large pool reflects light and holds seasonal rain, and a waterfall adds relaxing sound. Several spots seem specially designed for wedding photos, as the Stone World Bistro & Gardens are well sited for wedding banquets and celebrations. The stone garden is both raw and beautiful, reflecting the symmetry in design apparent throughout the architecture of the restaurant. It's a beautiful place to enjoy beer outdoors, in both shade and sun.

Wet Maximus and Stone Brewing Company for its Wet Arrogant Bastard, Hunt's ales completely fit the model of farmhouse brewing.

Sonoma County is famous for supporting small farmers, and Sheana Davis of the Epicurean Connection assists both brewers and small producers with agricultural marketing. Davis told me of an innovative experiment to bring together food and beer at the Lagunitas Brewing Company in Petaluma. "Small food producers bring samples to taste at the brewery, so that employees and friends of the brewery can meet the makers of specialty foods, growers, ranchers, and farmers and get an appreciation for local food in Sonoma County," Davis said.

The event ties into Lagunitas' owner Tony Magee's line of farmhouse ales, brews that reflect flavors balanced for tasting with food (although not all brewed in the *saison* style most identified with that name). Magee wants the people who brew and sell beer to understand what other producers are bringing to the table.

Other farmhouse ales that are exceptionally food-friendly include Bison Brewing Company's Organic Farmhouse Ale from the Butte Creek Brewing Cooperative in Chico, and Lost Abbey Avant Garde, brewed in San Marcos.

Brewer Tomme Arthur describes the farmhouse ale style in poetical terms, but hones in on the bready malt character that makes it so versatile with food, and the slight sourness of wild yeast fermentation that make it quenching and slightly vinous. Like a good sourdough bread, a well-crafted farmhouse ale can go with just about any style of cooking, from haute cuisine to hot pulled pork sandwiches.

Barbecue and hot pulled kalua pork roasted in ti leaves are specialties of Hawaii thanks to the presence of wild pigs on the islands. Pulled pork pupus or appetizers are among the many foods offered at the Kona Brewers Festival, held in Kona on the Big Island of Hawaii each March. As one of the top food and beer festivals in the hemisphere, more than fifty restaurants and breweries from Hawaii and the mainland offer tastings of specialties, including some brews made just for the festival.

Organizers include vice president of brewing operations Rich Tucciarone and his wife, Wendy, and Rebecca Villegas of the Kona Brewing Company. The festival also includes a large homebrew competition that draws judges from as far as Chicago and New York.

For a special beer dinner preceding one Kona Brewers Festival, the Outrigger Keauhou Beach Resort's Chef Bill Trask created a barbecue menu: grilled calamari and glazed salmon, grilled buffalo, barbecued pork, and more. Kona Brewing Company's Lilikoi Wheat Ale, flavored with passionfruit; Big Island Ginger, brewed with fresh yellow ginger root; and Pipeline Porter, made with real Kona coffee; were among the beers used to prepare the dishes.

Challenged by brewing on an island, Maui Brewing Company's Garrett Marrero and brewer Thomas Kerns have expanded the business to include a canning line, because their brews have to travel such great distances. The pub menu, expanded to offer more than just sandwiches and pizzas, features a wood rotisserie and grill to make authentic smoked kalua pig. But the best use of an indigenous ingredient has to be the flaked coconut added to the CoCoNut Porter, bringing out the sweet malt taste of the dark ale. A bourbon barrel-aged version called the Black Pearl is brewed to be a bit stronger, at about 7.5 percent alcohol by volume, and paired wonderfully with chocolate brownies at the Kona Brewers Festival dinner.

Roast kalua pig is a highlight of the twelve days of Oktoberfest that Gordon Biersch celebrates in Oahu at Haleiwa Joe's Haiku Gardens restaurant. Dan Gordon said he brings wooden kegs of beer to tap at each fest dinner, "usually five ten-liter kegs, and the manager, Tim York, goes all out for the fest."

Part of beer's flavor comes from aromas. "But one of the most lacking elements of our beer culture is the lack of proper glassware to present beer," Gordon said. "The design of a glass will deliver aromatics and flavor to the nose, so if you drink beer out of a bottle, you reduce the flavor by half, and if it's too cold, you lose flavor again. I'm big advocate of serving beer within the temperature range of 40 to 44 degrees, poured into glasses designed to deliver both taste and aromatics."

73

Another advocate for better beer and food is homebrew Chef Sean Paxton, who caters feasts for the Northern California Homebrewers Festival. "It's a fun challenge," said Paxton, who has worked with chefs such as Alan Sprints, the owner/brewer of Hair of the Dog Brewery in Portland, Oregon. "The sensory experience is much richer."

"Because homebrewers are becoming more sophisticated in creating recipes and styles and substyles, each incarnation can become bolder or more refined in flavors," Paxton said. "And the lost art of barrel-aging is finally returning, so that brewing has gone almost full circle to bring back the nuances of flavor that come with aging and how those flavors make the beer so much more food-friendly."

Craft beer is a fine medium for food, because it can be bitter, sour, creamy, and textural, or bready, malty, or sweet. As a chef, the question becomes, "How do you pull out those flavors best?"

APPETIZERS

Squash Shots with Hard Cider

Savor an appetizer-sized portion of puréed squash, very attractive when poured into shot glasses, and delicious with hard cider or brown ale, says Chef Justin Scardina, of La Rana Bistro, Decorah, Iowa.

2 pounds butternut squash, cut lengthwise, seeds and pith removed

12 ounces hard cider

⅓ cup brandy

1 ounce fresh ginger, crushed

2 cinnamon sticks

4 whole cloves

2 pieces of star anise

¼ teaspoon nutmeg, preferably freshly grated, plus more for garnish
Salt and ground white pepper (optional)
Grated zest from 2 oranges, juice reserved

1. Preheat oven to 400°F. Place squash cut side down on parchment-lined sheet pan and roast 30 to 40 minutes, until soft. Remove from oven; set aside.

2. Add cider, brandy, ginger, cinnamon sticks, cloves, and anise to large saucepan placed over low heat. Stir and bring to a slow simmer for 20 minutes, reducing by almost half, and remove from heat. Strain and set aside to cool.

3. When cool enough to handle, scoop squash out of skin and chop coarsely. Place 2 cups squash into a blender and purée until smooth. Slowly add the reserved cider-brandy mixture until the desired consistency is reached. Pour into saucepan and repeat processing until all squash is puréed. Mix in ground nutmeg, stir, and taste. (Add salt and ground white pepper, if desired.) Add 2 teaspoons orange zest and 2 tablespoons reserved orange juice.

4. Bring squash purée to a simmer and remove from heat. Pour into warmed shot glasses. Garnish with fresh nutmeg on the rim of each glass.

Makes 12 appetizer servings or 6 side dish servings

Beer Pairing Suggestion:

American brown ale

Bite-Sized Stout Burgers

You may prepare the patties ahead of time and cook just before serving. Do not overcook, or the beef will lose its flavor. For simple refreshment, serve with a crisp Pilsener, or use a dry stout as a complement to the caramel and bready notes.

3 brioche rolls, thinly sliced (total of 12 slices)
1 pound ground sirloin steak, ¼-inch grind
2 tablespoons panko bread crumbs
1 tablespoon minced garlic
3 tablespoons dry stout
1 teaspoon minced rosemary
1 tablespoon minced onion
   Salt and freshly ground black pepper
1 tablespoon canola oil
   Dijon mustard
   Dill pickles
   Baby greens
2 sliced Roma tomatoes
   Sauteed sliced onions

1. Preheat oven to 350°F. Arrange brioche slices in a single layer on a baking sheet. Bake until lightly toasted, about 3 minutes. Remove from oven and set aside.

2. In a medium stainless steel or glass bowl, mix ground beef with bread crumbs, garlic, stout, rosemary, onion, and salt and pepper to taste. Chill 15 minutes. Divide and shape mixture into 12 mini-burger patties.

3. Oil and preheat a skillet over medium-high heat. Cook patties in skillet for 1 to 2 minutes per side, until browned and cooked through. Remove to a warmed platter and cover.

4. Place brioche slices on large serving tray. Top each with a dab of Dijon mustard, drained dill pickle slice, and baby greens, and place a cooked beef patty on top. Finish with a slice of Roma tomato, sautéed onions, or other desired condiments. Serve immediately.

Makes 12 servings

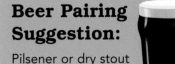

Beer Pairing Suggestion:
Pilsener or dry stout

77

Cheese-Stuffed Jumbo Shrimp with Bacon

Larry Bennett of Ommegang Brewery in Cooperstown, New York, serves these with Hennepin, a farmhouse ale.

18 slices pancetta
18 tail-on jumbo shrimp (16 to 20 count), peeled, deveined
1 cup grated Swiss cheese

1. Preheat oven to 400°F. In large skillet over medium heat, cook pancetta until half cooked but still pliable; set aside to cool.
2. Butterfly each shrimp (slice lengthwise, about two-thirds through largest section of shrimp) and fill cavity with 1 tablespoon cheese.
3. Pinch shrimp closed around stuffing and wrap with 1 strip par-cooked bacon in a spiral, securing ends with toothpick. Place on baking sheet and bake until golden, turning once, about 3 minutes per side. Do not overcook, as shrimp will continue to cook when removed from oven. Serve with Dijon *Saison* Sauce.

Makes 6 servings

Dijon *Saison* Sauce
6 ounces *saison*-style ale
1 tablespoon salted butter
2 tablespoons hot water
2 teaspoons mayonnaise
½ cup Dijon mustard
Juice of ½ lemon, about 2 tablespoons
½ teaspoon salt
½ teaspoon ground white pepper

1. Decant ale and let carbonation settle. In medium saucepan, combine ale, butter, water, mayonnaise, and mustard; bring to a simmer over medium heat. Simmer until reduced to a creamy consistency, about 30 minutes.
2. Add lemon juice and salt and pepper to taste. Serve with shrimp.

Makes 1 cup

Beer Pairing Suggestion:
Farmhouse ale

79

Lemon Thai Basil Sorbet

Chef Ian Morrison of the Royal Mile Pub, Wheaton, Maryland, enlisted the help of his mother, Joie, to develop this recipe. He paired it with Clipper City's Loose Cannon Hop[3] IPA as an intermezzo at a wonderful seafood and beer dinner. You'll need an ice cream maker to achieve the smoothest texture for the sorbet.

1 cup water
1 cup sugar
1 cup, packed, Thai basil
¾ cup fresh lemon juice
3 to 5 tablespoons lemon zest
    (about 4 large lemons)

1. In medium saucepan combine water and sugar over medium heat. Cook until sugar is dissolved. Raise heat and bring to a boil, then lower heat and simmer for 2 or 3 minutes.

2. Add basil and remove from heat; infuse for 5 to 8 minutes. Strain basil from mixture. Add lemon juice and zest. Refrigerate until very cold, at least 1 hour.

3. Add chilled mixture to ice cream maker, and freeze according to manufacturer's directions until firm.

Makes 1 pint

Beer Pairing Suggestion:

India pale or American pale ale

CHEF'S NOTE:

Thai basil is also known as royal basil and is much spicier and more fragrant than broadleaf Italian basil. You can find it at Asian markets, or substitute Italian basil and add a pinch of powdered ginger to the sorbet to capture the peppery taste.

Blue Heron Blue Cheese Spread

When Jason Noble Lee worked as the chef of the BridgePort Brewing Company pub in Portland, Oregon, he shared this recipe, which uses the classic Blue Heron Pale Ale, first introduced in 1987, as a key ingredient. It's perfect for dipping veggies, bread, or a sandwich spread with roast turkey.

---

1 pound crumbled blue cheese
1 pound cream cheese, softened
¼ cup sweet cream butter, softened
¾ cup pale ale
1 tablespoon minced tarragon
1 ½ teaspoons freshly ground black pepper
½ teaspoon Worcestershire sauce

1. Blend all ingredients in a food processor until a pasty lump forms. Divide mixture into small serving dishes and chill until ready to serve.

Makes 3 cups

Beer Pairing Suggestion:

India pale ale

81

Lager Steamed Thai Turkey and Shiitake Dumplings with Pale Ale Sweet and Sour Dipping Sauce

Chef Emil Topel of Phoenix City, Alabama, uses the classic Sierra Nevada Pale Ale to make the dipping sauce for these spicy dumplings, winners in the Cooking with Beer Challenge sponsored by the National Beer Wholesalers Association.

Dipping Sauce

- 12 ounces pale ale
- 1 teaspoon minced fresh ginger
- 1 teaspoon minced garlic
- ½ cup sweet chili sauce
- ¼ cup light brown sugar
- 1 teaspoon soy sauce

Dumplings

- 3 ½ ounces shiitake mushrooms
- 1 serrano or jalapeño chile, seeded**
- 1 ¼ pounds ground turkey
- 1 teaspoon minced garlic
  Juice from 1 lime
- ¼ cup chopped fresh cilantro
- ½ cup chopped scallions
- 2 tablespoons soy sauce
- 1 tablespoon sesame oil
- ½ teaspoon freshly ground black pepper
- ½ teaspoon ground cumin
- 1 package wonton wrappers, about 45
- ** *Use caution in handling hot peppers, and wash hands thoroughly before touching eyes*

Steaming Liquid

- 36 ounces Pilsener or amber lager
- 2 serrano chiles, halved lengthwise
- 1 lime, halved
- 3 cloves garlic, cut in half
- 1 tablespoon canola oil, divided

1. In small saucepan, make dipping sauce by bringing pale ale, ginger, and garlic to a boil and reducing liquid by half, about 5 or 6 minutes. Add chili sauce, brown sugar, and soy sauce, and bring to a slow boil for 5 minutes, stirring occasionally. Remove from heat and cool to room temperature.

2. Remove stems from mushrooms and place in food processor fitted with metal chopping blade, along with serrano or jalapeño. Pulse on HIGH until minced. Stir pepper mixture in a bowl with remaining dumpling ingredients (except wontons) and refrigerate.

Beer Pairing Suggestion:

American pale ale

82

3. In water holder of electric steamer, place lager, chiles, lime, and garlic. (Or, place ingredients in bottom of bamboo or metal steamer.) Lightly coat surface of steamer tray with canola oil.

4. Place heaping teaspoon of turkey mixture in center of wonton wrapper and pull 4 corners up to form a pouch. Pinch corners together and place in steamer tray. Repeat with other wrappers. Do not crowd the dumplings—steam in batches if necessary.

5. Steam dumplings for 20 minutes, being sure to replace liquid in steamer by adding additional beer. Oil tray again as needed to prevent dumplings from sticking. Serve with dipping sauce.

Note: Turkey mixture may be frozen for later use or formed into patties for turkey burgers using pale ale dipping sauce as a glaze.

Makes about 40 dumplings

Empanadas with Mango Salsa

Chef Brett Muellenbach of the Horse & Plow, The American Club, Kohler, Wisconsin, served these as an appetizer at a beer dinner featuring Tyranena Brewing Company of Lake Mills, Wisconsin.

Empanada Dough
- 1 cup masa harina (corn flour)
- 1 cup all-purpose flour
- 7 ounces *dunkel* or dark lager (use the beer you will be serving with this dish)
- ¼ cup vegetable shortening
- 1 large egg
- ¼ teaspoon ground turmeric
- ¼ teaspoon ground cumin
- ⅛ teaspoon cayenne pepper
  Pinch salt, or to taste

1. Combine empanada dough ingredients in a food processor, pulsing on HIGH until sticky ball forms. Remove and wrap in plastic; chill.

Filling
- 2 teaspoons olive oil
- 1 onion, finely diced
- 2 cloves garlic, minced
- 2 jalapeños, seeded and minced**
- 2 pounds lean ground beef
- 2 teaspoons ground cumin
- 1 tablespoon hot pepper sauce
- ½ cup chili sauce
- 2 tablespoons honey
- 1 beaten egg for egg wash
  Canola oil, to a depth of 1 inch in a deep Dutch oven

1. Sweat the onion, garlic, and jalapeños in the olive oil until the onion is translucent. Add the beef, and brown. Add remaining ingredients and simmer 5 minutes or until meat is no longer pink. Cool.
2. Roll the empanada dough and cut with a round cutter. Place a spoonful of filling on each round, and seal the empanada edges with a bit of egg wash, crimping dough. Bring canola oil in Dutch oven to 325°F. Deep fry empanadas on both sides until golden brown. Remove empanadas from oil and drain on parchment paper until cool enough to handle. Plate with Mango Salsa, and serve.

Makes about 2 dozen empanadas

Mango Salsa
- 2 teaspoons olive oil
- ⅓ cup red onion, finely diced
- 1 jalapeño, seeded and minced**
- 1 mango, pitted and diced
- 2 tablespoons cilantro, stems removed and leaves minced
- 1 teaspoon salt
- 1 teaspoon ground cumin
- ⅛ teaspoon cayenne pepper
- 1 tablespoon honey

Beer Pairing Suggestion:
Honey ale or wheat ale

** *Use caution in handling hot peppers, and wash hands thoroughly before touching eyes*

1. Heat olive oil in medium saucepan over medium heat; add onion and jalapeño and cook until soft. Remove from heat. Add mango, cilantro, salt, cumin, cayenne pepper, and honey. Stir until cooled. Scrape mixture into glass bowl and chill until ready to serve.

Makes about 1 cup salsa

85

SOUPS & SALADS

Bittersweet Salad

Pete Slosberg, entrepreneur and brewer, has collaborated with many chefs, among them Eddie Blyden, formerly of the 21st Amendment in San Francisco. I adapted their recipe for a bitter greens salad garnished with bittersweet chocolate by using my favorite nuts—pecans—and a tangy Wisconsin Asiago cheese.

Vinaigrette
- 1 tablespoon shallot, minced
- 2 tablespoons balsamic vinegar
- ¼ cup extra virgin olive oil
- ¼ teaspoon salt
  Freshly ground black pepper, to taste
- 1 teaspoon Dijon mustard

Salad
- 2 cups arugula
- 2 cups mixed greens
- 2 heads Belgian endive, trimmed and sliced
- 1 cup baby spinach leaves, stems removed
- ¼ cup grated Asiago cheese or crumbled *chèvre*
- ⅔ cup toasted pecans
- ⅔ cup fresh raspberries or sliced strawberries
  Salt and pepper
- 4 ounces bittersweet chocolate, shaved into curls

1. In large bowl, mix together vinaigrette ingredients, whisking well until emulsified. Add greens, cheese, pecans, and berries, and toss.
2. Divide among 4 plates. Season with salt and pepper and sprinkle with shaved chocolate.

Makes 4 servings

Beer Pairing Suggestion:

Belgian-style *tripel* ale

87

Brickskeller Carrot Ginger Curry Soup

Diane Alexander of the Brickskeller, Washington, D.C., shares this recipe developed for a Brooklyn Brewery beer dinner. Garrett Oliver paired the soup with Brooklyner Weisse and "it was one of his favorite pairings," Alexander said.

15 large carrots, chopped
3- inch piece of ginger, chopped
1¹/₂ quarts defatted chicken stock
¹/₃ cup dark brown sugar (or more to taste)
1 tablespoon hot Madras curry powder
2 teaspoons mild curry powder
Pinch garam masala
1¹/₂ cups heavy cream
Salt and ground white pepper

1. Place prepared carrots and ginger in a large 3-quart saucepan fitted with a lid. Add chicken stock and enough water to cover carrots and place over medium-high heat. Cover and bring to a boil; stir occasionally.

2. When carrots are completely tender, remove from heat and add brown sugar, curry powders, and garam masala. Use a stick immersion blender to purée cooked carrots with cooking liquid in the pot, or purée in batches in a standard blender. For safety, fill blender container only half full, and use a folded tea towel to hold the blender lid in place when puréeing the hot liquid. Steam may push the blender lid off if not held in place.

3. Return saucepan to stove, over low heat. Warm cream; slowly stir into puréed carrots to reach desired consistency. Taste and adjust seasonings with salt and ground white pepper to taste.

Makes 6 to 8 servings

Beer Pairing Suggestion:

Hefeweiss or American pale wheat ale

CHEF'S NOTE:

Garam masala is an Indian spice blend of ground cloves, cinnamon, cardamom, coriander, and black pepper. You may substitute a pinch of each of those spices if you can't find the premixed garam masala in Asian food sections of large supermarkets or ethnic groceries. You can make a low-cal vegan version of this soup with vegetable broth instead of chicken stock, and almond milk instead of cream.

88

Free State Brewing Company Fig and Balsamic Salad

Rick Martin, chef at Free State Brewing Company in Lawrence, Kansas, demonstrated this recipe at the culinary demo stage at the Great American Beer Festival, with rave reviews from the crowd.

15 dried black mission figs
1 pound baby arugula or mixed mesclun greens
3 tablespoons olive oil or basil oil
Sea salt
6 ounces crumbled Maytag blue cheese or similar blue cheese
½ cup toasted walnuts
6 ounces balsamic vinegar reduced to 2 ounces syrup, at room temperature
Freshly ground black pepper

1. Hold figs by the stem and slice into thin rings; discard stem. Set aside.
2. In large salad bowl, toss arugula greens with about 3 tablespoons oil until slightly coated, and sprinkle with salt to taste.
3. Arrange a tight mound of greens on 4 salad plates, then sprinkle each with figs, cheese, and walnuts. With a small spoon, drizzle a ribbon of balsamic reduction over each salad. Top with a grind of black pepper, if desired.

Makes 4 servings

Beer Pairing Suggestion:
American porter

89

Épluche-Culotte *Tripel* Marinated Grilled Vegetable Salad

Épluche-Culotte is a *tripel*-style ale brewed at Midnight Sun Brewing Company, Anchorage, Alaska. Brewer Ben Johnson says that "the smoky edge of the grill, blended with spices in the ale, makes this a perfect dish for a summer meal."

1 medium eggplant, sliced lengthwise

1 large zucchini, peeled and sliced lengthwise

1 large yellow squash, sliced lengthwise

1 large red bell pepper, seeded and sliced

1 large red onion, sliced at least ½-inch thick

½ cup *tripel*

¼ cup olive oil

2 cloves garlic, minced

1 teaspoon minced fresh thyme

½ teaspoon ground coriander

1 teaspoon lemon juice
Salt and freshly ground black pepper

3 large Roma tomatoes, diced

1. Place eggplant, zucchini, yellow squash, red bell pepper, and onion in a large bowl. Mix beer, olive oil, garlic, thyme, coriander, lemon juice, salt, and pepper in a blender on HIGH until emulsified. Pour over vegetables and toss to coat. Cover and chill 1 hour.

2. Prepare grill to medium-hot. Drain vegetables and reserve marinade. Grill vegetables in a grill basket or on a grill screen until just tender. When cool enough to handle, chop cooked veggies and place back into bowl with marinade. Add tomatoes and adjust seasoning with salt and pepper. Serve warm.

Makes 4 servings

Beer Pairing Suggestion:

Belgian-style *tripel*

Tyranena Three Beaches Blonde Buttermilk Dressing

Chef Brett Muellenbach of Wisconsin's Horse & Plow uses Tyranena's Three Beaches Blonde Ale to make this creamy dressing, which tastes wonderful on a slaw made of grated carrot, thinly sliced red cabbage, and baby spinach.

½ cup blonde ale
½ cup buttermilk
¼ cup apple cider vinegar
1 tablespoon pasteurized liquid egg
2 tablespoons Dijon mustard
1 small shallot
1 garlic clove
1 teaspoon salt
1 teaspoon freshly ground black pepper
1 teaspoon celery seed (optional)
1½ cups grapeseed (or safflower) oil

1. Place beer, buttermilk, vinegar, egg, mustard, shallot, garlic, salt, pepper, and celery seed (if using with slaw) in blender. Cover and bring the blender to high speed.
2. With the lid firmly in place to prevent splashes, carefully remove the cap. Slowly drizzle the oil into the opening of the blender lid until the mixture is creamy and fully incorporated. Taste and adjust seasonings. Use dressing on root vegetable slaw or spinach salad.

Makes about 3 cups dressing

CHEF'S NOTE:

Muellenbach advises that his recipe works best if you own a powerful blender with a sharp mixing blade and a removable cap inset into the lid. If not, simply mince the garlic and shallot and combine everything in a bowl and whisk to emulsify.

91

Jicama, Apple, Fennel, Sweet Pepper, and Orange Salad with an Éphémère Ale and Mint Vinaigrette

Brew Chef Tim Schafer says, "Jicama is a tuber, much like a potato with the crispness of an apple. The marriage of these ingredients makes not only a colorful salad, it make a wonderfully crunchy accompaniment to tender barbecue. Éphémère is an apple-scented ale made by the great Unibroue brewery in Chambly, outside Montreal, Quebec."

Salad

- 1 small jicama, peeled and thinly sliced
- 1 Granny Smith apple, cored, seeds removed, and thinly sliced
- 1 Rome or Red Delicious apple, cored, seeds removed, and thinly sliced
- 1 small bulb fennel, greens trimmed, split, and thinly sliced
- 1 sweet red bell pepper, cored, seeds removed, and thinly sliced
- ½ small red onion, thinly sliced
- 2 navel oranges, seeds removed and segmented

Dressing

- 2 ounces apple cider vinegar
- ½ teaspoon Dijon mustard
- 10 fresh mint leaves, sliced
- 4 ounces olive oil
- 2 ounces apple ale or hard cider
- 2 teaspoons sugar
  Kosher salt
  Freshly ground black pepper

1. Place jicama, apples, fennel, pepper, and onion into mixing bowl; add orange segments and set aside.
2. To make dressing, blend vinegar, mustard, mint, oil, ale, and salt and pepper to taste in a blender, holding lid in place with folded tea towel. Toss salad with dressing and serve immediately.

Makes 6 servings

Note: If Éphémère is not available, use 2 ounces of mild ale mixed with a splash of apple juice concentrate, or hard cider.

Beer Pairing Suggestion:
American spiced strong ale or apple ale

93

Granite City's Strawberry Chicken Salad

Art Nermoe, director of the culinary center for the fast-growing pub chain Granite City Food & Brewery, which is head-quarted in St. Cloud, Minnesota, shares one of the brewmaster's favorite recipes.

1 pound boneless skinless, chicken breasts
3 tablespoons soy sauce
2 tablespoon mirin
3 cups Romaine lettuce
3 cups mixed spring greens or mesclun lettuce
1 cup fresh sliced strawberries
½ cup canned pineapple, drained and chopped
½ cup canned Mandarin oranges, drained
⅓ cup fresh red onion, thinly sliced
1 medium peeled and seeded cucumber, halved lengthwise and sliced
⅓ cup shredded carrot

3 large whole pieces of leaf lettuce
2 ounces sliced toasted almonds

1. Flatten chicken breasts with a meat pounder or rolling pin. Grill chicken over medium heat, turning twice for cross-hatched grill marks, and brush with soy sauce mixed with mirin during last 5 minutes of cooking. Cook until internal temperature reaches 160°F. Set aside to cool.

2. Place chopped Romaine, spring greens, strawberries, pineapple, Mandarin oranges, red onion, cucumber, and carrot in large, stainless steel mixing bowl. Add Strawberry Vinaigrette to taste. Toss ingredients until evenly coated with dressing.

3. Line both ends of a medium-sized oval platter with leaf lettuce and fill with tossed salad. Arrange sliced chicken on top of salad. Garnish with toasted almonds.

Makes 4 servings

Strawberry Vinaigrette
½ cup melted strawberry fruit-only spread (no sugar added)
6 fresh strawberries, hulled
⅓ cup raspberry vinegar
⅓ cup olive oil
1 teaspoon minced shallot
Pinch sugar
¼ teaspoon salt
Pinch ground white pepper

1. Place all ingredients in blender; cover and pulse on HIGH until emulsified.

Makes 1 ¼ cups

Beer Pairing Suggestion:
Unfiltered wheat ale or hefeweiss

94

Garlic Chicken Rail Mail Rye Split Pea Soup

Chef Will Deason of the Willimantic Brewing Company and Main Street Café in Willimantic, Connecticut, says the flavor of this thick soup improves on the second day.

1 pound dried split green peas
3 ½- to 4-pound roasting chicken
5 cups water
¼ cup olive oil
3 tablespoons minced garlic
3 tablespoons unsalted butter
2 ounces spicy chorizo or hot Italian sausage
¼ pound finely diced celery
¼ pound finely diced carrots
2 teaspoons minced fresh thyme
¼ pound finely diced white onions
Dash of hot pepper sauce
Bouquet garni—a small piece of cheesecloth containing 2 medium bay leaves, parsley stems, 3 whole cloves, and 5 tri-color peppercorns, wrapped and tied at the top
4 cups water
1 quart lightly hopped rye ale
Salt and pepper
Juice of 1 lemon

1. Rinse peas in a colander and pick out any debris. Soak in water to cover for 8 hours or overnight.
2. Preheat oven to 375°F. Rub chicken with olive oil and 2 tablespoons garlic, place in roasting pan and cook 1 hour. Remove from oven and let cool. When cool enough to handle, pull off chicken meat, reserving bones and skin for broth. Reserve chicken pan drippings. Dice meat into $1/2$-inch pieces. Make chicken broth by placing bones and scraps in a large pot with 5 cups water. Bring to a boil and cook 10 minutes. Strain before use.
3. Melt butter with reserved chicken drippings in a large soup pot set over low heat, and add chorizo or hot sausage, celery, carrots, thyme, onions, remaining tablespoon garlic, and hot pepper sauce. Sauté 5 minutes, stirring occasionally. Add the bouquet garni, peas, and chicken broth; turn heat to medium and bring to a boil. Skim foam from the pot, reduce heat to low and simmer 1 hour. When peas are tender, add the chopped chicken and ale to reach desired consistency, and simmer 30 minutes. Remove the bouquet garni. Add salt and pepper to taste. Stir in lemon juice and serve.

Makes 6 to 8 servings

Beer Pairing Suggestion:
American rye ale

95

Ommegang Ale Onion Soup

Larry Bennett of Ommegang Brewery in Cooperstown, New York, shares this recipe for a caramelized onion soup, topped with toasted cheese and bread, perfect for pairing with the brewery's Hennepin farmhouse ale.

8 tablespoons salted butter
6 pounds small yellow onions, thinly sliced
1 tablespoon minced garlic
1 tablespoon dark brown sugar
2 quarts beef or veal stock
1 tablespoon minced fresh parsley
1 teaspoon dried thyme
2 bay leaves
Sea salt and freshly ground black pepper
8 ounces Belgian-style *dubbel* or *quadrupel* ale
8 slices baguette or similar crusty white bread
8 ounces Gruyère cheese, grated

1. Melt butter in large Dutch oven or deep saucepan over medium-high heat. Add onions and sauté 30 minutes, stirring occasionally. As onions soften and start to caramelize, add garlic and sugar and stir. Add 2$\frac{1}{2}$ cups broth, $\frac{1}{2}$ cup at a time, stirring after each addition. Add remainder of broth with parsley, thyme, and bay leaves.

2. Reduce heat and simmer 20 minutes; add salt and pepper to taste. In separate pot, simmer ale until warmed. Slowly stir warmed ale into soup. Taste and adjust seasonings.

3. Sprinkle toast slices with grated Gruyère, salt, and pepper and place in hot oven or under broiler. When cheese is melted, divide soup among 8 bowls and serve with toasted cheese slice placed on top.

Makes 8 servings

Beer Pairing Suggestion:

Belgian-style brown ale or farmhouse ale

96

Spicy Lentil Salad

The Spoetzl Brewery has participated in numerous cooking classes, and this recipe pairs well with the Shiner Bock. The salad is healthful and simple to make, so don't be put off by the long list of ingredients.

1 (16-ounce) bag dried lentils
3 cups vegetable broth
3 cups water
2 tablespoons olive oil
2 cups diced sweet onion
3 tablespoons chopped garlic
1 cup diced roasted red bell peppers
1 cup diced plum tomatoes
1 cup diced roasted green chiles (such as pasilla chiles)
Juice of 1 lemon
1 teaspoon freshly ground black pepper
½ teaspoon salt
1 teaspoon ground chile powder
1 teaspoon smoked paprika (see p. 197)
¼ teaspoon ground cumin
¼ teaspoon powdered oregano
8 Romaine lettuce leaves
3 tablespoons minced fresh cilantro or parsley (optional)
1 tablespoon grated lemon zest (optional)

1. Rinse and pick over lentils. Place vegetable broth, water, and lentils in 2-quart saucepan; cover and bring to a boil over high heat. Reduce heat to medium; cook 15 to 20 minutes, stirring often, until tender.

2. Place large skillet over medium heat and add oil; stir in onion and garlic. Cook and stir 3 minutes; reduce heat to low. Add bell pepper, tomatoes, and chiles. Cook and stir 3 minutes, and remove from heat.

3. Drain lentils and return to saucepan. Stir onion mixture, lemon juice, and spices into lentils. Cook and stir over low heat, until mixed well.

4. Remove lentils from heat and let cool to room temperature. Spoon into lettuce leaf cups. Garnish with cilantro or parsley and lemon zest, if desired.

Makes 8 servings

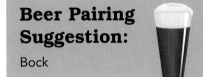

Beer Pairing Suggestion:
Bock

97

Salad of Celery Hearts, Pancetta, Tart Apples, Hazelnuts, and Blue Cheese

Brugge Brasserie of Indianapolis shares this nutty, crunchy salad, developed by Chef Greg Hardesty of Elements Restaurant, also of Indianapolis. Ted Miller, managing partner and brewer, says: "We chose to pair this salad with our Sacre Fleur *saison*. Chef Greg and I thought the use of lavender in our *saison*, along with its natural spiciness, would complement this salad. The acidity of the ale cuts through the pancetta, and the earthiness stands up to the blue cheese without much struggle."

Vinaigrette

- 3 tablespoons rice wine vinegar or Champagne vinegar
- 1 teaspoon Dijon mustard
  Pinch salt
- ¼ cup hazelnut oil
- ¼ cup extra virgin olive oil

1. Place vinegar, mustard, and salt in bowl, whisk oils into vinegar until emulsified; set aside.

Salad

- ¼ cup pancetta, cooked until crisp, drained on paper towel
- 6 white celery stalks from inside bunch, sliced ⅛-inch thick
- 6 ounces blue cheese, softened at room temperature
- 1 large tart green apple, sliced thin on mandoline or with a sharp knife
- 1 large shallot, finely chopped
- 8 basil leaves, sliced thin
- ¼ cup whole hazelnuts, toasted and coarsely chopped
- ½ pound baby arugula leaves, stems removed
  Salt and pepper

1. Place all salad ingredients in a bowl and toss with just enough Vinaigrette to coat salad. You may not need all the dressing. Taste and adjust seasonings, then divide evenly between four salad plates.

Makes 4 servings

Beer Pairing Suggestion:

Saison-style ale

98

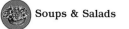

Garlic Cheddar & Stone Ruination IPA Soup

Creamy and intensely garlicky, this soup, as presented at the Stone World Bistro & Gardens in Escondido, California, tastes wonderful with a glass of Stone Ruination IPA.

⅓ cup canola oil
⅓ cup all-purpose flour
½ cup finely chopped yellow onions
½ cup minced garlic
3 cups vegetable stock
10 ounces India pale ale, at room temperature
1 cup heavy cream, warmed
½ cup roasted and mashed garlic (3 bulbs garlic, coated in oil, wrapped in foil, and baked at 325°F until tender, about 30 minutes)
2 teaspoons kosher or finely ground sea salt
1½ teaspoons ground white pepper
1 teaspoon hot Hungarian paprika
2½ pounds white cheddar cheese, grated, at room temperature

1. In a large saucepan over medium heat, whisk together oil and flour. Cook and stir until a paste forms and mixture begins to bubble and turns golden. Add onions and garlic and cook until golden roux is formed.
2. Slowly add vegetable stock by the half cupful, followed by ale and cream, whisking constantly. Whisk in roasted garlic, salt, pepper, and paprika. Reduce heat to low and bring to simmer.
3. Remove pan from heat. Whisk in cheese, about ½ cup at a time, whisking after each addition until smooth. If soup seems too thick, thin with a bit of warmed ale to reach desired consistency. Serve immediately.

Makes 6 to 8 servings

Beer Pairing Suggestion:

American Imperial India pale ale

100

Tuscarora Mill Asiago Soup with Smoked Ham

Shawn Malone of Tuscarora Mill Restaurant in Leesburg, Virginia, offers a fragrant Asiago cheese soup with smoked ham, which would be delicious with shredded American country ham or in a pinch, pan-fried crumbles of sage and pepper country sausage.

1 white onion, diced
3 stalks celery, diced
1 tablespoon salted butter
½ teaspoon sherry vinegar
24 ounces Belgian-style wheat ale, divided
⅓ cup dry sherry
4 cups chicken broth
3 cloves garlic, toasted in 1 tablespoon olive oil
1 teaspoon dried thyme
Pinch cayenne pepper
3 bay leaves
2 cups heavy cream
2 large russet potatoes, peeled and diced
1 ½ cups grated Asiago cheese, at room temperature
½ cup grated Parmesan, at room temperature
1 ½ cups diced smoked ham

1. In large saucepan over medium heat, cook onion and celery in butter and vinegar for 2 minutes. Add 12 ounces ale, sherry, chicken broth, garlic, thyme, cayenne, bay leaves, cream, and potatoes. Bring to a simmer and cook until potatoes are tender, about 25 minutes. Remove from heat and use a stick immersion blender to purée soup. Add more of the reserved ale to reach desired consistency. Let cool to lukewarm.

2. Pour soup through mesh strainer and return to soup pot placed over medium-low heat. Bring mixture to just a simmer, and, by the quarter-cupful, slowly stir in grated Asiago and Parmesan, and 1½ cups diced ham. Taste and adjust seasonings. When cheese is melted and ham is heated through, serve immediately. Do not boil, or cheese will curdle.

Makes 6 servings

Beer Pairing Suggestion:

Belgian-style *witbier*

101

Chinoise Chicken Salad with Ginger Beer Vinaigrette

Chef Larry Perdido of the Moonshine Patio Bar & Grill in Austin, Texas, shares one of his favorite salads, which is accompanied by a tangy Ginger Beer Vinaigrette. Try it with a bock or a spicy ale brewed with lemongrass or star anise.

1 pound boneless chicken breast
Vegetable oil
½ teaspoon salt
½ teaspoon freshly ground black pepper
¼ cup hoisin sauce
4 cups Napa cabbage, julienned
1 cup sugar snap peas, blanched and shucked
1 cup red bell pepper, seeded and cut into 1-inch strips
½ cup white onion, julienned
1 cup Mandarin orange segments
½ cup dry-roasted almonds
2 teaspoons fresh tarragon leaves
2 teaspoons fresh cilantro leaves
2 teaspoons basil leaves, cut into slivers
1 tablespoon white sesame seeds, lightly toasted
1 tablespoon black sesame seeds

1. Prepare grill. Clean chicken, trim off excess skin, rub lightly with oil, and season with mixture of salt and pepper. Cook over medium heat, turning twice to obtain cross-hatch of grill marks. Brush with hoisin sauce for last 3 minutes of cooking. Remove from heat and let cool. Chop chicken into bite-sized slices.

2. In large bowl, toss cabbage, peas, pepper, onion, oranges, almonds, and herbs. Toss with Ginger Beer Vinaigrette, as desired. Divide among 4 serving plates. Garnish with sesame seeds and serve immediately.

Makes 4 servings

Ginger Beer Vinaigrette

1 tablespoon freshly grated ginger
½ cup ginger beer or bock
1 tablespoon minced shallot
¾ cup rice wine vinegar
1 teaspoon Dijon mustard
2 ounces low-sodium soy sauce
1 tablespoon honey
1 ½ cups canola oil
¼ cup toasted sesame oil
Sea salt and freshly ground pepper

1. In small saucepan over low heat, mix ginger and beer; simmer and reduce by one-third, about 15 minutes. Let cool.

2. In a medium bowl, whisk ginger, shallot, vinegar, mustard, soy sauce, honey, and reduced beer. Whisk in canola oil until emulsified, then whisk in sesame oil. Taste and add salt and pepper if needed. Whisk until emulsified before tossing into salad.

Makes 2 cups

Beer Pairing Suggestion:

Spiced ale or bock

CHEF'S NOTE:

Black sesame seeds, often used as a garnish for seafood and sushi, can be found in the Asian food sections of large supermarkets, in Asian ethnic markets, and by mail order. If not available, substitute toasted sesame seeds.

EGGS, PASTA & SAUCES

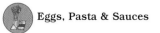

Sunday Mornin' Haystack French Toast

Colorado craft beer maven Jeff Mendel prepares this with Left Hand Brewing Company's Haystack Wheat, but any unfiltered wheat ale with citrus hops character may be used to prepare this for brunch.

12 ounces bottle-conditioned wheat ale
6 eggs
¼ cup whole milk
½ teaspoon ground cinnamon
¼ teaspoon vanilla extract
¼ teaspoon ground nutmeg
6 slices bread (any type)
Nonstick cooking spray (preferably canola oil)
½ cup powdered sugar
Warmed maple syrup, blueberries, strawberries, raspberries for garnish (optional)

1. Let bottle of ale sit out at room temperature at least 6 hours to allow the yeast to settle to the bottom of the bottle. Carefully decant the first 10 ounces (1¼ cups) of the bottle into 2 glasses and reserve. The remaining 2 ounces in the bottle should be very yeasty and opaque. Swirl the bottle to mix the yeast.
2. Combine the eggs, yeasty ale, milk, cinnamon, vanilla, and nutmeg in a mixing bowl. Whip with an electric beater until the mixture is smooth and aerated, with lots of bubbles.
3. Place bread slices in large jelly roll pan with a deep rim and pour egg mixture over it. Turn bread to coat evenly and let soak until almost all of the mixture is absorbed. Prepare a greased griddle or large skillet with 2 to 3 sprays of oil, and place over medium heat. Use a spatula to place soaked bread on hot griddle. Cook and turn bread pieces 2 or 3 times until both sides are golden brown.
4. Arrange French toast on warmed plate. Pour powdered sugar into a sifter or strainer and tap over toast. Top with syrup and fruit to taste.

Makes 4 to 6 servings

Beer Pairing Suggestion:
American pale wheat ale

104

Brew Chef Beernaise Sauce

Beernaise is "Brew Chef" Tim Schafer's rendition of one of the classic "mother" sauces, *béarnaise*. The reduction of beer and vinegar gives this versatile sauce a wonderful aroma and flavor. Serve slightly warm, but be sure not to overheat or the sauce will curdle. Spoon over steamed vegetables, eggs, or grilled beef tenderloin, as Schafer does at his Lake Norman restaurant, Sherrills Ford, North Carolina, and choose a pairing to suit the ensemble.

½ cup pale ale
1 ½ teaspoons malt vinegar
1 tablespoon minced shallot
3 large egg yolks
4 ounces unsalted butter, melted and cooled to lukewarm (must be liquid)
1 teaspoon tarragon leaves, chopped
¼ teaspoon hot pepper sauce
⅛ teaspoon Worcestershire sauce
½ teaspoon kosher salt
Pinch ground white pepper
Lemon juice (optional)

1. In small saucepot over low heat, simmer pale ale, vinegar, and shallots until reduced by half. Set aside.

2. In the top of a double boiler over simmering water, whisk egg yolks until pale and slightly thick. Using ladle, slowly drizzle melted butter, a third at a time, into the yolk mixture, whisking constantly. Be sure the mixture is smooth and emulsified before adding more butter. Use a spatula to scrape sides of pot.

3. Whisk in the beer-shallot mixture, hot pepper sauce, and Worcestershire sauce. Season with salt and white pepper, and serve immediately. To add a slightly different flavor, add several drops of lemon juice to the sauce.

Makes 1 scant cup

Creamy Cavatappi with Fresh Corn, Fennel and Wild Mushrooms

Chef Bruce Paton of the Cathedral Hill Hotel in San Francisco pairs this warm, creamy pasta salad with Twist of Fate Bitter from Moonlight Brewing of Santa Rosa, California. You could pair it with your favorite extra-special bitter.

1 tablespoon olive oil
1/2 teaspoon red pepper flakes
2 tablespoons minced garlic
2 cups fresh corn kernels (about 6 ears)
2 bulbs fennel, sliced very thin
1 cup shiitake mushrooms, trimmed and diced
1 cup cremini or chanterelle mushrooms, trimmed and diced
1/4 teaspoon ground fennel
  Salt and ground black pepper
1 1/2 cups light cream
1 pound cavatappi pasta, cooked *al dente*
1 medium red bell pepper, minced

1. Heat oil in a large saucepan over medium heat, add pepper flakes and garlic and cook, stirring often, 2 minutes. Add corn and sliced fennel, stir well, and cook 5 minutes. Add mushrooms, ground fennel, and salt and pepper to taste, and cook until tender, about 5 minutes.

2. Add cream and bring to a boil. Reduce heat and simmer 20 minutes. Drain pasta and toss with vegetables and cream. Garnish with red bell pepper and freshly ground black pepper.

Makes 4 to 6 servings

Beer Pairing Suggestion:

Extra-special bitter or pale ale

106

Smoky Haystack Omelet

Jeff Mendel, craft brew maven for Left Hand Brewing Company in Longmont, Colorado, suggests the brewery's Haystack Wheat ale for this easy omelet, but you can substitute any unfiltered wheat ale with spicy yeast notes.

12 ounces bottle-conditioned wheat ale
3 large eggs
1 large egg white
2 tablespoons milk
¼ teaspoon freshly ground black pepper
Several drops hot pepper sauce
1 tablespoon minced chives
1 tablespoon salted butter
2 slices Black Forest smoked ham
¼ cup shredded Gruyère cheese
¼ cup shredded smoked Gouda cheese

1. Let bottle sit at room temperature to allow yeast to settle to the bottom. Carefully decant 11 ounces into 2 glasses and set aside. The remaining ale in the bottle should be very yeasty and opaque. Swirl to mix.

2. Combine the eggs, yeasty ale, milk, pepper, hot pepper sauce, and chives in a mixing bowl. Whip until the mixture is smooth and aerated. Place butter in medium skillet over medium heat. When butter melts, add the egg mixture.

3. When the eggs bubble around the edges, lift the edges with a spatula and swirl the skillet to let runny eggs set. Add the ham and cheeses. When the cheeses begin to melt, fold the omelet in half and flip. Cook until light golden brown on both sides and cheese is melted. Serve on warmed plates with toast.

Makes 2 servings

Beer Pairing Suggestion:

Pale wheat ale

108

White Bean Custards with Mirror Pond Pale Ale Caramelized Onion Vinaigrette

A make-ahead appetizer or brunch dish to impress guests, adapted from a recipe served at Deschutes Brewery beer dinners. For ease, prepare the custards ahead and reheat just before serving. You'll need 6 ramekins and a large casserole dish to bake the custards.

1 can (15.8 ounces) white beans, drained
2 tablespoons roasted garlic
1 ½ cups heavy cream
  Freshly ground black pepper
½ teaspoon freshly grated nutmeg
3 large eggs
  Pinch salt
1 Meyer lemon, zest grated and pulp juiced
1 cup diced sweet onion (such as Maui, Vidalia, or Walla Walla)
6 ounces pale ale
2 tablespoons Dijon mustard
½ cup extra virgin olive oil
1 tablespoon honey
3 ounces thinly sliced pancetta
5 cups mixed baby greens, baby spinach, and watercress, stems removed

6 ramekins, 6-ounce capacity, lightly buttered

Large casserole dish with deep rim

1. Purée the white beans with roasted garlic in a food processor until smooth; set aside. Preheat oven to 300°F. Fill teakettle with 6 cups water and bring to a simmer.
2. Heat cream, ¼ teaspoon freshly ground pepper, and nutmeg in a small saucepan over low heat until steaming. Remove from heat. Mix ½ cup cream mixture with white beans in food processor on HIGH until smooth; set aside.
3. In a large bowl, whisk the eggs with a pinch of salt until pale yellow and fairly thick. Slowly add the remaining hot cream mixture to the eggs, ¼ cup at a time, stirring constantly. Add bean purée and whisk well. Push mixture through a mesh sieve for perfectly smooth custard. Add the grated lemon zest and pour into 6 lightly buttered 6-ounce custard cups or ramekins.
4. Place the cups in a deep baking dish and add hot water so it reaches halfway up the outside of the cups. Bake until the custard is set (it should jiggle slightly in the middle) about 30 minutes. Remove and chill.

Beer Pairing Suggestion:

Pale ale

CHEF'S NOTE:

Roasted garlic is easy to make. Rub a head of garlic with olive oil to coat, wrap in foil, and place in a toaster oven on MEDIUM heat to bake 20 minutes, or until tender. Cooking time will vary according to the size of the garlic cloves, so bake a bit longer if the cloves are very large. Remove from oven and when cool enough to handle, squeeze the cooked garlic out from the papery skins. Place in a resealable container and keep chilled; use within 1 week.

109

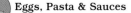

5. To make vinaigrette, sauté the onion with pinch of salt in 2 tablespoons olive oil (reserve remaining oil) in large skillet over low heat until caramelized. Add mustard, honey, lemon juice, salt, and pepper to taste. Deglaze pan with pale ale, stirring well to mix ingredients. Let cool and scrape mixture into a 1-quart bowl. Slowly whisk in remaining olive oil until smooth. Taste and adjust with salt and pepper if desired.

6. Sauté pancetta until crisp in a nonstick skillet over medium heat. Drain on paper towels and chop into bite-sized bits. In a large bowl, toss mixed greens with 1 cup vinaigrette; divide evenly between 6 plates. Invert ramekin of custard onto center of each plate. Sprinkle crispy pancetta over each custard. Drizzle with remaining vinaigrette, if desired.

Makes 6 servings

Piece Pasta

Piece Brewery & Pizzeria in Chicago, serves an appetizer dip with fresh diced tomatoes and spinach in a garlicky mozzarella alfredo sauce. I adapted it to make a topping for pasta.

3 tablespoons salted butter
2 tablespoons minced garlic
2 tablespoons minced onion
1 teaspoon flour
1¼ cups heavy cream
¼ teaspoon cayenne pepper, or to taste
⅓ cup grated Parmesan cheese, room temperature
1 cup grated mozzarella cheese, room temperature
4 cups cooked pasta
1 teaspoon olive oil
2 cups chopped spinach
1 cup chopped plum tomatoes

1. Melt butter in medium saucepan over low heat. Add garlic, onion and flour, and simmer 1 minute. Slowly stir in cream and cayenne pepper, whisking well. Bring to a simmer, cooking until onion is tender.
2. Reduce heat and add the Parmesan cheese. Simmer and stir until melted. When sauce thickens, add the mozzarella cheese by the ¼ cupful, whisking after each addition.
3. Prepare pasta according to package directions while sauce cooks. Drain pasta, and toss with olive oil, chopped spinach, and tomatoes. Cover the pasta pot and let spinach wilt from the heat of the cooked pasta.
4. Divide pasta and vegetables into 4 warmed serving bowls and top each with about ½ cup mozzarella cream sauce. Serve immediately.

Makes 4 servings

Beer Pairing Suggestion:
American pale ale

111

FISH & SEAFOOD

Bacon-Wrapped Bluefish with Brown Ale Hot Sauce

This recipe is adapted from one by Chef Brian Morin of Toronto's beerbistro restaurant. While you could also make this with shrimp, I preferred the stronger taste of bluefish with the intense heat of the Brown Ale Hot Sauce. Choose a blonde ale for pure refreshment, or a strong dark ale to highlight the peppers.

2 pounds bluefish, cleaned and boned
1 pound sliced bacon (applewood smoked is best), cut in half lengthwise
2 tablespoons garlic, chopped
1 ½ cups Brown Ale Hot Sauce
1 lemon, cut into wedges

8 short wooden skewers, soaked in water

1. Preheat oven to 300°F. Trim bluefish into bite-sized chunks and chill.
2. Arrange bacon on a parchment-lined baking sheet. Lightly par-cook bacon in oven 10 minutes, until fat is translucent but slices are still flexible. Remove from oven and let cool.
3. When bacon is cool enough to handle, wrap each chunk of fish in half a slice, and thread several chunks through each wooden skewer. Grill on medium-high heat until bacon is crisp and fish is just cooked. Serve with lemon wedges and Brown Ale Hot Sauce.

Makes 4 to 6 servings

Brown Ale Hot Sauce
¼ cup vegetable oil
1 yellow onion, diced
1 tablespoon minced garlic
2 tablespoons tomato paste
1 cup habañero peppers, roasted and puréed**
¼ cup dark brown sugar
Juice of 2 limes
¼ cup malt vinegar
2 cups Belgian-style brown ale
¼ cup Dijon mustard
½ cup brown raisins

** *Use caution in handling hot peppers, and wash hands thoroughly before touching eyes. To roast the peppers, brush with canola oil and broil until soft and golden. For less intense heat, remove the seeds.*

1. Place oil in large saucepan over medium heat, and sweat onions until soft. Add garlic and cook for several minutes. Add tomato paste and cook 2 minutes.
2. Add remaining ingredients, bring to boil and skim. Reduce heat and simmer until thickened. Strain and cool.

Beer Pairing Suggestion:

Blonde ale or Belgian-style strong dark ale

Makes about 2 cups

113

Wood-Grilled Trout with Mission Fig Compound Butter

The Stone World Bistro & Gardens serves wood-grilled trout with black mission fig butter to make it taste even milder and sweeter. Mission figs are available in the dried fruit section of most large supermarkets. Untreated wood planks for grilling are available in grilling and barbecue sections of hardware stores as well as some supermarkets. CEO Greg Koch suggests pairing the trout with a pint of Stone IPA or an amber ale.

10 dried mission figs, stems removed and coarsely chopped
1 stick (½ cup) butter
Pinch ground cardamom
½- inch piece ginger root, minced
1 teaspoon sea salt
½ teaspoon grated lemon zest
2 tablespoons extra virgin olive oil
Coarse salt and black pepper
4 trout, cleaned, skin on, 6 to 8 ounces each
Fresh herbs, such as parsley and chives, for garnish

2 large wood planks

1. Place figs in food processor and pulse on HIGH until pasty. Melt butter in large skillet. Add cardamom, ginger root, salt, and zest. Sauté over low heat until ginger is tender. Add chopped figs and stir well. Simmer 1 minute and remove from heat. Set aside.

2. Prepare grill for medium heat. Soak wood planks in water for 15 minutes. Rinse trout fillets and rub with oil and salt and pepper to taste. Place 2 trout on each plank and arrange on grill. Cover and cook 5 minutes until the wood begins to char. Turn fillets over, and cook 2 to 3 minutes more, depending on thickness of fish and planks. Do not overcook.

3. Remove trout and planks from grill. Arrange trout on a serving platter with fresh herbs to garnish. Spoon 2 tablespoons of fig compound butter onto each fillet and serve immediately.

Makes 4 servings

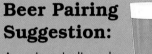

Beer Pairing Suggestion:

American India pale ale or amber ale

115

Grilled Scallops with Roasted Shallots, Vermouth, and Shiitake Sauce, and Tomato Couscous

Chef Marcel Lavallee of Dogfish Head's pub in Rehoboth Beach, Delaware, shares this recipe. It looks impressive, assembled in several stages, and tastes even more divine, yet requires little more effort than a timer. Choose large sea scallops graded "U-10," which means that there should be about 10 scallops per pound. Lavallee recommends serving the dish with Dogfish Head Pangaea, as its spicy notes meld with the dish's sweet vermouth flavor, but taste-testers also liked *witbier* as a pairing.

Roasted Shallots

18 medium shallots, whole and
    unpeeled
½ cup olive oil
1 tablespoon sea salt
1 tablespoon freshly ground
    black pepper

1. Preheat oven to 350°F. In large mixing bowl, toss shallots with olive oil until coated; season with salt and pepper. Arrange on sheet pan and bake until soft, about 30 minutes. Keep warm until ready to serve.

Israeli Couscous

1 ½ cups dry Israeli couscous
1 tablespoon salt
1 cup chopped sun-dried
    tomatoes
3 cups hot water

1. In medium saucepan, blend couscous, salt, and tomatoes. Add hot water and place over medium heat; bring to a simmer, uncovered, for 10 minutes or until most of the water is absorbed. Remove from heat and cover pan. After 5 minutes, uncover and fluff with fork.

Scallops and Sauce

12 large (U-10 grade) sea scallops
    Nonstick cooking spray
    Freshly ground black pepper
4 tablespoons unsalted butter,
    cut into 4 pieces
¼ pound sliced shiitake
    mushrooms
1 shallot, minced
2 cups sweet vermouth
¼ cup heavy cream
    Salt
    Fresh minced parsley (optional)

1. Prepare grill to medium-high heat. Lightly spray both sides of sea scallops with cooking spray and sprinkle with pepper, and place on grill. Sear on both sides, about 3 minutes. Do not overcook. Remove from grill and set aside.

2. Place large, deep skillet over low heat and add 1 tablespoon butter;

Beer Pairing Suggestion:

American spiced ale or *witbier*

CHEF'S NOTE:

Israeli couscous is also known as pearl couscous, with a larger heft and more substantial flavor than traditional North African couscous. In a pinch, you could substitute *acini de pepe*—small peppercorn-sized pasta—or *pastini*.

when melted, sauté with mush-rooms and shallot. When they are soft, add vermouth.

3. Simmer over low heat until volume is reduced by three-fourths, with about $\frac{1}{2}$ cup liquid left in pan. Warm heavy cream, and slowly drizzle into sauce. Let sauce simmer until thickened. Turn heat off but leave skillet on stovetop.

4. Add 3 tablespoons butter, 1 tablespoon at a time, whisking after each addition. Season with salt and pepper to taste. Return scallops to sauce to warm through, turning twice to heat completely. Check interior of scallop with small knife cut—the scallop should be milky and opaque.

5. Place a scoop of cooked couscous in center of plates, top with 2 to 3 scallops, drizzle sauce over all, and garnish with roasted shallots and fresh minced parsley, if desired.

Makes 4 to 6 servings

Spicy Steamed Mussels

Vince Marsaglia of the Pizza Port Pub in Carlsbad, California, blends equal amounts of *gueuze* and Chardonnay to make these mussels fragrant and adds Cajun spices for heat. Brewer Tomme Arthur suggests a farmhouse ale in the Flemish tradition to pair with the mussels.

2 pounds fresh mussels
¼ pound tomatoes
¼ pound green bell pepper
¼ pound red onion
1 small ancho chile**
2 cloves garlic, chopped
3 tablespoons unsalted butter
1 ½ tablespoons Cajun spice blend
4 ounces *gueuze*
4 ounces Chardonnay
Grated zest and juice of 1 lemon
¼ cup fresh cilantro or Italian parsley leaves, chopped
Salt and freshly ground black pepper

** *Use caution in handling hot peppers, and wash hands thoroughly before touching eyes*

1. Wash and debeard mussels; discard any mussels with shells that will not stay closed. Dice the tomatoes, bell peppers, red onions, and chile.
2. In a sauté pan fitted with a lid and large enough to hold mussels (at least 2 quarts) add half the butter, and sauté the vegetables, chile, and garlic over medium-low heat until onions are translucent. Add Cajun spice blend and mussels, and stir to coat.
3. Add *gueuze* and Chardonnay and cover with lid. Steam 5 minutes; remove from heat and pick over mussels to discard any that have not opened. Use tongs to place remaining mussels in warmed serving bowl, and reserve cooking liquid in pan.
4. Add remaining butter, lemon, and zest to reserved pan juices and bring to a simmer for 5 minutes. Add chopped cilantro or parsley and pour sauce over mussels.

Makes 4 servings

Beer Pairing Suggestion:
American sour wheat ale or farmhouse ale

SERVING SUGGESTION:

Serve with bread and salad. Or, cook ½ pound linguine, toss with ½ teaspoon red pepper flakes, and top with mussels and broth. Garnish with grated Parmesan cheese.

118

Dogfish Head Crabcakes

Chef Marcel Lavallee from the Rehoboth Beach, Delaware, pub shares Sam Calagione's favorite crabcake recipe, which blends the pricey jumbo lump crab with the less expensive "special" meat plucked from other parts of the crab.

1 tablespoon unsalted butter
¼ cup minced red bell peppers
¼ cup minced green bell peppers
¼ cup minced onion
2 tablespoons minced shallot
¼ cup minced celery
1 tablespoon Old Bay Seasoning
1 scallion, sliced thin
1 cup mayonnaise
1 tablespoon Worcestershire sauce
1 tablespoon chopped parsley leaves, stems removed
1 teaspoon Dijon mustard
1 egg
2 tablespoons panko bread crumbs
1 pound jumbo lump crab meat
½ pound special crab meat
Fresh parsley and lemon wedges for garnish

1. Preheat oven to 350°F, and grease large baking sheet. Place butter in small sauté pan over medium heat. When butter melts, add peppers, onion, shallot, and celery; sauté until translucent. Stir in Old Bay Seasoning and remove from heat. Let cool.

2. In large mixing bowl, blend scallions, mayonnaise, Worcestershire sauce, parsley, mustard, and egg. When vegetable mixture is cool, add to the bowl with the bread crumbs and stir. Add crabmeat and gently fold it together until uniformly mixed. Chill 10 minutes.

3. Place mixture, by ¼ cupfuls, 2 to 3 inches apart on prepared baking sheet (8 cakes). Flatten mounds slightly into cake shapes, and bake until the crabmeat starts to brown, about 8 minutes. Remove pan from oven, turn cakes over, and bake on other side until brown, about 8 minutes. Do not overcook, as crab will continue to cook after removed from oven. Serve warm on platter garnished with parsley and lemon wedges.

Makes 8 to 10 cakes

Beer Pairing Suggestion:
American brown ale

CHEF'S NOTE:

Our taste-testers recommended adding a few spoonfuls of bread crumbs to this mixture to keep crabcakes together as they bake. Lavallee suggests panko bread crumbs, found in the Asian food section or ethnic markets.

120

Angry Lobster

Feeling ambitious? This show-stopping recipe features the artistry of Chef David Burke, of Burke & Donatella in New York City, who is a big fan of the Sam Adams line of brews. Who knew that a floral decoration item called a frog could stand in for a food presentation piece? You'll also need a clean hand saw, or a sturdy and sharp serrated knife, to cleanly cut the lobsters in half, as a cleaver will crush the shell. Prepare this creation with a friend or partner and reward yourselves with a lovely pint upon completion. I recommend pairing this spicy, briny creation with a quenching American pale ale with enough hops character to match the cayenne.

---

2 live lobsters (2 lobsters at 1½ to 2 pounds each for 4 portions), killed just before preparing

2 cups instant flour (Burke uses Wondra)

¼ cup chili powder

2 tablespoons ground cayenne pepper
Finely ground sea salt

¼ cup canola oil

1½ tablespoons minced garlic

1 tablespoon red pepper flakes

½ cup fresh basil leaves

¼ cup chili oil **

2 tablespoons sun-dried tomatoes packed in oil, drained, julienned

1 tablespoon lemon zest, julienned, simmered in simple syrup, and drained

½ cup lobster or chicken stock

2 tablespoons unsalted butter

1 tablespoon lemon juice

4 lemons, cut into eighths
Fresh basil leaves, deep fried (for garnish)

4 metal floral frogs (a metal disc with spikes to hold flowers)

Clean small hand saw

** *You may use a bottled brand of chili oil, or make your own by sautéing dried red or ancho chiles, to taste, in ¼ cup canola oil. Strain before using oil in the recipe.*

1. Separate knuckles/claws from each lobster; split knuckles/claws with the saw and reserve. Split lobster from head to tail with the saw; separate body halves from tail halves. Clean guts but if preparing a female lobster retain tomalley and roe in each body half.

2. Heat oven to 475°F. Mix instant flour, chili powder, cayenne, and salt on a plate. Dredge lobster in flour mixture, shaking off excess; reserve.

3. Heat oil in large skillet set over medium-high heat; add lobster, cut side down. Cook until it begins to color; flip; place in oven and cook 7 to 8 minutes. Remove from oven and place lobster on a platter; keep warm.

4. Set skillet used to cook lobsters over medium heat; add garlic, red pepper flakes, basil, and chili oil; cook 2 minutes. Add sun-dried tomatoes and lemon zest; cook 1 minute. Stir in stock and bring to a boil; reduce heat to low. Simmer 5 minutes.

5. Add butter to skillet; swirl skillet until butter is incorporated. Remove from heat, taste, and add 1 tablespoon lemon juice; reserve (keep warm).

6. To serve, set each round frog on large plate; impale lemon eighths around perimeter of the frog; set lobster half in the center of the frog. Spoon sauce over lobsters and garnish with fried basil leaves.

Makes 4 servings

121

Beer Pairing Suggestion:

American Imperial India pale ale

Slow Roasted Wild Salmon with Caramelized Belgian Endive and Almond Piccata

Chef Bart Seaver of the Washington, D.C., seafood restaurant Hook shares a recipe that pairs well with American pale ale or a crisp, hoppy Pilsener.

4 (6-ounce) pieces wild salmon, skin on and pin bones removed
⅓ cup extra virgin olive oil, divided
Ground black pepper
Sea salt
4 heads white Belgian endive, sliced in half lengthwise
½ cup blanched almonds, toasted until golden brown
2 cloves garlic, finely minced
2 tablespoons parsley, finely chopped

1. Preheat oven to 250°F degrees. Brush salmon filets with 1 tablespoon oil and season generously with salt and pepper. Place salmon fillets skin side down in large baking dish. Roast in oven until medium doneness, about 25 minutes.

2. Heat 2 tablespoons olive oil in a cast iron pan over high heat. Place endive cut side down and cook until light golden brown. Add ½ cup water and reduce heat to a low simmer. Season with salt and cook until all water is evaporated, about 10 minutes.

3. Using a mortar and pestle, crush almonds with 1 tablespoon olive oil and garlic until nuts are reduced to the size of rice grains. Place crushed almonds in a bowl and stir in remaining olive oil and parsley. Season with sea salt.

4. To serve, remove salmon from oven. Gently turn over. Skin should peel off very easily; discard. Place 2 pieces of caramelized endive on each plate. Place 1 piece of salmon on top of endive and divide almond garlic piccata evenly over the salmon fillets.

Makes 4 servings

Beer Pairing Suggestion:

Light India pale ale or Pilsener

123

Gritty's Summer Shellfish Grill

Chef Dave French of Gritty McDuff's pubs in Maine makes this "tasty snack" to share with friends, although he says he keeps the Gritty's VacationLand tasty ale for himself. This recipe is easy to double or triple to serve a crowd. Although brands dubbed "summer ales" abound, the suggested beer pairing should be a lightly hopped blonde ale or wheat ale, to avoid overwhelming the taste of the shellfish.

16 ounces blonde ale
8 cloves garlic, crushed, divided
1 onion, chopped
2 bay leaves
1 pound Maine mussels, picked to remove beards and scrubbed
1 pound steamer clams, rinsed and scrubbed
4 freshly cooked lobster claws
1½ pounds salted butter
1 lemon, sliced into 6 even wedges
1 tablespoon hot pepper sauce (or to taste)

4 sauce dishes

1. Place large, deep skillet over hot grill. Add ale, 4 cloves crushed garlic, onion, and bay leaves and bring to a simmer. Add shellfish.
2. In a separate skillet, melt butter. Divide melted butter among 3 sauce dishes. Add remaining crushed garlic to 1 dish and stir. Squeeze juice from 2 lemon wedges into another dish of melted butter and stir. Stir hot pepper sauce into remaining dish of melted butter.
3. Remove shellfish from skillet, reserving 1 cup ale steaming liquid, and place on a serving platter. Strain reserved ale into fourth sauce dish. Serve shellfish immediately with assorted dipping sauces.

Makes 4 servings

Beer Pairing Suggestion:

American pale wheat ale or blonde ale

124

Savannah Grits and Shrimp

Spicy shrimp and grits can be found in innumerable variations across the South. This recipe originated at the Boathouse Restaurant in Charleston, South Carolina, and was adapted by Beryl and Don Zerwer, owners of the Foley Inn in Savannah, Georgia, using a roux base for the sauce. The recipe is assembled in three stages, so read through it all to make your shopping list. John Cochran, founder of Terrapin Beer Company of Athens, Georgia, said that he enjoyed it best with the Terrapin Rye Pale Ale, which complements the tangy sauce and creamy grits.

Hot Pepper Sauce
- 3 tablespoons salted butter
- 2 tablespoons flour
- 2 tablespoons minced shallot
- ¼ cup green hot pepper sauce
- 1 tablespoon rice wine vinegar
- 1 tablespoon fresh lemon juice
- ½ teaspoon lemon zest
- 1 cup heavy cream

1. Place butter in a large heavy skillet over low heat until melted and sprinkle in flour, 1 tablespoon at a time, whisking to make a paste. Cook and stir over low heat until mixture turns light gold and smells like popcorn. Stir in shallot and simmer 1 minute.
2. Add hot pepper sauce, vinegar, lemon juice, and zest, whisking well. Simmer 1 minute. Slowly pour cream into mixture, whisking constantly. Simmer until mixture is thickened and set aside. (May be made ahead of time and chilled until ready to use.)

Grits
- 4 cups water
- 3 cups whole milk
- 1 cup light cream
- 3 tablespoons unsalted butter
- 2 cups corn grits
  Salt and pepper

1. Bring water, milk, cream, and butter to a simmer in a large saucepan. Gradually whisk in grits. Cook over low heat, stirring often, until creamy and thickened, about 1½ hours. Taste for tenderness and adjust seasoning with salt and pepper, if desired.

Shrimp Topping
- ¼ cup olive oil
- 8 ounces smoked andouille sausage, sliced
- ¾ cup chopped red bell pepper
- ¾ cup chopped yellow bell pepper
- ⅓ cup minced sweet onion
- 2 tablespoons minced garlic
- 30 large (16 to 20 count) raw shrimp, cleaned and peeled
- 4 plum tomatoes, chopped (about 1 cup)
- 1 teaspoon Cajun seasoning blend
- 1 teaspoon Old Bay Seasoning

  Minced fresh chives

1. When grits are almost tender, heat olive oil in large heavy skillet over medium heat. Add sausage, peppers, onion, and garlic; sauté until vegetables are tender. Add shrimp, tomatoes, and seasonings. Sauté until shrimp are cooked, about 4 to 6 minutes, depending on thickness. Remove from heat and set aside.
2. Warm pepper sauce. Divide grits among 6 serving plates. Spoon shrimp mixture over grits, allowing 5 shrimp per portion, and drizzle with pepper sauce. Garnish with minced chives, if desired.

Makes 6 servings

Beer Pairing Suggestion:
Rye ale or pale ale

125

Seafood Gumbo-Abita Style

Kathy Tujague of Abita Brewing Company shares a favorite recipe made with Abita Amber, a Munich-style lager that adds a crisp taste to the caramelized roux base of this gumbo, which she pairs with Turbodog or a dark lager.

⅓ cup butter
¼ cup flour
2 cups chopped onion
1 tablespoon minced garlic
1 cup chopped bell peppers
1 cup chopped celery
1 tablespoon salt
1 teaspoon cayenne pepper (or to taste)
5 bay leaves
6 cups seafood broth or vegetable broth
12 ounces amber lager
1 pound medium shrimp, peeled and deveined
1 pound lump crabmeat, shells and cartilage removed
2 dozen oysters, shucked, liquor reserved
¼ cup chopped scallions
¼ cup chopped parsley
Filé powder

1. Combine butter and flour in large cast iron or enameled cast iron Dutch oven. Cook over medium heat, stirring slowly and constantly for 20 to 25 minutes, until dark brown roux, the color of chocolate, forms.

2. Add onions, garlic, bell peppers, celery, salt, cayenne, and bay leaves. Cook, stirring occasionally, about 10 minutes or until very soft. Add broth and stir to blend; simmer 15 to 20 minutes.

3. Add lager, shrimp, and crabmeat and cook 10 minutes. Reduce heat to low. Add oysters, reserved oyster liquor, scallions, and parsley. Cook 2 to 3 minutes, or until edges of oysters curl. Remove pan from heat. Discard bay leaves.

4. Pass filé powder at the table for guests to thicken the gumbo to taste.

Makes 6 servings

Beer Pairing Suggestion:
American dark lager

127

Grilled Wild Striped Bass Over Toasted Almond Potatoes and Lemon-Garlic Gremolata

Chef Bart Seaver left Café St.-Ex in 2007 to open a new restaurant, Hook, devoted to serving sustainable seafood in Washington, D.C. His talents with seafood shine in this dish. Seaver uses a microplane to make paper-thin slices of garlic, but you may also try it with a very sharp paring knife. Almond oil may be found in the cooking oil or natural foods sections at large supermarkets or specialty stores. If not available, substitute canola oil to toast the almonds. A pale wheat ale will bring out the nutty flavors of the toasted almonds and highlight the Lemon Gremolata garnish over the bass.

¼ cup salt
1 tablespoon sugar
2 cups water
2 pounds wild striped bass fillet
Oil for brushing
1 lemon, sliced very thin, seeded
1 clove garlic, sliced very thin
Salt
2 tablespoons chopped parsley
1 tablespoon extra virgin olive oil
¼ cup sliced, blanched almonds
1 pound red-skinned organic potatoes, diced
1 teaspoon natural almond extract
¼ cup almond oil

1. In stockpot or large container, dissolve salt and sugar in water; add fish and brine for 15 minutes. Remove fish from brine and dry carefully with paper towels. Lightly brush with oil and grill skin side down about 3 minutes over high heat. Turn and cook flesh side down for 1 minute on low heat. Set aside.

2. To make gremolata, grill lemons until slightly caramelized and edges are black. Chop very finely and mix with parsley, olive oil, and garlic. Season with salt.

3. Heat almond oil. Toast almond slices in oil until just golden brown. Using slotted spoon, remove almonds from oil and reserve. Add diced potato and cook until just barely done, about 10 minutes. Season generously with salt and add reserved almonds and almond extract. Toss to incorporate.

4. To serve, place small pile of almond potatoes on plate and gently lay fish, skin side up, angled off the potatoes. Garnish with gremolata around plate.

Makes 4 servings

Beer Pairing Suggestion:

American pale wheat ale

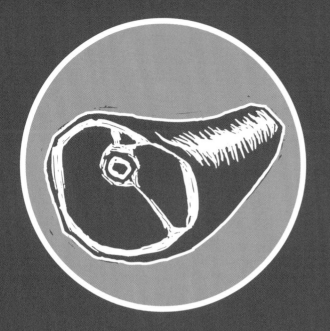

OFF THE HOOF

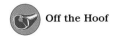

Poor Richard's Molasses Marinade

This sweet and tangy marinade, developed by Tony Simmons, head brewer at Pagosa Brewing Company in Pagosa Springs, Colorado, is best used to marinate wild game such as venison, wild boar, and duck. It also goes well with beef, pork, and especially smoked pork chops. The added molasses complements the taste of Poor Richard's Ale wonderfully.

---

1 cup dark ale
2 tablespoons dry English mustard
¼ cup dark molasses
¼ cup malt vinegar
⅓ cup finely chopped onion
1 tablespoon Worcestershire sauce
¼ teaspoon powdered red pepper or cayenne pepper
1 bay leaf

1. Blend ale and mustard in small saucepan over low heat. Gradually stir in remaining ingredients. Bring to a simmer and cook for 2 minutes. Cool before using.
2. For most flavorful results, use to marinate wild game overnight in refrigerator. For ham or pork, marinate up to 6 hours in refrigerator.

Makes 2 cups

130

Bock-Braised Pork Shoulder

Chef Nathan Berg of Native Bay Restaurant and Lounge in Chippewa Falls, Wisconsin, serves this as a base for pulled-pork sandwiches. Serve it with roasted potatoes and garlic sauerkraut.

1 cup flour
    Salt and freshly ground black pepper
4 to 5 pounds pork shoulder (about 3 inches thick)
4 tablespoons grapeseed (or safflower) oil
1 large yellow onion, halved and sliced thick
2 medium carrots, peeled and chopped
2 stalks celery, trimmed and chopped
4 cups pork or beef stock
3 (12-ounce) bottles bock or *doppelbock*
10 black peppercorns
2 bay leaves
3 sprigs fresh thyme
2 sprigs fresh rosemary
1 teaspoon sherry vinegar
1 tablespoon truffle oil

1. Preheat oven to 200°F. Place flour in a shallow pan or plate, and season liberally with salt and pepper. Dredge broad sides of shoulder roasts in seasoned flour, and shake to remove excess.

2. Heat oil in large, nonstick frying pan over medium-high heat. Sear all sides of the pork roasts until brown and crispy. Place the onion, carrots, and celery in the bottom of a deep casserole or Dutch oven, and place meat on top. Add stock and beer until meat and vegetables are fully submerged, and add peppercorns, bay leaves, thyme, and rosemary. Cover with a tight-fitting lid or aluminum foil (to prevent meat from drying out and burning). Bake at least 6 hours (or use slow cooker set on LOW).

3. Remove pan from oven and remove lid, taking care not to let steam hit face or hands. Taste a small piece of pork and check its texture. It should be falling straight off the bone or coming apart easily when pulled. If the meat isn't fully tender, return to pan or slow cooker for another 1 to 2 hours.

4. Remove meat from liquid, set it on a plate or in a shallow pan, and place it in the refrigerator to cool slightly. In the meantime, strain cooking pan juices and place in a saucepan over medium-high heat; bring it to a rolling boil on the stovetop. Reduce liquids by 70 percent, to about 2 cups. When fully reduced, taste and adjust seasonings with salt and pepper and the sherry vinegar.

5. When cool enough to handle, pick through the pork to remove all bones and as much of the fat as possible. To finish, combine pork and sauce in a large saucepan and heat until warmed throughout. Stir in truffle oil just before serving.

Makes 6 to 8 servings

Beer Pairing Suggestion:
Bock or *doppelbock*

131

Deschutes Lamb Chops with Roasted Fennel and Portobello Mushroom Risotto

Originally prepared with Black Butte Porter, this lamb dish also pairs well with any American porter.

8 thick-cut lamb chops, trimmed well
Finely ground sea salt
Finely ground black pepper
4 ounces dried tart cherries
12 ounces porter
2 fresh fennel bulbs, greens trimmed
Olive oil
3 cups chicken broth
1 cup Arborio or sticky rice
1 large Portobello mushroom cap, stem removed, minced
1 large shallot, minced (about 2 tablespoons)
4 tablespoons salted butter
1 tablespoon minced garlic
½ cup shredded Parmesan cheese

1. Preheat oven to 450°F. Rub both sides of lamb chops with salt and pepper.
2. Put cherries in small bowl with 6 ounces of porter to cover; set aside to macerate.
3. Cut fennel bulbs in half. Coat lightly with olive oil, about 2 tablespoons, and season with salt and pepper. Place cut side down in ovenproof dish and place on middle rack of oven. Bake 30 minutes, or until golden brown and soft.

4. Heat chicken broth to a simmer in 1-quart saucepan. Meanwhile, place another saucepan over medium heat. When hot, add 3 tablespoons olive oil and add rice, stirring to coat with oil.
5. When rice has begun to sizzle, carefully pour in ½ cup hot broth. As liquid is absorbed, add more broth and stir until rice is *al dente*. Rice will take about 30 minutes to cook. Remove from heat and keep warm.
6. In medium skillet, sauté mushroom and shallot with a pinch of salt and pepper in 1 tablespoon olive oil and 1 tablespoon butter over medium-high heat. When almost done, add garlic and sauté 2 minutes. Add this mixture, Parmesan cheese, and 2 tablespoons butter to risotto and stir. Taste and adjust seasonings.
7. Heat an ovenproof sauté pan over high heat. When hot, add a pinch of salt to pan and add lamb chops. Place pan immediately on lowest rack or floor of hot oven. Roast lamb chops 5 minutes; remove from oven and turn. Return to oven and roast 5 minutes longer. Move to a warmed plate and tent with foil. Reserve juices in cooking pan.

8. Place pan with reserved lamb drippings over medium-high heat and pour in porter-macerated cherries. Stir and let reduce until thickened, about 5 minutes. Remove pan from heat and whisk in 1 tablespoon cold butter until butter is evenly melted.
9. Plate one halved roasted fennel bulb, 2 lamb chops, and large spoonful of risotto on each plate. Offer cherry sauce on the side in ramekins or poured over lamb.

Makes 4 servings

Beer Pairing Suggestion:
American porter

132

Glazed Pork with Pineapple-Black Bean Salad

Jim Bradley of Chicago was a finalist in the National Beer Wholesalers Association's Cooking with Beer Challenge with this gently spiced dish that uses the all-American amber lager as a key ingredient.

Marinade
1 teaspoon grated fresh ginger
½ teaspoon hot curry powder
¾ teaspoon ground allspice
2 tablespoons plus ⅛ teaspoon light brown sugar
6 ounces amber lager
2 tablespoons Worcestershire sauce
2 tablespoons fresh lime juice
2 tablespoons finely chopped garlic
6 lean boneless pork loin chops, cut ¾-inch thick

Glaze
6 ounces amber lager
3 tablespoons hoisin sauce
2 tablespoons light brown sugar
2 tablespoons low-sodium soy sauce
1 tablespoon plum sauce
1 teaspoon grated fresh ginger

Pineapple-Black Bean Salad
2 cups diced pineapple
1 cup canned black beans, rinsed and drained
⅔ cup diced red bell pepper
¼ teaspoon salt
Freshly ground black pepper
3 tablespoons sliced scallions

2 tablespoons fresh mint
1 tablespoon lime juice
1 tablespoon canola oil
Salt
Freshly ground black pepper
Lime wedges and mint sprigs, for garnish

1. In large resealable plastic bag, combine ginger, curry powder, allspice, and ⅛ teaspoon brown sugar. Reserve ½ teaspoon spice mixture for salad. Add beer, Worcestershire sauce, lime juice, remaining 2 tablespoons brown sugar, and garlic to remaining spice mixture; seal bag and shake to blend. Place pork chops in bag; reseal bag and turn to coat. Refrigerate 2 hours.
2. For glaze, combine beer, hoisin sauce, brown sugar, soy sauce, plum sauce, and ginger in large saucepan over medium-high heat. Bring to simmer; reduce heat to medium-low. Simmer 20 minutes or until reduced and thickened to a glaze.
3. Meanwhile, combine all salad ingredients with reserved ½ teaspoon spice mixture in medium bowl. Cover and refrigerate until ready to cook pork.
4. Remove pork from bag and discard marinade. Sprinkle pork chops with salt and pepper and place in 12-inch nonstick skillet over medium heat. Cook chops 3 minutes on each side. Brush chops with some glaze; cover skillet and cook over low heat 6 minutes.
5. Using tongs, turn chops, brush with more glaze. Cover skillet and cook 5 minutes longer, or until instant-read thermometer inserted in center of chop reads 150°F. Transfer chops to platter; brush with more glaze. Top glazed chops with salad. Garnish with lime wedges and mint sprigs.

Makes 6 servings

Beer Pairing Suggestion:
Amber lager

Fennel Crusted Rack of Lamb with Barley Risotto and Brugge Black Ale Niçoise Sauce

Three recipes go into making this flavorful rack of lamb dressed in black ale and oil-cured Niçoise olives, from chef Greg Hardesty of Elements Restaurant, Indianapolis. Managing partner and brewer Ted Miller says, "Brugges Black is a Belgian strong dark ale. (It) evokes thoughts of licorice, dried fruits and has a lightly roasted quality. The licorice notes of the ale playfully acknowledge the fennel and harmonize with the roasted lamb."

Pearl Barley Risotto

- 4 tablespoons salted butter
- 1 medium yellow onion, minced
- 1 ½ cups pearl barley
- 4 cups chicken or vegetable stock
- ½ cup grated Parmesan cheese
- 1 tablespoon fresh thyme leaves, stems removed
- 1 tablespoon fresh flat leaf parsley, chopped
  Salt and pepper

1. Melt butter in large saucepan over medium heat. Add onion to butter and cook until soft. Add the barley and stir to coat with the butter.
2. Add 1 cup stock and stir frequently until almost dry. Add another cup of stock and repeat with third and fourth cups stock until barley is completely cooked. Use just enough stock to cook the barley until it is fluffy and tender.
3. Remove cooked barley from heat and stir in Parmesan cheese, thyme, and parsley. Add salt and pepper to taste. Cover pan and keep warm.

Niçoise Black Ale Sauce

- 3 tablespoons olive oil
- 1 pound button mushrooms, sliced
- 2 cloves garlic, sliced
- 1 small onion, chopped
- 2 Roma tomatoes, chopped
- 2 cups black ale
- 4 cups chicken or veal stock
- 2 tablespoons salted butter
- 1 cup oil-cured, pitted Niçoise olives
  Salt and freshly ground black pepper

1. Warm oil in medium saucepan over medium-low heat. Add mushrooms and sauté until golden brown and dry. Add garlic, onion, and tomatoes to pan. Continue to cook over medium heat until vegetables begin to caramelize.
2. Deglaze pan with beer and reduce until syrupy. Strain mushrooms and vegetables out of the sauce about halfway through the reduction process; discard or save for a soup or stock. Add the chicken or

Beer Pairing Suggestion:

Strong black ale

135

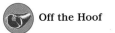

veal stock and reduce, skimming as necessary, to 1 cup. Stir Niçoise olives into reduced, strained sauce; season with salt and pepper to taste. Remove from heat and cover to keep warm.

Lamb

1 rack of lamb (8 bones)
3 tablespoons toasted fennel seeds, ground in a spice or coffee grinder
  Salt and pepper
2 tablespoons olive oil
2 tablespoons butter

1. Preheat oven to 400°F. Season lamb with ground fennel, salt, and pepper. Heat oil in large, oven-proof sauté pan over high heat and sear lamb rack on all sides.

2. Place lamb in oven and roast for 12 to 16 minutes, or until medium rare. Remove lamb from oven and place on a plate to rest for 5 minutes. Meanwhile, divide risotto among 4 plates. Rewarm beer sauce and whisk in butter, 1 tablespoon at a time. Spoon sauce around the risotto. Slice the lamb into 8 single bone chops and place 2 chops on each plate. Sprinkle any remaining fennel powder over lamb.

Makes 4 servings

Pan-Seared Pilsener Sirloin Tips with Herbed Pecan Orzo and Shiitake-Blue Cheese Sauce

Another finalist in the National Beer Wholesalers Association's first Cooking with Beer Challenge, Veronica Callaghan of Glastonbury, Connecticut, produced this rich beef dish that pairs well with nut brown ale or dark lager.

Sirloin Tips
1 ½ pounds beef sirloin tips
1 cup Pilsener
1 cup beef broth
2 tablespoons Worcestershire sauce
1 teaspoon hot red pepper sauce
1 teaspoon kosher salt
½ teaspoon freshly ground black pepper

Herbed Pecan Orzo
1 cup orzo
2 tablespoons unsalted butter
1 teaspoon salt
½ teaspoon freshly ground black pepper
2 tablespoons finely chopped fresh rosemary
2 tablespoons finely chopped flat leaf parsley
1 tablespoon finely chopped fresh thyme
½ cup chopped pecans, lightly toasted

1 tablespoon olive oil
1 tablespoon butter
1 large shallot, finely chopped
2 cups shiitake mushrooms, stems removed and thinly sliced

3 ounces Pilsener
½ teaspoon kosher salt
2 tablespoons flour
½ cup crumbled blue cheese
Rosemary sprigs for garnish

1. Place sirloin tips in large zipper-lock plastic bag. Add Pilsener, beef broth, Worcestershire sauce, hot pepper sauce, salt, and pepper. Marinate at least 20 minutes.
2. Cook orzo in boiling water according to package directions. Drain and toss with butter, salt, and pepper. Stir in herbs and pecans. Cover with foil and set aside.
3. Heat olive oil in large heavy skillet or cast iron pan over medium-high heat. Remove sirloin tips from marinade, reserving marinade for later use. Add meat to pan and cook 3 to 4 minutes on each side until slight crust is formed and meat is just browned. Remove meat to a plate and cover with foil.
4. Melt butter in same pan used for meat. Add shallot and mushrooms. Sauté for 2 to 3 minutes or until just tender. Stir in Pilsener and cook until almost completely absorbed. Sprinkle salt and flour over mushrooms, stirring to coat. Pour in reserved marinade. Bring to a boil and cook 1 minute. Reduce heat and cook, stirring frequently, 3 to 4 minutes, or until liquid is reduced by half.
5. Return meat to pan, pouring in any accumulated juices from the plate, and cook 4 to 5 minutes for medium-rare, or until desired doneness.
6. Arrange Herbed-Pecan Orzo on large serving platter. Fan sirloin tips over orzo and pour sauce over top. Sprinkle with blue cheese and garnish with fresh rosemary.

Makes 4 to 6 servings

Beer Pairing Suggestion:
American dark lager or nut brown ale

137

Porcini Pork Medallions

This dish was designed to pair with Belgian-style brown ales with slight sour notes and fine carbonation, says Chef Rick Martin of Free State Brewing Company in Lawrence, Kansas. The earthy flavor of the dried porcini melds with the spicy Mexican chocolate. Serve the medallions with mashed potatoes and wilted greens.

¼ cup dried porcini mushrooms
2 tablespoons ancho chile powder
1 teaspoon sea salt
1 teaspoon ground black pepper
1 pork tenderloin, about 2 pounds, trimmed of silver skin (white connective tissues)
3 tablespoons butter
2 tablespoons flour
2 cups veal stock, warmed
2 ounces grated Mexican chocolate, such as Ibarra brand
1 tablespoon molasses
Strips of orange zest, for garnish

1. Toast mushrooms on baking sheet in toaster oven on HIGH for 3 to 5 minutes, until crispy. Cool to room temperature. Grind to a fine powder with a mortar and pestle or a mini food processor. Place powder in shallow dish with chile powder, salt, and pepper and mix well. Coat tenderloin with mixture. Set aside.

2. In medium saucepan, melt butter and whisk in flour. Over medium-low heat cook butter-flour mixture, stirring often, until the color of peanut butter. Cool immediately by setting pan base inside sink partially filled with 1 inch of cool water. Very slowly, drizzle in warmed veal stock, stirring or whisking out any clumps after each addition. Remove pan from water and wipe bottom dry; return pan to low heat. Add chocolate and molasses; bring to a simmer to thicken.

3. Cook tenderloin over a medium-hot grill, rotating often, until it reaches internal temperature of 140°F. Remove from heat to warmed platter to rest for 10 minutes. Slice into ½-inch thick medallions and serve over chocolate-chile sauce. Garnish meat with orange zest strips.

Makes 4 servings

Beer Pairing Suggestion:

Flanders-style sour brown ale

139

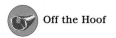

Goose Island Brown Ale Braised Beef Ribs

Goose Island Beer Company president and founder John Hall shares this recipe, which is a favorite at the brewery's pub on North Clybourn Avenue in Chicago.

8 beef short ribs, visible fat removed
Salt and pepper
½ cup all-purpose flour
½ cup canola oil
4 large onions, diced
10 cloves garlic, 4 sliced and 6 whole
¼ cup butter
3 bottles brown ale
4 cups chicken stock
¼ cup molasses
2 tablespoons tomato paste
3 sprigs fresh thyme
2 bay leaves

1. Season the short ribs generously with salt and pepper and lightly dust with flour. In a large sauté pan, warm the canola oil over medium-high heat until it starts to smoke. Add the short ribs and reduce the heat slightly. Brown the ribs on all sides, about 3 minutes per side. After browning, transfer ribs to a large stew pot.

2. In a separate pan, sauté onions and sliced garlic in the butter until onions become translucent. Add the garlic and onions to the ribs. Add the beer and simmer, uncovered, over low heat until the beer is reduced by one-third. Cover the ribs with stock and add the molasses and tomato paste, whole garlic, thyme, and bay leaves. Simmer covered 1-½ to 2 hours or until meat is tender. Shake the pot periodically to prevent sticking.

3. Transfer ribs to a serving dish and cover to retain heat. Skim excess fat from the broth, discard the herbs, and pass liquid through a sieve. Return liquid to a saucepan over medium heat. Reduce until thickened and pour over ribs.

Makes 4 to 6 servings

Beer Pairing Suggestion:

American brown ale or dark lager

Plantain Crusted Pork Loin

Plantain chips add color to the pork loin, which goes well with traditional Caribbean side dishes such as black beans and rice. A malty lager accents the sweetness of the orange-rum sauce.

2 cups plantain chips
1 teaspoon salt
1 teaspoon freshly ground black pepper
1 teaspoon dried thyme
1 teaspoon minced garlic
¼ cup heavy cream
1 egg white
4 large boneless top loin pork chops, ¾-inch thick
2 tablespoons extra virgin olive oil
¼ cup dark rum
¼ cup orange or lime marmalade
1 tablespoon hot pepper sauce

1. Crush plantain chips in food processor fitted with metal blade, or place in resealable plastic bag and pound with rolling pin to crush finely and evenly. Mix salt, pepper, and thyme in a small bowl.

2. Whisk together garlic, cream, and egg white until smooth in a square 9-by-9-inch pan (so pork can be dipped to the proper depth for coating) and dip pork chops on both sides in the mixture. Place crushed plantains on large plate. Place pork chops on top of plantains, and sprinkle half of the crushed plantains evenly over pork chops; turn and sprinkle chops on other side. Press firmly so crumbs will stick. Sprinkle chops with salt mixture.

3. Place oil in large skillet over medium heat; swirl to coat. Heat until almost smoking. Add pork chops, using tongs, and reduce heat to medium-low. Cover and cook 7 minutes on each side or until internal temperature reaches 155°F (medium). Turn once with large spatula to keep crumb crust intact.

4. Mix rum, marmalade, and hot pepper sauce in a small bowl. Remove chops from skillet and place on warmed serving platter. Deglaze skillet with rum mixture and serve warm over pork chops.

Makes 4 servings

Beer Pairing Suggestion:
Strong amber lager or *doppelbock*

Roast Pork Tenderloin in Brown Ale-Raspberry Chipotle Cream Sauce

Chris Swersey, competition manager for the World Beer Cup and river guide, says, "This recipe works as well in a Dutch oven over a charcoal fire as in a conventional oven. It's an easy preparation that takes little time and makes you look like a genius!" Our taste-testers used Bell's Brown Ale in this very tasty sauce, but you could use your favorite American brown ale. Serve with rice pilaf or mashed potatoes. A recipe for Raspberry Chipotle BBQ Sauce follows, if you can't find a suitable bottled version.

4 pounds pork tenderloin, 2 to 3 pieces
2 teaspoons salt
2 teaspoons freshly ground black pepper
2 teaspoons garlic powder
1 teaspoon smoked paprika (see p. 197)
1 teaspoon dried thyme
2 tablespoons olive oil
2 tablespoons butter, softened
10 ounces brown ale
1 cup heavy cream, warmed
½ cup Raspberry Chipotle BBQ Sauce

Charcoal, if using Dutch oven

Instant read meat thermometer (crucial to preventing pork from overcooking)

1. Preheat oven to 375°F. Rub pork with salt, pepper, garlic powder, paprika, and thyme. Heat olive oil in heavy, ovenproof skillet (cast iron is good) or Dutch oven over medium-high heat. Sear pork on all sides until browned.

2. Remove pan from heat. Dab butter over pork in the pan, cover and roast 20 to 25 minutes. Roast until pork reaches 140°F (check each piece in 3 places with meat thermometer, and average readings). When done, remove meat to plate to rest; tent with foil. Don't overcook pork loin—once it hits 135°F, it cooks quickly.

3. Pour ale into roasting pan placed over medium-high heat. Bring beer to simmer and scrape bottom of pan with whisk or spatula to release spices and juices. Reduce to about half volume, stirring constantly, about 5 minutes. Reduce heat to low, add warmed cream and Raspberry Chipotle BBQ Sauce, and simmer and stir 2 to 3 minutes.

4. Remove sauce from heat and let sauce rest about 5 minutes before plating. Slice pork in thick slices, place on plate, and cover with sauce.

Makes 6 to 8 servings

Beer Pairing Suggestion:
American brown ale

CHEF'S NOTE:

Prepare the pork tenderloin by removing the shiny membrane known as silver skin from the exterior; otherwise, the tenderloin will toughen and curl as it cooks.

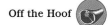

Raspberry Chipotle BBQ Sauce

If you can't find a bottled raspberry chipotle sauce, here's a recipe that may be prepared up to 2 weeks before use.

1 tablespoon olive oil
½ cup minced Vidalia onion
1 tablespoon minced garlic
2 chipotles en adobo, chopped**
1 large jar (at least 14 ounces) seedless raspberry all-fruit spread (no sugar added)
1 teaspoon Worcestershire sauce
1 teaspoon lemon juice

** *Use caution in handling hot peppers, and wash hands thoroughly before touching eyes*

1. In large saucepan over medium heat, mix oil, onion, and garlic. Cook and stir about 3 minutes. Add chipotles and raspberry spread. Cook and stir until spread is melted. Add the Worcestershire sauce and lemon juice, stir well, and taste and adjust seasonings.
2. Remove from heat and let cool. Pack in resealable container and use within 2 weeks.

Makes about 2 cups

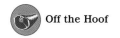

Port Pomegranate Short Ribs

Vince Marsaglia braises these short ribs in Port Brewing's Old Viscosity Ale, aged for six months in old bourbon barrels at the San Marcos, California, brewery. If you can't get your hands on a barrel-aged beer (or, like me, want to save the Old Viscosity for drinking alongside the prepared ribs), use a strong ale such as barley wine and add a splash of bourbon. Pair with a Belgian-style *quadrupel* ale to match the pasilla peppers and tangy sauce.

2 pounds boneless beef short ribs
2 tablespoons spicy rib rub seasoning blend, or salt and pepper
¼ cup canola oil
¼ pound yellow onions, chopped
¼ pound carrots, chopped
¼ pound celery, chopped
1 large roasted pasilla chile, peeled, seeded, and chopped**
¼ cup minced garlic
2 tablespoons balsamic vinegar
20 ounces unsweetened pomegranate juice
2 ½ cups defatted chicken or veal stock
2 cups barrel-aged strong ale (or 2 cups barley wine and 1 tablespoon bourbon)
** *Use caution in handling hot peppers, and wash hands thoroughly before touching eyes*

Finishing Sauce
1 tablespoon salted butter
¼ pound yellow onion, chopped
1 tablespoon tomato paste
  Reserved and strained, skimmed braising liquid from ribs

Garnish
¼ cup pomegranate seeds
2 tablespoons minced chives
¼ cup roasted corn kernels

1. Trim excess fat from short ribs and rub with beef rub seasoning, or sprinkle with salt and pepper.
2. Place a large cast iron pot or Dutch oven over medium-high heat, and add canola oil. When oil is hot, sear ribs on all sides until well browned. Remove ribs and reserve on plate. Preheat oven to 350°F.
3. Turn heat to low and add onion, carrots, celery, and chile to pot. Cook and stir until onion turns golden. Add garlic and deglaze with balsamic vinegar. Add pomegranate juice and stock. Scrape any browned bits from bottom of pan. Add beer and bring to a simmer. Add ribs and submerge in liquid. Cover with lid or a double layer of foil, crimped tight around edges of pan, and bake 2 ½ hours.
4. Remove ribs from oven and carefully drain off pan juices; set juices aside to let fat rise to the surface. Set ribs on a large warmed platter, cover and keep warm. Skim off and discard fat; strain juices.
5. In a large saucepan over medium-low heat, melt butter and sauté onions until caramelized. Stir in tomato paste and cook until browned. Add skimmed sauce from ribs and reduce over medium heat until sauce is thickened and coats back of spoon, about 30 minutes.
6. Arrange ribs on platter, and add sauce to taste. Garnish with mixture of pomegranate seeds, chives, and roasted corn kernels.

Makes 4 servings

Beer Pairing Suggestion:
American quadrupel ale

CHEF'S NOTE:

Find fresh pomegranates in season from October through March, and freeze them whole for use year 'round. Pomegranate juice is available in the juice sections at large supermarkets and specialty food stores. Small bottles, such as the POM brand, are sometimes sold in drink coolers.

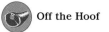

Samuel Adams Winter Lager Glazed Ham and Pineapple Tart Tatin

The Boston Beer Company offers this recipe for a spiced ham prepared with the winter seasonal Winter Lager, which is styled after a *weizenbock* with fruity aromatics from the yeast. The Pineapple Tart Tatin may be prepared in advance.

36 ounces dark lager or bock
¾ cup sugar
¾ cup Dijon mustard
1 pinch each cinnamon, orange peel, and ginger
1 (12- to 14-pound) fresh ham, trimmed of excess fat and rind
  Coarse salt
  Freshly ground black pepper

1. In large saucepan, bring lager to a boil over medium-high heat. Reduce. Add sugar and mustard and reduce volume by half. Stir in cinnamon, orange peel, and ginger; remove from heat and cool about 10 minutes.
2. Generously baste ham with glaze and sprinkle with salt and pepper. Marinate at least 3 hours.
3. Preheat oven to 375°F. Place marinated ham on rack in roasting pan. (It is important to place ham on rack so fat can drip down.) Roast ham, uncovered, about 5 hours or until instant-read thermometer inserted into center of ham near but not touching bone registers 160°F.

4. Remove ham from oven and transfer to serving platter. Place Pineapple Tart Tatin on platter and carve ham, family style, at the table.

Makes 1 large ham, enough to serve 6 with leftovers for sandwiches

Pineapple Tart Tatin
1 large pineapple
3 tablespoons coarsely ground black pepper
3 tablespoons green peppercorns
1 tablespoon unsalted butter, softened
1 large egg yolk
¼ cup plus 1 tablespoon water
2 cups sugar
2 tablespoons unsalted butter, chilled
6 (3-inch) round puff pastry circles

1. Cut off each end of pineapple, peel, and core. Cut crosswise into ½-inch-thick rings. Season each pineapple ring with ¼ teaspoon pepper and 4 green peppercorns. Set aside. Using softened butter, lightly coat 6 3-inch round, non-stick molds. Set aside.
2. Preheat oven to 350°F. To make egg wash, place egg yolk and 1 tablespoon water in small bowl and whisk to blend. Set aside.
3. Combine sugar and remaining ¼ cup of water in medium, heavy-duty saucepan over high heat. Bring mixture to a boil, then lower heat, and simmer about 15 minutes, or until sugar has begun to caramelize and temperature registers 350°F on candy thermometer. Remove mixture from heat and immediately beat in chilled butter until well incorporated.
4. Spoon ½ cup caramel into each mold; place seasoned pineapple ring on top. Bake about 10 minutes.

5. Remove molds from oven and place puff pastry circle on top of each roasted pineapple slice. Using pastry brush, lightly coat pastry with reserved egg wash. Return molds to oven and bake 25 minutes, or until puff pastry has risen and turned golden brown. Remove pastry from oven and let rest for several minutes.

6. Invert molds and tap tarts free. Serve warm.

Makes 6 servings

Beer Pairing Suggestion:
Strong dark lager or winter ale

147

Shallot and Stout-Glazed Steak with Cumin-Pepper Onions

I like an American stout, such as the Rogue Shakespeare Stout, that's got a hint of sweetness to complement the shallots and garlic. However, some taste-testers preferred a dry stout, so choose according to your taste. The recipe for the Cumin-Pepper Onions may be made spicier with a pinch of cayenne.

5 large shallots, thinly sliced
5 cloves garlic, thinly sliced
2 tablespoons salted butter
2 bay leaves
12 ounces American dry or sweet stout
¼ cup tomato paste
1 teaspoon Worcestershire sauce
Sea salt and freshly ground black pepper
2 pounds skirt steak, trimmed
1 teaspoon balsamic vinegar
2 tablespoons fresh orange juice

1. Combine shallots, garlic, and butter in large saucepan over low heat. Sauté until garlic turns golden. Add bay leaves, stout, tomato paste, and Worcestershire sauce. Whisk until smooth. Simmer until reduced by one-third, about 20 minutes. Remove from heat and cool. Remove bay leaves.
2. Pour 1 cup cooled sauce in large, resealable plastic bag. Add meat to bag, seal, and turn to coat evenly. Marinate meat on a tray in refrigerator 6 to 8 hours. Chill remaining sauce (about ¼ cup) in covered container.

3. Remove steaks from marinade, place on platter, and discard bag. Preheat grill to medium-hot. If desired, rub steaks with freshly ground pepper and sea salt. Let reserved sauce come to room temperature, and whisk in balsamic vinegar and orange juice.
4. Grill steaks to desired doneness, turning twice to get a cross-hatch of grill marks on both sides, brushing with sauce during last 2 minutes of cooking. Serve with Cumin-Pepper Grilled Onions.

Makes 4 servings

Cumin-Pepper Grilled Onions
3 large yellow onions, sliced into ½-inch-thick slices (about 20 slices)
2 tablespoons olive oil
1 tablespoon ground cumin
1 ½ tablespoons ground coriander
¼ teaspoon cayenne pepper
¼ teaspoon onion powder
¼ teaspoon garlic powder
¼ teaspoon sugar
1 tablespoon paprika
Salt and pepper

Beer Pairing Suggestion:
American Pilsener or dark lager

1. Prepare grill. Brush onion slices with olive oil and grill until tender, turning twice. Place onions on platter. Mix cumin, coriander, cayenne, onion powder, garlic powder, sugar, paprika, and salt and pepper to taste. Lightly sprinkle spice blend over grilled onions and serve.

Makes 4 to 6 servings

148

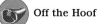

Allagash White Sausage with Roasted Red Pepper Polenta and Smoky White Sauce

This recipe by student Alexander Pope won the 2005 award at the Allagash culinary competition at the Institute for Culinary Education in New York City. Over the past four years, Allagash Brewing Company of Portland, Maine, has spurred the creativity and interest of hundred of culinary students—a terrific incentive for craft beer appreciation! Though the recipe is elaborate, you may prepare it in two stages, making the sausage and sauce a day ahead.

Sausage

- 1 cup Allagash White or other Belgian-style white ale, frozen in an ice cube tray
- 1½ pounds pork butt, cut into 1-inch cubes
- 1 tablespoon salt
- ½ teaspoon ground mace
- ½ teaspoon dried mustard
- ½ teaspoon dried oregano
- 1 teaspoon fresh-cracked black pepper
- ½ teaspoon sugar
- 6 ounces fatback, cut into 1-inch cubes
- 3 ounces dried cranberries, chopped
- 2 ounces fresh sage, chopped
- 4 ounces macadamia nuts, roasted and halved
- 5 feet sausage casing

1. Chill a large mixing bowl for 30 minutes. Combine cubed pork with salt, mace, mustard, oregano, pepper, and sugar in the chilled bowl. Mix well. Remove frozen ale cubes from tray. Pass pork, fatback and frozen ale in equal portions through sausage grinder fitted with coarse (¼-inch grind)

plate, and place in chilled 1-gallon bowl from an electric stand mixer.

2. Combine cranberries, sage, and macadamia nuts with meat mix. Mix in electric stand mixer with 1-gallon bowl fitted with paddle attachment for 20 seconds on MEDIUM; scrape bowl and mix again. Place bowl in a sink filled with ice to keep meat cold. Stuff into casings to make 6 to 8 sausages. Refrigerate.

Polenta

- 2 tablespoons butter
- 4 ounces shallots, minced
- 2 large red peppers, roasted, peeled, chopped to medium dice
- 1 tablespoon fresh rosemary leaves, chopped
- 5 cups whole milk
- ½ pound corn grits or polenta

1. In a large 2-quart saucepan, melt butter, and add shallots, peppers, and rosemary. Sauté for 4 to 5 minutes.
2. Add milk and bring to just under a boil. Add polenta in thin stream, whipping constantly. Cook polenta

Beer Pairing Suggestion:

Belgian-style wheat ale or unfiltered pale wheat ale

over medium heat, stirring constantly with a wooden spoon or heat-safe spatula, until mixture is thick and begins pulling away from sides of pot.

3. Line a half-sheet pan with buttered parchment paper. Pour polenta into pan, cover with another sheet of parchment and refrigerate.

Sauce

16 ounces American *witbier*
½ cup heavy cream
1 ounce smoky slab bacon, chopped
⅓ cup adobo sauce
1 chipotle en adobo, stemmed and chopped
½ cup chopped banana
2 teaspoons finely ground sea salt
Canola oil

24 ounces *witbier*, for simmering

Dried cranberries (optional)
Sage leaves (optional)

1. In a large, heavy saucepan placed over low heat, cook the *witbier* slowly until reduced by three-quarters, to yield about 4 ounces. It should not boil. In a separate skillet over low heat, sauté bacon with pepper and banana until bacon is crispy and golden.

2. Whisk in cream, simmer to reduce by one-third, and whisk in adobo sauce. Add pepper and banana. Purée with stick immersion blender in saucepan and keep warm. Adjust seasoning if necessary.

To assemble dish:

1. Bring 24 ounces *witbier* to a low simmer. Add sausages. Simmer in beer for 10 minutes.

2. Remove sausages and transfer to a hot grill, searing on all sides until just fully cooked.

3. Cut cooled polenta into rectangles. Sauté 3 pieces in oil until golden brown and hot. Cut 3 sausages into halves on an angle, and serve draped over polenta with warm sauce around. Add a small bunch of sage and a few dried cranberries to garnish.

Makes 6 to 8 servings

CHEF'S NOTE:

Sausage casings and fatback are available through specialty butcher stores, as well as by mail order through sausage supply websites. Fatback is the layer of hard fat that runs along the sides and belly of a hog, and is sold fresh at specialty butchers. Do not substitute lard or salt pork. To make it easier to cube the pork butt and fatback, place the meats in the freezer for 20 minutes before cutting.

SAFETY TIP:

Keep meat as cold as possible throughout the sausage-making process. Chill all bowls used to mix and hold raw meat, and chill stuffed uncooked sausages immediately.

151

Wild Game and Mushroom Stroganoff

Chris Swersey, brewer and avid outdoorsman, says this recipe takes a blue-collar, pedestrian dish and turns it into something decadent. "I prefer elk and moose, but venison will work in a pinch, as will beef. If you use venison, insist on a tenderloin cut. Seek out and pay for morels, if you can find them—they are worth it. The nutty flavor in morels complements the smoke flavors in the beer, and their meaty texture stands up to any meat you use. If you can't find morels, go with creminis, or button mushrooms in a pinch."

---

2 pounds elk, moose, or beef sirloin roast, well-trimmed (or if preferred, substitute lean ground beef)
2 tablespoons olive oil
Salt
2 tablespoons butter
1 cup diced yellow onion
⅓ cup minced shallot
½ pound sliced cremini mushrooms, or a mixture of cremini and morel mushrooms
12 ounces smoked porter
1 ½ cups beef broth (may be made from low-salt bouillon or beef base)
1 pint sour cream, lightly warmed
Freshly ground black pepper
1 pound egg noodles or pasta, cooked *al dente*

1. Cut meat across grain into thin slices about 1 inch long (skip this step if using ground beef). In large skillet, heat olive oil over medium-high heat. Add meat and salt to taste; sauté just until browned. Remove meat and reserve juices in skillet.

2. Add butter to juices in skillet and cook over medium-high heat until bubbly; add onion and shallot and sauté until translucent, about 3 minutes. Add mushrooms and sauté 2 minutes. Add meat and collected juices on platter back to skillet.

3. Meanwhile, heat beer in bowl in microwave or in small saucepan on stove until steaming. Add beef broth, stirring until dissolved. Add broth to meat mixture. Bring to a simmer, lower heat, and simmer loosely covered or uncovered for 30 minutes. Add warmed sour cream and gently stir until mixed. Simmer, covered, over low heat 8 to 10 minutes. Season with salt and pepper to taste. Serve over cooked pasta.

Makes 6 servings

Beer Pairing Suggestion:
Smoked porter

153

Seaver's Grilled Lamb Top Round Steaks with Caramelized Tomato Risotto

Chef Bart Seaver served this dish at a Clipper City beer dinner in Washington, D.C. He used tomato leaves for flavor, but you may substitute fresh rosemary leaves. Make the Flavored Oil and Caramelized Tomato Purée ahead of time, and allow 4 hours to marinate the lamb.

Flavored Leaf Oil

- 4 tablespoons extra virgin olive oil
- 2 tablespoons fresh organic tomato or rosemary leaves

Lamb

- 4 lamb top round steaks, about 8 ounces each
- 3 cloves garlic
- 2 anchovy fillets
- ½ cup canola oil
- 1 tablespoon brown sugar
- 1 tablespoon salt

Caramelized Tomato Purée

- 8 large plum tomatoes, puréed
- 2 teaspoons salt
- 2 tablespoons butter

Risotto

- 3 tablespoons olive oil
- 1 large yellow onion, diced
- 1 pound risotto (carnaroli) rice
- 2 tablespoons sea salt

Flavored Leaf Oil

1. Heat olive oil in small sauté pan until 180°F. Place tomato or rosemary leaves in hot oil and remove from heat.

2. Steep for at least 2 hours and up to 24 hours in advance of plating. Strain and discard leaves before use.

Lamb

1. Place lamb in a deep glass dish. Purée garlic, anchovy, canola oil, brown sugar, and salt in a blender until smooth. Pour mixture over lamb, cover and chill at least 4 hours, turning twice to marinate evenly.

2. Remove lamb from refrigerator 30 minutes before grilling. Place lamb steaks on hot grill and cook until desired doneness, about 12 to 15 minutes, depending on thickness. Let rest 5 minutes before serving.

Caramelized Tomato Purée

1. Place fresh tomato purée with salt in top of a double boiler over boiling water. Cook over high heat for about 3 hours, adding water as needed to bottom pan. Stir purée often, scraping down sides of pan.

2. After 3 hours, add butter and stir well to mix. Purée should be a dark, rusty red color, with a nutty aroma and thick texture.

Risotto

1. Heat oil in large saucepan over medium heat and sauté onion until tender. Add rice, stir to coat with oil, and cook for 2 to 3 minutes to toast rice.

2. Add 1 quart hot water and salt. Stir continuously over high heat until most of the water is absorbed. Add 1 more quart of hot water.

3. Turn heat down to medium and stir often until the rice is creamy and al dente. Just before serving, add in Caramelized Tomato Purée and stir to mix. Taste and adjust seasonings. Divide risotto evenly among 4 plates. Thinly slice lamb and arrange around risotto. Garnish with flavored oil and chopped herbs.

Makes 4 servings

Beer Pairing Suggestion:

English-style dry stout

Asian Ginger Beer Ribs

Adapted from a recipe by Detroit chef Jimmy Schmidt, these ribs make good use of ginger-spiced strong ale. Substitute an amber ale mixed with a teaspoon of freshly grated ginger root if you can't find a suitable spiced ale.

¼ cup canola oil
¼ cup minced fresh ginger root
8 cloves garlic, minced
¼ cup smoked paprika
(see p. 197)
¼ cup palm sugar (found in ethnic food stores, or substitute dark cane sugar)
Red pepper flakes, as desired
1 ½ tablespoons freshly ground black pepper
¼ cup low-sodium soy sauce
½ cup spiced beer (ginger or allspice)
1 tablespoon powdered Chinese mustard
1 ½ cups chopped scallions, divided
2 slabs baby back ribs, about 1 ½ pound each, trimmed
Nonstick cooking spray

1. In a large nonstick skillet, heat oil over medium-low heat. Add ginger and garlic; cook until tender, about 4 minutes. Stir in paprika, palm sugar, red pepper flakes to taste, and black pepper. Add soy sauce, beer, and mustard; stir to combine and bring to a simmer. Remove from heat; scrape mixture into a food processor fitted with a metal chopping blade. Add 1 cup scallions. Cover and pulse until mixture turns pasty; let cool.

2. Prepare baking sheet lined with heavy-duty foil; spray foil with nonstick cooking spray. Arrange ribs on foil; rub both sides with cooled spice paste. Wrap ribs in foil and chill in refrigerator at least 8 hours or overnight.

3. Preheat grill to medium heat. Place foil-wrapped ribs on grill; cover. Turn heat to low and cook 3½ hours. Test ribs (meat should be falling off bones). Move ribs to a large, deep-rimmed platter and remove foil carefully, as cooking juices collect inside foil. If desired, place ribs over direct heat for several minutes to allow exterior to become crispy and browned, turning 2 or 3 times to prevent the onions from burning. Place ribs on platter and garnish with remaining ½ cup chopped scallions.

Makes 6 appetizer servings or 3 to 4 entrée servings

Beer Pairing Suggestion:

Strong golden ale or ginger-spiced ale

155

Boscos Pork Chops with Guajillo Coffee BBQ Sauce

Make a pot of red beans to serve alongside this hearty, moderately spiced dish, suggests Chuck Skypeck, head brewer at Boscos, a chain of pubs headquartered in Memphis, Tennessee.

2 tablespoons kosher salt
¼ cup loosely packed brown sugar
1 tablespoon ground black pepper
¼ cup dark honey
2 tablespoons minced garlic
¼ cup minced onion
1 tablespoon fresh, chopped rosemary leaves
1 cup water
1 cup amber ale
4 large loin pork chops, trimmed

1. Mix salt, sugar, pepper, honey, garlic, onion, rosemary, water, and ale in large saucepan over medium heat. Bring to a simmer and stir until salt and sugar are dissolved. Remove from heat and let cool.
2. When brine has cooled, pour into a large resealable container and add pork chops. Seal and chill overnight or at least 3 hours.
3. Prepare a charcoal grill. Remove chops from brine and cook over low heat on charcoal grill until done, turning twice to obtain cross-hatch grill marks. Serve with red beans and Guajillo Coffee BBQ Sauce.

Guajillo Coffee BBQ Sauce

3 dried guajillo chiles (may substitute chipotles en adobo, if desired)**
½ cup strong coffee or espresso, cooled
1 cup diced yellow onion
1 tablespoon canola oil
1 cup ketchup
¼ cup malt vinegar
2 tablespoons brown sugar
2 tablespoons molasses
1 teaspoon Worcestershire sauce
2 tablespoons prepared yellow mustard
4 ounces brown ale
** *Use caution in handling hot peppers, and wash hands thoroughly before touching eyes*

1. Soak guajillo chiles in hot water to cover until rehydrated and pliable. (If substituting chiles en adobo, skip soaking in water.) Drain chiles and place in blender with coffee; cover blender and hold lid in place while pulsing on HIGH until smooth.
2. Place onion and oil in large saucepan over medium heat; cook until onions are tender. Add chile-coffee mixture, ketchup, vinegar, brown sugar, molasses, Worcestershire sauce, mustard, and brown ale. Reduce heat to low and simmer, uncovered, for 30 minutes. Do not let boil. Remove from heat and strain through fine mesh sieve. Warm sauce before serving with grilled pork chops.

Makes 4 servings

Beer Pairing Suggestion:

American brown ale or *dubbel*-style ale

156

Brewer's Pie

From Jason Fox, head brewer for Custom BrewCrafters in Honeoye Falls, New York, comes this recipe for a shepherd's pie. It has been adapted to the tastes of an American brewer and was originally made with the brewery's Wee Heavy Ale, a Scottish ale. It yields a huge casserole, so be sure to share with friends, Fox says.

3 pounds white potatoes, peeled and cubed
⅓ pound smoked bacon, chopped
1 medium onion, diced
3 medium carrots, chopped
3 stalks celery, chopped
2 tablespoons minced garlic
2 cups mushrooms, chopped (use a mixture of button, cremini, and Portobello)
2 ½ tablespoons chopped fresh thyme
2 ½ tablespoons chopped fresh rosemary
1 tablespoon hot Hungarian paprika
1 ½ teaspoons smoked paprika (see p. 197)
¼ cup chopped parsley
Salt
Freshly ground black pepper
⅔ pound ground veal
⅔ pound ground lean beef
⅔ pound ground pork
1 cup frozen peas
12 ounces smoked porter or strong ale
3 tablespoons flour
¼ cup whole milk
2 tablespoons butter
¼ teaspoon ground white pepper

2 cups shredded white cheddar cheese
Parsley sprigs, for garnish

1. Boil potatoes in large stockpot with salted water to cover them for 15 to 20 minutes.
2. Brown bacon in a large skillet placed over medium heat. Remove bacon with slotted spoon and set aside on paper towel to drain. Drain all but 2 tablespoons bacon fat and reserve in skillet. Preheat oven to 400°F. Sauté onion, carrots, and celery in reserved bacon fat over medium heat until soft. Add garlic, mushrooms, thyme, rosemary, paprikas, parsley, and salt and pepper; cook and stir 2 minutes.
3. Add meats and cook until no longer pink. Stir in peas, beer, and flour and simmer until slightly thickened.
4. When potatoes are tender, drain and return to pot. Place over low heat and dry cook for 1 minute to remove all water. Add milk, butter, salt, and white pepper. Mash until spreadable. Stir in cheese. Pour meat mixture into large, deep, ovenproof casserole, and spread potatoes evenly over top. Place baking sheet under casserole to catch drips and bake 25 minutes.
5. Crumble bacon over top of dish and bake for another 3 to 5 minutes, or until potatoes are browned. Garnish with parsley and serve hot.

Makes 8 to 10 servings

Beer Pairing Suggestion:

Dry stout or Scottish ale

CHEF'S NOTE:

To spread mashed potatoes over the filling without spilling, place large spoonfuls of the potatoes at 2-inch intervals dotted across the top of the casserole. Use a lightly oiled spatula to spread evenly.

Pear and Lamb Kebabs with Harpoon Winter Warmer-Rosemary Pan Sauce

Boston-based Chef Andy Husbands cooks and enjoys Harpoon ales all year 'round. To make the kebabs, you'll need 8 (10-inch) wooden or bamboo skewers, soaked in water for 20 minutes. Metal skewers may overcook the lamb, so use only if you like your meat well done.

⅓ cup olive oil
½ teaspoon cinnamon
Juice of 1 lemon
1 teaspoon fresh rosemary leaves, stems removed and minced
1 clove garlic, minced
2 pounds boned leg of lamb, trimmed and cut into 1-inch cubes
3 ripe, firm pears, cored and cut into 1 ½-inch chunks
2 red bell peppers, seeded and cut into 1 ½-inch squares
1 teaspoon kosher salt
1 teaspoon freshly ground black pepper
1 tablespoon canola oil
½ cup strong winter warmer ale
2 tablespoons brown sugar
2 tablespoons cold butter, cut into pieces
Salt and freshly ground black pepper

1. In large bowl, whisk together olive oil, cinnamon, lemon juice, rosemary, and garlic. Add lamb and toss to coat. Marinate in refrigerator at least 3 hours. Discard marinade.

2. In large bowl, combine lamb, pears, bell peppers, salt, and pepper. Thread lamb, pears, and peppers alternately on skewers.

3. Preheat oven to 250°F. Preheat large skillet over medium-high heat and grease with canola oil. When pan is hot, sear kebabs until dark golden brown, 2 to 4 minutes per side. Transfer kebabs to warmed platter, cover and keep warm in oven.

4. Add ale to skillet, scraping up browned bits with wooden spatula, and simmer until reduced by half, about 2 minutes. Turn heat to low and add brown sugar, stirring until smooth. Remove pan from heat and whisk in butter until fully incorporated. Season with salt and pepper. Spoon sauce over lamb kebabs and serve immediately.

Adapted from The Fearless Chef, *copyright 2004 by Andy Husbands and Joe Yonan. Used by permission of Adams Media. All rights reserved.*

Makes 6 to 8 servings

Beer Pairing Suggestion:

Seasonal winter ale or highly hopped brown ale

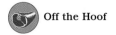

Lamb with Ratatouille and Hefeweiss Sauce

Adam Siegel, executive chef of Bartolotta's Lake Park Bistro in Milwaukee shares this recipe created for a dinner with the Sprecher Brewery of Glendale, Wisconsin.

Sauce

3 cups beef stock
1 tablespoon veal or beef demiglace
2 bay leaves
1 teaspoon juniper berries
2 cups diced mushroom caps and stems
3 sprigs thyme
8 ounces *hefeweiss* (preferably Sprecher)
1 teaspoon rice wine vinegar

Ratatouille

4 ounces extra virgin olive oil
1 medium onion, chopped
1 small red bell pepper, seeded and diced
1 small green bell pepper, seeded and diced
1 small zucchini, trimmed and diced
1 small yellow squash, trimmed and diced
1 small eggplant, trimmed and diced
2 tablespoons minced garlic
1 large tomato, seeded and diced
3 medium yellow Yukon Gold potatoes, peeled, diced, and parboiled until just tender
1 ounce basil leaves, julienned
1 bay leaf
Salt and black pepper
8 lamb chops

1. For the sauce, mix beef stock, demiglace, bay leaves, juniper berries, mushrooms, and thyme, and reduce by half in large stainless steel pot placed over medium heat. Reduce heat to low; add the beer and rice wine vinegar and simmer 10 minutes. Season to taste and strain; sauce should be thin in consistency and strong in flavor. Keep warm until ready to use.

2. Heat skillet over medium heat and add 1 ounce olive oil, onions, and peppers. Cook until the onions are soft and translucent, or about 7 minutes. Add zucchini and squash and cook 5 minutes. Place a separate skillet over medium heat and add the remaining oil and eggplant; sauté until golden brown. Add cooked eggplant to onion-squash mixture. Add garlic, tomato, and potatoes and cook 2 minutes. Add basil and bay leaf, and season with salt and pepper. Simmer 5 minutes.

3. Rub lamb chops with salt and pepper. Place lamb on grill over medium heat; cook each side for 4 to 5 minutes, depending on thickness, to reach preferred degree of doneness. Remove bay leaf. Serve with sauce and warmed vegetables.

Makes 4 servings

Beer Pairing Suggestion:

American dark wheat ale

CHEF'S NOTE:

Demiglace is a key ingredient for many sauces. It is a stock that has been simmered and reduced to a thick, gelatinous syrup. You can find packaged demiglace in specialty food stores, or make your own by simmering 2 cups of veal or beef stock with 1 pound veal or beef bones over very low heat until it turns into a thick syrup, about 3 hours. Strain and discard bones and keep covered in a sterile glass jar. Demiglace will keep for up to 2 weeks, chilled.

160

Green Peppercorn Crusted Beef Tenderloin

Chef Will Deason of the Willimantic Brewing Company, Willimantic, Connecticut, sears the beef medallions in a heavy skillet or sauté pan to capture the browned bits. Pan brownings make an excellent sauce when deglazed with a splash of Lagunitas Brewing Company's Brown Shugga or other strong ale. The technique is easy: add the ale to the pan with reserved brownings, and whisk well to incorporate all the browned bits. Let the mixture simmer over medium heat, and spoon over the plated beef. Serve with baked sweet potatoes and spinach salad.

½ cup green peppercorns
12 ounces barley wine, divided
6 thick slices beef tenderloin **
2 teaspoons sea salt
1 tablespoon minced garlic
2 tablespoons butter
2 tablespoons olive oil

** *Prepare the tenderloin by trimming away the white connective tissues known as silver skin, and freeze the tenderloin for 20 minutes before slicing into 1 ½-inch thick pieces. You may also rub the peppercorn paste over the whole tenderloin and slice after cooking, if serving a larger group.*

1. Rinse peppercorns in cold water and drain. Simmer in 8 ounces barley wine in small saucepan over low heat for 30 minutes. Drain and grind softened pepper to a paste in a food processor.
2. Line a baking sheet with parchment paper. Place beef tenderloin medallions on sheet pan. Rub with the sea salt and garlic. Smear on the peppercorn paste. Let rest for 15 minutes.
3. Place butter and olive oil in a large skillet over medium-high heat. When butter is bubbly and hot, sear beef, turning twice, until medium rare. Deglaze pan with a few spoonfuls of the remaining barley wine, if desired.

Makes 4 servings

Beer Pairing Suggestion:

Barley wine or Imperial porter

161

Indonesian Beef Rendang

Hawaii-born brewer Fal Allen was featured in *TIME Magazine*, seeking out Asian pantry ingredients to flavor new brews, such as the Archipelago Trader Brown Ale made with gula melaka (palm sugar) and fresh young ginger root. "Alamak, so good, it broke da mout," says Allen of this recipe. Serve with steamed rice.

2 tablespoons canola oil
6 cloves garlic, minced, about ¼ cup
6 large shallots, chopped, about 1 cup
3 ounces red chile peppers, seeded and finely chopped**
3 tablespoons freshly grated galangal (or 2 tablespoons freshly grated ginger root)
2 tablespoons freshly grated turmeric root (or 1 tablespoon powdered turmeric)
1 tablespoon freshly grated coriander root (or 1 teaspoon powdered coriander)
1 teaspoon freshly ground black pepper
1 teaspoon fresh ginger root, grated
2 stalks lemongrass, bruised and chopped
2 bay leaves
5 Kaffir lime leaves
1 tablespoon sea salt
4 cups coconut milk
4 ounces tamarind paste
2 ½ pounds beef chuck roast, well trimmed and cut into 1-inch cubes
Fresh minced cilantro leaves

** *Use caution in handling hot peppers, and wash hands thoroughly before touching eyes*

1. In large Dutch oven or 3-quart saucepan, heat the oil over medium heat; add garlic, shallots, and chiles as soon as oil heats, and sauté 2 to 3 minutes. Add galangal, turmeric, coriander, black pepper, ginger, lemongrass, bay leaves, lime leaves, and salt; sauté 2 to 3 more minutes.
2. Stir in coconut milk and tamarind paste and simmer until liquid becomes oily. Add beef cubes and stir frequently.
3. Reduce heat to low and simmer 3 to 4 hours, stirring occasionally. Coconut milk mixture should reduce to a thick gravy and turn dark brown. Serve with steamed rice and garnish with freshly minced cilantro leaves.

Makes 6 servings

Beer Pairing Suggestion:

Spiced ale or Imperial brown ale

CHEF'S NOTE:

You can find galangal (a cousin to ginger root), palm sugar, kaffir lime leaves, tamarind paste, and other Asian ingredients at specialty food stores, or by mail order. Choose your chili peppers according to your spice tolerance, as the original recipe uses bird or pequin peppers, which are very hot.

163

Cedar Planked Beef Brisket with Chocolate Ancho Rub

Rich chocolate with the earthy flavors from dried ancho chiles add a unique twist to a barbecued beef brisket, says Chef Sean Paxton. Use the Stout BBQ Sauce to play up all the wonderful flavors the cedar plank will add. You'll need a meat thermometer or electronic temperature probe to check the brisket as it cooks. If using a gas grill, position a drip pan filled with water and stout below the cedar plank, to block direct flame from the wood. Untreated wood planks for grilling are available in grilling and barbecue sections of hardware stores as well as some supermarkets.

Chocolate Ancho Rub

    1 cup cocoa
    ½ cup ground ancho chile powder
    ½ cup organic cane sugar
    ½ cup finely ground sea salt
    ¼ cup ground black pepper
    ¼ cup ground cumin

1. Place all ingredients in a quart-sized jar fitted with a lid. Seal tightly and shake to mix. Keeps covered up to 1 month.

Makes 3 cups

Brisket

    5 pounds beef brisket, whole, fat not removed
    1 cup Chocolate Ancho Rub

    1 large cedar plank, soaked 20 minutes in water to cover

    12 ounces stout

1. Rinse brisket under cold water to remove loose fat pieces, and pat dry with paper towel. Line a baking pan with 24 inches of plastic wrap, edges hanging over sides of pan, and sprinkle half of the Chocolate Ancho Rub in center of pan. Place brisket on top of rub, and sprinkle remaining rub evenly over the top of the meat. Turn meat to coat all sides of brisket. Cover brisket by bringing up edges of plastic wrap to press rub into meat; chill 2 hours. After 2 hours, remove from refrigerator and let meat rest while preparing grill.

2. Prepare grill by piling 2 mounds of charcoal at the farthest ends, with room for a drip pan in center. This will prevent the cedar plank from burning. Place drip pan in center, and fill halfway with mixture of water and 12 ounces stout. Ignite charcoal.

3. When coals are hot, remove plank from water and place on grill grate over coals. Let plank dry for 2 minutes. Turn over plank and set in the middle of the grill. Add more water to drip pan if needed. Unwrap brisket and place in center of plank. Cover grill. Place an electronic thermometer probe in top vent on lid and turn vent to almost closed. Over the next 4

hours, add charcoal as needed to keep heat near 250° F.

4. When brisket turns dark brown, remove from grill. Tent with foil and let meat rest 5 minutes per inch of thickness. Slice thinly, against the grain of the meat, and serve with Barrel-Aged Stout BBQ Sauce.

Makes 8 servings
    2 tablespoons olive oil

Barrel-Aged Stout BBQ Sauce

1 large yellow onion, chopped
1 tablespoon sea salt
2 tablespoons Chocolate Ancho Rub
¼ cup blackstrap molasses
12 ounces barrel-aged stout or dark ale
¼ cup malt or cider vinegar
1 can (15 ounces) tomato sauce, preferably organic
1 ounce brewed espresso

1. Place olive oil, onion, and salt in medium saucepan over medium heat. Cook, stirring occasionally, until onions are caramelized. Add Chocolate Ancho Rub and molasses, stir 30 seconds, then add beer to deglaze pan, whisking well.

2. Add vinegar and tomato sauce, stir and reduce heat to medium-low. Simmer, stirring occasionally, until sauce is reduced and thickened.

3. When sauce is brown and thick, add espresso and remove from heat. When cooled to lukewarm, transfer sauce to a blender, cover with lid, and hold lid in place with a folded tea towel. Purée on HIGH until smooth, about 1 minute. Use with the brisket, or keep refrigerated in a resealable glass or nonreactive container.

Makes 2 cups

Old Chub Chocolate Mole

This recipe is adapted from one created by Denver Chef Charles Edson using the Oscar Blues Old Chub brand of Scotch ale. We adapted it to be thicker and sweeter by adding caramelized onion and garlic to offset the hoppy bitterness of the ale.

1 tablespoon canola oil
⅓ cup minced Vidalia onion
1 tablespoon minced garlic
1 ¼ cups chicken stock
1 cup golden raisins
3 dried ancho chiles, crushed**
1 teaspoon garam masala
1 teaspoon sea salt
½ cup pine nuts, toasted
½ cup almonds, toasted
1 cup Scotch ale
3 ounces Mexican chocolate (such as Ibarra brand), grated
** *Use caution in handling hot peppers, and wash hands thoroughly before touching eyes*

1. Heat oil in large saucepan over low heat. Stir in onion and garlic and cook until caramelized, about 10 minutes. Add chicken stock, raisins, and chiles; simmer 10 minutes. Add garam masala and salt and remove from heat.
2. When cool, place mixture in food processor fitted with metal chopping blade and add toasted nuts. Cover and pulse on HIGH until mixture turns pasty.
3. Return mixture to saucepan and place over low heat. Slowly add Scotch ale until desired consistency is reached, best as a thick gravy. Add grated chocolate and stir until melted. Taste and adjust seasonings. Use over roasted and shredded turkey or chicken.

Makes 2 ½ cups

CHEF'S NOTE:

Garam masala is an Indian spice blend of ground cloves, cinnamon, cardamom, coriander, and black pepper. You may substitute a pinch of each of those spices if you can't find the premixed garam masala in Asian food sections of large supermarkets or ethnic groceries.

Beer Pairing Suggestion:

Chocolate stout or black lager

Marsaglia's Truffled Potatoes

Vince Marsaglia of Pizza Port in Carlsbad, California, makes these incredibly rich potatoes with truffle cheese—an Italian specialty that infuses the curds of farmhouse cheese with shaved black or white truffles—before glazing the final plating with a gilding of white truffle oil. It's worth the splurge and makes a rich accompaniment to meats of all kinds. You can find truffle cheese and truffle oil in specialty food stores or Italian markets.

---

1 tablespoon softened butter
3 pounds Yukon Gold potatoes, peeled
⅓ cup heavy cream
3 tablespoons minced garlic
¼ pound grated Pecorino cheese
1 pound truffle cheese, cubed
Salt and freshly ground black pepper
2 tablespoons white truffle oil

1. Preheat oven to 375°F. Grease large casserole dish with softened butter. Thinly slice potatoes with mandoline into a large bowl filled with heavy cream and minced garlic. Stir sliced potatoes to coat evenly with cream to avoid discoloration.

2. Arrange layers of potatoes, Pecorino, truffle cheese, salt and pepper ending with a layer of potato, to a height of about 1½ inches, in the prepared casserole dish. Cover with foil. Bake 1¼ hours. Let rest for 5 minutes before slicing into 8 portions and serving. Finish by drizzling about ½ teaspoon white truffle oil on top of each serving.

Makes 8 servings

Beer Pairing Suggestion:

Belgian-style golden ale or Dortmunder lager

ON THE WING

Chicken Breast à la Blanche de Chambly

Chef François Pellerin of Fourquet Fourchette in Chambly, Quebec, shares a classic French dish, *Poitrine de Poulet en Velouté*, enhanced with a splash of Blanche du Chambly. Pellerin suggests serving it with roasted summer vegetables and rice. For ease, you may prepare the Velouté in advance.

2 tablespoons salted butter
2 tablespoons olive oil
6 boneless, skinless chicken breasts
¼ cup white ale
Pinch saffron
1 tablespoon mashed ripe banana
2 tablespoons lemon zest
2 tablespoons orange zest
1 tablespoon crushed pineapple
Pinch ground coriander
2 cups Chicken Velouté
Salt and pepper

1. Preheat oven to 300°F. Place butter and olive oil in a large skillet over medium heat. When butter is bubbly, add chicken and sear on both sides. Transfer chicken to a roasting dish and bake 25 minutes. Reserve skillet.

2. While chicken bakes, prepare the Chicken Velouté. Deglaze the reserved skillet placed over medium heat with white ale, add saffron, and simmer 1 minute. Add banana, zests, pineapple, and coriander. Simmer 2 minutes. Add Velouté, reduce heat to low, and simmer, whisking often, about 8 to 10 minutes. Add salt and pepper to taste.

3. Press the Velouté through a sieve and discard solids. Serve chicken with sauce and desired accompaniments.

Makes 6 servings

Chicken Velouté

2 cups chicken stock
2 tablespoons butter
1 tablespoon plus 1 teaspoon flour
¼ teaspoon salt
¼ teaspoon ground white pepper

1. Bring stock to a simmer in a small saucepan over medium heat. Remove from heat and set aside.

2. Melt butter in medium saucepan over low heat. When butter is bubbly, whisk in flour and cook until mixture turns golden and smells like popcorn, whisking often.

3. Slowly whisk in hot stock by the ¼ cupful, whisking until smooth. Bring to a simmer. Reduce heat to very low and simmer, uncovered, 5 minutes or until thickened. Season to taste with salt and white pepper. Use immediately, or cover and chill.

Beer Pairing Suggestion:

Witbier or summer ale

169

Pan-Seared Duck Breast with Door County Cherry Sauce and Gruyère Mashed Potatoes

Chef Brett Muellenbach of the Horse & Plow, of the American Club, Kohler, Wisconsin, offers monthly beer dinners featuring American craft brewers. Here's one of his favorite recipes using duck; in a pinch, you could use other game birds or chicken.

1 cup dried tart cherries
4 trimmed and boned duck breasts
2 tablespoons salted butter
2 large shallots, minced (about ¼ cup)
2 cups unsweetened tart cherry juice
¼ cup brown sugar
2 teaspoons cornstarch dissolved in 1 tablespoon cold water
Salt and ground white pepper

1. Place the cherries and 2 cups of hot water in a stainless steel bowl. Soak cherries for 30 minutes to an hour. Drain cherries and reserve for sauce.
2. In a large skillet placed over medium heat, sear duck breasts, skin side down, until the skin turns brown. Turn over and sear until breasts are cooked to medium rare. Remove from heat, and cover to keep warm.
3. Melt the butter in a medium saucepan over medium-low heat. Simmer shallots in butter until soft. Add the cherry juice, rehydrated cherries, and sugar, and bring to a boil. Add enough of the cornstarch slurry to thicken the sauce so it coats a spoon. Adjust the seasoning with salt and white pepper if necessary. Slice the cooked duck breasts on a bias. Serve with cherry sauce and Gruyère Mashed Potatoes.

Makes 4 servings

Beer Pairing Suggestion:
Cherry stout

170

Gruyère Mashed Potatoes

An ideal accompaniment to roasted meats and dark ale, from Chef Brett Muellenbach of the Horse & Plow, the American Club, Kohler, Wisconsin.

6 russet potatoes, peeled and diced
½ cup heavy cream
¼ pound salted butter
¼ cup sour cream
½ cup Gruyère cheese, shredded
Salt and ground white pepper

Beer Pairing Suggestion:
Amber ale

1. In a medium saucepan bring potatoes and 3 quarts salted water to a boil. Cook until potatoes are soft.
2. Heat butter and cream over low heat until the butter is completely melted; set aside. Drain potatoes and press through a food mill or mash until fluffy. Stir in the cream/butter mixture, the sour cream, and the Gruyère. Taste and adjust seasonings with salt and white pepper.

Makes 4 servings

172

Chicken and Artichoke Hearts in Anchor Steam Beer

Diane Alexander served this dish at a Brickskeller celebration with Anchor Brewing Company, using Anchor Steam beer and fresh figs to enhance the braising liquid. Alexander suggests serving it over steamed rice.

3 pounds fryer chicken pieces, trimmed (6 to 8 pieces)
½ cup flour
1 teaspoon salt
½ teaspoon freshly ground black pepper
1 teaspoon hot paprika
2 tablespoons unsalted butter
2 tablespoons olive oil
2 pounds frozen artichoke hearts, thawed and drained
8 ounces fresh mushrooms, cleaned and sliced
12 ounces steam beer
2 ounces fresh figs, diced
1 Meyer lemon, cut into 6 wedges
Fresh minced parsley

1. Preheat oven to 325°F. Dredge chicken pieces thoroughly in mixture of flour, salt, pepper, and paprika. Heat butter and oil in large deep skillet over medium heat. Brown each piece of chicken on all sides, without crowding the skillet.

2. As the chicken browns, transfer the pieces to a large casserole. Set skillet aside. When the bottom of the casserole is covered with chicken, add half the artichokes and half the mushrooms. Add any remaining browned chicken, then the remaining artichokes and mushrooms.

3. Deglaze the skillet with steam lager and a whisk to emulsify pan drippings. Mix in fresh figs and simmer over medium heat 1 minute, scraping skillet well to mix in all of pan brownings. Pour warm fig-beer sauce over chicken. Cover casserole with foil and bake 50 to 60 minutes or until tender. Serve with steamed rice, garnished with lemon wedges and minced parsley.

Makes 6 servings

Beer Pairing Suggestion:
American steam beer

173

Braised Pheasant *Saison*

Chef Rick Martin of Free State Brewing Company in Lawrence, Kansas, uses pheasant, but you can use duck breasts, or chicken breasts in pinch. The blackberry sauce also goes well with pork. You'll need a mesh sieve or the cone-shaped metal chinois to remove the blackberry seeds—or pick seedless berries to make the sauce.

½ cup fresh blackberries
¼ cup balsamic vinegar
2 teaspoons cornstarch
1 tablespoon cold water
¼ cup olive oil
4 wing-on, cleaned pheasant breasts
½ cup flour, mixed with 1 teaspoon salt and pepper
2 shallots, chopped
3 fresh thyme sprigs
2 cloves
1 orange, thinly sliced, peel on
1 apple, cored and sliced
1 cup pressed apple cider
1 cup chicken stock
1 cup *saison*
1 cup heavy cream

1. Cook blackberries with vinegar until berries dissolve. Strain out seeds and pulp; return purée to heat. Mix cornstarch with cold water to make a slurry, and add to the warmed fruit. Whisk and heat until thickened. Remove from heat and set aside to cool to room temperature.

2. In a large sauté pan, heat olive oil over medium-high heat. Dredge pheasant breasts in flour mixture and shake off excess. Brown breasts in oil, turning often until golden on all sides. Add shallots, thyme, clove, apple, and orange slices. Allow shallots and fruit to lightly caramelize. Add cider, stock, and *saison*. Cover and cook over low heat. Remove pheasant breasts when done. Uncover pan and allow sauce to reduce by half.

3. Once sauce is reduced, add cream 1 tablespoon at a time, whisking well after each addition. Reduce sauce until syrupy enough to coat a spoon. Strain the sauce through a mesh sieve or chinois, being sure to push all of the liquid out of the solids, and return liquid to pan. Return pheasant breasts to the sauce and reheat if necessary. Drizzle blackberry sauce over pheasant and garnish with fresh thyme sprigs.

Makes 4 servings

Beer Pairing Suggestion:
Fruit ale or *saison*

174

Roast Turkey with Samuel Adams Old Fezziwig Ale Bread Pudding

Ask your butcher to halve and debone the turkey, except for the leg bones. The turkey will cook quickly as a result. The bread puddings may be prepared ahead of time and reheated just before serving.

8 tablespoons unsalted butter
3 tablespoons fresh lemon juice
2 tablespoons minced fresh
  thyme leaves
  Coarse salt
  Freshly ground white pepper
1 (14-pound) turkey, halved and
  de-boned, with only leg bone
  attached, rinsed well and dried
  Freshly ground black pepper
3 cloves garlic, cut into slivers

1. Preheat oven to 350°F.
2. In bowl of food processor fitted with metal cutting blade, combine butter, lemon juice, thyme, salt, and white pepper to taste. Cover and pulse on HIGH until mixture is well blended. Form flavored butter into 2 equal pieces, wrap in plastic and place in refrigerator to chill until firm.
3. Season turkey with salt and black pepper. Place a piece of flavored butter and some garlic slivers under skin of each turkey half. Arrange on large roasting pan at least 3 inches deep.

4. Place turkey in oven and roast about 55 minutes to 1 hour, or until instant-read thermometer inserted into thickest part of bird registers 160°F.
5. Place turkey halves on large serving platter and serve with Samuel Adams Old Fezziwig Ale Bread Pudding.

Makes enough to serve 6, with leftovers for sandwiches

Beer Pairing Suggestion:

Winter strong ale

Samuel Adams Old Fezziwig Ale Bread Pudding

    2 tablespoons unsalted butter,
      softened
    4 large eggs, beaten
    1 cup heavy cream
    1 cup winter strong ale
    ½ pound cooked lean bacon,
      crumbled
    2 tablespoons minced flat-leaf
      parsley
    2 tablespoons thinly sliced
      scallions
    1 tablespoon pureed roasted
      garlic
      Coarse salt
      Freshly ground black pepper
    6 cups (½-inch cubes) fresh
      white bread crumbs

1. Preheat oven to 350°F. Lightly coat interior of six 6-ounce ramekins with softened butter. Set aside.

2. Whisk eggs, cream, and beer together in large mixing bowl. Stir in bacon, parsley, scallions, and garlic purée. Season mixture with salt and pepper. Fold in bread cubes, and allow bread to soak up egg mixture.

3. When bread mixture is very moist, spoon equal portion into each of prepared ramekins. Place filled ramekins into roasting pan and pour warm water in to come halfway up sides of ramekins.

4. Place pan in oven and bake 25 to 35 minutes, or until edges begin to brown and center is almost set. Increase oven temperature to 400°F, and bake puddings an additional 5 minutes, or until browned. (These can be baked early in the day and reheated in a microwave oven, or baked for 15 minutes in a 325°F oven just before using.) Remove from oven and serve immediately.

Makes 6 servings

Waterzooi

Sean Paxton, a homebrewer and chef based in Northern California, says, "The flavor of Waterzooi will warm the soul." A traditional Flemish dish from Ghent, Belgium, it may be prepared for everyday dinners with chicken, and as a splurge, with shellfish.

4 tablespoons unsalted butter
1 tablespoon olive oil
2 pounds chicken breasts, boned and chopped
3 large shallots, minced
3 large leeks, trimmed, washed free of grit, and sliced
1 large bulb fennel, trimmed and julienned
2 carrots, julienned
2 stalks celery, sliced
4 potatoes, peeled and cut into 1-inch cubes
4 cups chicken stock
1 cup *tripel* or strong golden ale
2 bay leaves
1 tablespoon fresh thyme leaves
1 cup heavy cream
¼ cup Italian flat leaf parsley, minced

1. Put butter and olive oil in a large Dutch oven or stockpot and place over medium heat until the butter bubbles. Add chicken and stir. Let chicken brown 3 minutes, then reduce heat to low. Add shallots and cook 3 minutes.

2. Add sliced leeks and fennel, and cook 3 minutes or until leeks turn soft. Add carrots, celery, potatoes, stock, beer, bay leaves, thyme, and cream, bringing mixture to a simmer. Cover and cook 25 to 30 minutes, or until chicken is cooked through and vegetables are tender. Do not bring to a boil, just a light simmer, or cream will curdle. Remove bay leaves before serving. Ladle Waterzooi into warm bowls and garnish with parsley.

Makes 4 to 6 servings

Beer Pairing Suggestion:

American *tripel*-style ale, strong golden ale

179

DESSERTS

Native Bay Dark Chocolate Porter Cake

Chef Nathan Berg of Native Bay Restaurant and Lounge in Chippewa Falls, Wisconsin, uses the Viking Brewing Company's Whole Stein porter, but testers found the cake was more chocolaty than beery. Try making a powdered sugar glaze with the porter of your choice for a bolder beer flavor. Serve layers filled with whipped cream, or softened caramel or nut-flavored ice cream, and topped with mocha or berry sauce.

8 ounces porter
12 ounces dark chocolate, finely chopped
1 ½ teaspoons vanilla
1 stick (8 tablespoons) unsalted butter, cubed
5 eggs
3 ½ cups all-purpose flour
2 ½ cups sugar
1 teaspoon baking powder
1 tablespoon baking soda
1 teaspoon finely ground sea salt

1. Preheat oven to 350°F. Coat two 9-by-9-inch cake pans with oil and line with parchment paper; spray lightly with cooking spray.
2. In heavy-bottomed saucepan, bring beer to a full boil. Slowly whisk in dark chocolate until completely melted. Remove from heat, add vanilla and butter, and stir until butter is melted.
3. In medium mixing bowl, lightly beat eggs. Slowly drizzle chocolate-beer mixture into eggs while whisking. Set aside.
4. In large mixing bowl, combine remaining dry ingredients and mix well. Using rubber spatula, slowly fold chocolate mixture into dry ingredients, mixing as little as necessary. Batter should drip slowly from spatula.
5. Fill prepared pans evenly with batter. Place on middle rack in oven and bake about 45 minutes or until a knife inserted in the cake comes out clean. Allow cake to cool for 60 minutes before serving.

Makes 2 9-by-9-inch cakes

Beer Pairing Suggestion:
Fruit beer or American brown porter

181

Vermont Maple Syrup and Porter-Poached Apples

As prepared by Chef Will Deason of the Willimantic Brewing Company and Main Street Café in Willimantic, Connecticut, these apples are gently spiced and good for brunch as well as dessert.

6 baking apples (Rome, Cortland, Macintosh, or Golden Delicious)
3 (12-ounce) bottles porter or other dark ale
1 cup Vermont maple syrup
Juice of 1 lemon, plus additional for adding to water
¼ teaspoon mace
1 cinnamon stick
Fresh seasonal berries for garnish

1. Wash and core apples. Place in cold water mixed with lemon juice to prevent browning.
2. Bring porter, maple syrup, lemon juice, mace, and cinnamon stick to a boil. Reduce to a simmer; submerge apples in poaching liquid. Poach 8 to 10 minutes, or until apples begin to soften and look shiny.
3. Remove from liquid, plate, and garnish with Maple Whipped Cream, Cinnamon Toasted Oats, and fresh seasonal berries.

Makes 6 servings

Maple Whipped Cream
2 cups heavy cream
2 tablespoons granulated sugar
2 tablespoons Vermont maple syrup

1. Place ingredients in a cold, stainless steel bowl. Whip slowly until stiff peaks form. Use immediately or refrigerate until needed.

Makes 2 cups

Cinnamon Toasted Oats
1 cup whole oats
3 tablespoons melted butter
¼ cup packed dark brown sugar
Pinch salt
1 tablespoon cinnamon
Pinch freshly grated nutmeg

1. Preheat oven to 350°F. Combine ingredients and spread on a lined baking sheet. Toast oats until golden brown, about 20 minutes, stirring occasionally.

Makes 1 cup

Beer Pairing Suggestion:
Porter

182

Obsidian Stout Chocolate Tiramisu

The flavor of this dessert depends upon the freshest possible ingredients, so check the date of the pasteurized eggs. If you prefer an egg-free tiramisu, omit the eggs and sugar, and substitute 1 cup sweetened whipping cream, whipped to stiff peaks, folded into the softened mascarpone cheese. Use a dry or sweet stout, depending on your taste.

½ cup stout
½ cup strong espresso
16 ladyfinger sponge cakes
3 egg yolks
¾ cup sugar
1 pound mascarpone cheese, brought to room temperature
⅓ cup pasteurized egg whites (found in refrigerated dairy case) or 1 cup sweetened whipped cream
¼ teaspoon vanilla extract
4 ounces bittersweet dark chocolate

1. Mix stout with espresso and set aside.
2. Soak ladyfingers in stout-coffee mixture for a few minutes and fit 4 each along sides and bottom of each of 4 8-ounce ramekins.
3. Beat egg yolks and sugar until smooth and lemony in color. Place in top bowl of double boiler over simmering water, with heat at low. Whisking constantly, cook mixture until it just begins to thicken and reaches 160°F. Immediately remove from heat. Scrape into large bowl, and whisk in the lukewarm mascarpone cheese, 1 tablespoon at a time.
4. Whip egg whites until soft peaks form, and fold into cheese mixture. Stir in vanilla extract and divide filling evenly among ramekins. Cover and chill 4 hours.
5. Just before serving, shave 1 ounce chocolate over each ramekin (a potato peeler works well for this).

Makes 4 servings

Beer Pairing Suggestion:

Dry or sweet stout

Obsidian Stout Chocolate Cherry Scones

Renata Stanko of Lebanon, Oregon, uses Deschutes Obsidian Stout in these tender scones. You may use a sweet or dry stout and adjust sugar, if desired. This recipe was a finalist in the National Beer Wholesalers Association's Cooking with Beer Challenge.

5 ounces dried Bing cherries
¾ cup stout
2 cups unbleached flour
1 tablespoon baking powder
3 tablespoons sugar
½ teaspoon salt
5 tablespoons cold unsalted butter, cut into ¼-inch cubes
4 ounces dark chocolate chunks
¼ cup heavy cream
1 tablespoon powdered sugar

1. Prepare cookie sheet for baking by covering with parchment paper; set aside.
2. Chop cherries coarsely and soak in beer 30 minutes. Preheat oven to 425°F.
3. Combine flour, baking powder, sugar, and salt in mixing bowl. Cut in butter with pastry blender until mixture resembles coarse meal. Add cherries with beer, chocolate, and cream. Quickly mix until dough forms a ball.
4. Place dough on top of another sheet of parchment paper and pat into 8-inch circle. Cut into 8 wedges.
5. Place wedges on prepared baking sheet and bake 12 to 15 minutes. Remove from oven and cool 4 minutes. Dust with powdered sugar and serve immediately.

Makes 8 scones

Beer Pairing Suggestion:

Chocolate stout or cherry ale

185

Fudge Stout Brownies

It has been almost twenty years since I first poured stout into a batch of brownies, but one taste of the Original Hawaiian Chocolate Company's best bittersweet chocolate drove me to experiment. I had agreed to bring dessert to the Kona Brewers Fest barbecue and decided to bake with the local ingredients—Kona Brewing Company's Da Grind Buzz Stout and the artisanal chocolate. The resulting stout brownies were moist, fudgy, and deeply chocolaty. The flavor was so rich most guests of the Brewers Luau at the Kona Brewers Fest savored them like truffles.

Butter for coating pan
1 tablespoon cocoa powder
1 stick (½ cup) unsalted butter
4 ounces chopped bittersweet chocolate
1 cup granulated sugar
2 tablespoons brown sugar
2 large eggs
2 egg yolks
1 teaspoon vanilla extract
⅓ cup coffee stout
2 tablespoons bourbon
¾ cup sifted all-purpose flour
¼ teaspoon salt

1 cup chopped nuts, such as macadamia, pecans, or walnuts (optional)

1. Preheat oven to 325°F. Prepare a 9-inch metal baking pan by buttering it well and dusting inside with 1 tablespoon cocoa powder. Set aside. In a large 2-quart saucepan, melt stick of butter over low heat until liquid. Add chopped chocolate, stirring often, until melted and smooth. Remove saucepan from heat and let cool to lukewarm (still liquid but not hot).

2. Stir in sugars and mix well. Beat together 2 eggs, yolks, vanilla, stout, and bourbon in a large measuring cup until smooth. Sift flour with salt. Stir stout mixture into saucepan by thirds, alternating with flour by ⅓ cupfuls, and stirring after each addition until batter is just blended. Stir in nuts if desired. Do not overbeat.

3. Scrape batter into prepared 9-inch-square metal pan and bake at 325°F for about 1 hour. Let cool to lukewarm before slicing. Use a knife dipped in warm water and wiped clean with each slice (otherwise, because of the very fudgy texture, the brownies will clump).

Makes 16 fudgy brownies

Beer Pairing Suggestion:

Coffee stout or barrel-aged stout

CHEF'S NOTE:

Coffee stouts are made by breweries across North America, but if you can't find one, substitute 2 ounces sweet stout mixed with 1 ounce brewed espresso.

187

Pike's XXXXX Chocolate Sauce

Rose Ann Finkel, an extraordinary chef and partner in the Pike Brewery, cautions not to substitute chocolate chips for the chopped chocolate in this recipe "because chips are too waxy" and the sauce won't be as smooth.

---

1 cup heavy cream
½ cup dry stout
8 ounces bittersweet chocolate (60% to 72% cocoa), finely chopped
1 teaspoon Madagascar Bourbon vanilla extract

Beer Pairing Suggestion:

Dry stout

1. Combine the cream and stout in a saucepan and bring it to a simmer over medium-high heat. Pour it over the chopped chocolate and gently whisk until the chocolate is melted and the sauce is smooth. Whisk in the vanilla and serve warm, or cool completely and store in airtight container in refrigerator. Keeps for up to 1 week.

Makes 1 ²/₃ cups

188

Pelican Wee Heavy Marshmallows

These ale-fluffed confections, originally made with Pelican Pub's Wee Heavy, will add a bit of beer flavor to mugs of hot cocoa, or use them as the filling for adult S'mores, made with graham crackers and bittersweet chocolate. Use organic powdered sugar for the best taste and texture. Adjust the water to soften gelatin according to humidity and elevation. The texture should be thick and smooth, not grainy.

1 ounce plain gelatin
4 to 5 ounces cold water
    Unsalted butter for pan
¼ cup sifted organic powdered
    sugar for pan
4 ounces Scottish ale
2 cups pure cane sugar
¼ teaspoon finely ground sea
    salt
6 ounces corn syrup
½ teaspoon Madagascar
    Bourbon vanilla extract
2 cups organic powdered sugar
    sifted with 2 tablespoons corn-
    starch

1. Bloom or soften gelatin in 4 to 5 ounces water in the bowl of a stand mixer (adjust according to humidity and elevations, gelatin should be soft, not grainy). Set aside for 10 minutes. Prepare a 9-by-13-inch glass baking pan by greasing it with butter on base and sides and sprinkling it with powdered sugar to cover base and sides. Rotate pan so sugar is evenly applied. Set aside.

2. Combine ale, sugar, salt, and corn syrup in a saucepan over medium-high heat, and bring to soft-ball stage, 238°F to 240°F on a candy thermometer.

3. Place bowl with bloomed gelatin into a stand electric mixer fitted with the whisk attachment. Turn mixer to MEDIUM-LOW and slowly pour in hot sugar mixture, whisked into bloomed gelatin until it starts to fluff. Do not whip too fast or the hot syrup will splatter. Stop mixer and scrape sides. Restart mixer on MEDIUM-HIGH and whip until mixture becomes white and fluffy, about 10 minutes, adding vanilla extract during final minute of mixing.

4. Scrape mixture into powdered sugar-lined pan and spread evenly to desired thickness (about 1 inch). Sprinkle top with powdered sugar-starch mixture and set aside. When cooled and set (from 30 minutes to 3 hours depending on humidity), turn slab out onto a cookie sheet covered with half of the sifted powdered sugar mixture. Slice into cubes with sharp knife or scissors dipped in warm water between each slice. Roll cubes in remaining powdered sugar mixture so all sides are coated. Let air-dry until not sticky (time varies according to humidity), and place in covered container. Will keep up to 10 days.

CHEF'S NOTE:

Vanilla extracts range in taste from artificially flavored extracts to top-quality Madagascar Bourbon vanilla extract. For these marshmallows, splurge on the pricier vanilla, since the flavor makes a difference. You can find Madagascar Bourbon vanilla extract in the baking section of specialty food stores and online by mail order.

189

Makes about 50 marshmallows

Flourless Chocolate Cake with Molten Ganache

Executive Chef Jeff Foresman of the Hyatt Regency Hill Country Resort and Spa in Texas prepared this special dessert with Shiner Dunkelweizen for a dinner hosted by Jaime Jurado and the Spoetzl Brewery of Shiner, Texas.

---

12 ounces unsalted butter
8 ounces quality bittersweet chocolate, chopped (Callebaut recommended)
4 eggs
4 egg yolks
⅓ cup granulated sugar
¼ cup dark wheat beer

8 (4-ounce) buttered ramekins or small soufflé cups

1. Preheat oven to 350°F. Melt butter in a large saucepan over low heat, add chopped chocolate and stir until melted and smooth. Remove from heat. Or, place chopped chocolate and butter in microwave-safe bowl, cover and heat on MEDIUM for 30 seconds. Remove from microwave, stir, and heat again on MEDIUM 30 seconds. Stir until melted. Do not overcook.
2. Combine eggs, yolks, and sugar in mixing bowl of standing electric mixer fitted with paddle attachment. Beat until ribbon forms, 8 to 10 minutes. Fold in chocolate-butter mixture. Stir in beer and scrape sides of bowl. Divide equally between ramekins. Bake 8 to 10 minutes.

3. Remove from oven and place 2-ounce scoop of Ganache in center of each ramekin. Replace in oven and bake 30 minutes. Remove from oven, let cool for 5 minutes and serve immediately.

Ganache

¾ cup heavy cream
4 ounces unsalted butter
¼ cup granulated sugar
8 ounces good quality bitter-sweet chocolate, chopped (Callebaut recommended)

1. In medium saucepan, heat cream, butter, and sugar over medium heat. Bring to a simmer. Remove from heat, add dark chocolate and whisk well until melted. Let cool until set.

Makes 8 servings

Beer Pairing Suggestion:

American dark wheat beer or dark lager

191

Paxton's Chocolate Stout Pudding

Why is it that stout and chocolate go so well together? Proof is in this pudding, a wonderful dessert that is rich in flavor, smooth, and not overly sweet, allowing the dark ale to stand up to the strong chocolate notes. Chef Sean Paxton uses a chocolate stout from Bison Brewing Company of Berkeley, California, but a sweet milk stout would be just as delicious.

4 tablespoons cornstarch
1 tablespoon organic cocoa powder
¼ teaspoon finely ground sea salt
½ cup organic pure cane sugar
⅓ cup packed light brown sugar
¾ cup whole milk
1 ¼ cups heavy cream
1 cup chocolate stout or sweet stout
4 ounces bittersweet chocolate**, chopped fine
1 teaspoon Madagascar Bourbon vanilla extract

** *Paxton recommends Scharffen Berger 70% Cacao Bittersweet, Valrhona 85% Dark Bittersweet, or Lindt 70% Dark Extra Fine*

1. In large bowl or top of double boiler, whisk cornstarch, cocoa, sea salt, and sugars until smooth and no cocoa lumps remain. Slowly whisk in cold milk and place over a pot of boiling water. Slowly stir in cream and stout until well combined. Add chopped chocolate and stir occasionally until mixture is thick and smooth, about 12 to 15 minutes. Remove from heat and stir in vanilla.

2. Pour pudding into 6 individual serving cups or a large serving dish. Refrigerate at least 4 hours or until chilled.

3. Alternatively, pour the pudding into a shallow bowl and chill 2 to 4 hours. Then place mixture into an ice cream maker and freeze, following the manufacturer's instructions. Remove the ice cream from the machine and transfer to an airtight container; freeze overnight for smoothest texture.

Makes 6 servings

Beer Pairing Suggestion:

Raspberry or cherry ale

Harpoon Winter Warmer-Spiced Pumpkin and Cranberry Bread

For a great holiday gift, our taste-testers suggest baking the batter in 4 mini-loaf pans for 55 minutes, and wrapping the loaves in baskets with bottles of your favorite winter ale.

3 cups all-purpose flour
2 teaspoons ground cinnamon
1 teaspoon baking powder
1 teaspoon baking soda
1 teaspoon salt
½ cup winter ale
¼ cup heavy cream
¾ cup unsalted butter, softened
2 cups sugar
1 teaspoon vanilla extract
3 eggs
1 cup canned or fresh pumpkin purée
1 cup dried cranberries, coarsely chopped
1 tablespoon minced fresh ginger (about 1-inch piece)
½ cup coarsely chopped pecans

1. Preheat oven to 350°F. Grease two 9-by-5-by-3-inch loaf pans or 12-cup muffin tin.
2. Whisk flour, cinnamon, baking powder, baking soda, and salt in medium bowl; set aside. Combine ale and cream in glass measuring cup; set aside.
3. In large bowl of electric mixer, cream butter and sugar until fluffy, about 3 minutes. Add vanilla and eggs, one by one, scraping down bowl and blending well after each addition.
4. Mix in pumpkin, cranberries, and ginger. Add dry ingredients in 3 additions, alternating with ale and cream mixture. Mix well and scrape down bowl between additions. Blend 30 seconds longer on medium. Divide batter between pans.
5. Sprinkle pecans on top, and bake until toothpick inserted in the center comes out clean, 1 hour to 70 minutes for loaves, 25 to 30 minutes for muffins. Turn out onto wire racks; cool at least 30 minutes before slicing. Serve warm.

Beer Pairing Suggestion:
Winter strong ale

Adapted from The Fearless Chef, *copyright 2004 by Andy Husbands and Joe Yonan. Used with permission of Adams Media. All rights reserved.*

Makes 2 9-by-5-inch loaves or 12 muffins

Summer Berry and Phyllo Tart with Balsamic-Barley Wine Sabayon

Chef Greg Higgins of Higgins Restaurant in Portland, Oregon, is a pioneering influence in pairing craft beer with organic foods. He shares a favorite summer dessert, which tastes wonderful with a berry-flavored beer or a *witbier*.

4 sheets phyllo dough
¼ cup unsalted butter, melted
2 cups sugar
1 cup water
¼ cup balsamic vinegar
Freshly ground black pepper
4 egg yolks
¼ cup barley wine
2 pints mixed berries, washed and stemmed

1. Preheat oven to 375°F. Brush a sheet of phyllo dough with melted butter. Form a square by folding 1 edge of the pastry back. Turn the corners into the center, forming a square approximately 6 inches by 6 inches. Set this square into an individual tart pan and crimp the corners under to form a rustic tart shell. Repeat with each sheet of phyllo to make 4 pastry shells. Bake shells until golden brown, about 4 to 8 minutes. Remove from oven and set aside.

2. Bring sugar and water to a boil in a stainless steel saucepan. Boil until the syrup beings to turn golden, about 15 to 20 minutes. When the syrup turns a rich golden caramel color, remove the pan to a sink and add the vinegar and several grinds of black pepper. Let caramel syrup cool.

3. In a copper bowl or double boiler, combine the egg yolks, 4 tablespoons caramel syrup, and barley wine. Whisk constantly over medium heat until the sabayon froths, turns pale, and thickens, about 10 to 12 minutes.

4. Drizzle each of 4 dessert plates with the black pepper caramel. Place a tart shell on each plate, fill each shell with warm sabayon, and top with mixed berries. Serve immediately.

Makes 4 servings

Beer Pairing Suggestion:
Fruit ale

194

Asian ingredients such as panko bread crumbs, black bean chili paste, and toasted sesame oil can be found online or via telephone mail order.

Asian Food Grocer
www.asianfoodgrocer.com
Toll Free: (888) 482-2742
Phone: (650) 873-7600, Ext. 107
Fax: (650) 871-9154
Address: 131 West Harris Ave.,
San Francisco, CA 94080
Email: info@asianfoodgrocer.com

Mail Order Sources

The Oriental Pantry
www.orientalpantry.com
Phone: (978) 264-4576
Fax: (781) 275-4506
Address: 423 Great Road (2A), Acton, MA 01720
Email through a contact form on the website

Chiles, Herbs, and Spices
Guajillo and other chiles, plus whole or ground spices, can be found via mail order and online through several sources. If seeking smoked paprika, you can find it through the Spice House and Vann's and even McCormick's. MoHotta also has lots of pepper sauces, if you don't want to handle raw or dried chiles.

MoHotta MoBetta—specializes in chiles and hot sauces
www.mohotta.com
Phone: (800) 462-3220
Fax: (800) 618-4454 or 912-748-1364
International: (912) 748-2766
Address: P.O. Box 1026, Savannah, GA 31402
Email: mohotta@mohotta.com

The Spice House—smoked paprika
www.thespicehouse.com
Phone: (414) 272-0977
Fax: (414) 272-1271
Address: 1031 North Old World Third St., Milwaukee, WI 53203
Email through a contact form on the website

Vann's Spices Ltd.
www.vannsspices.com
Phone: (410) 358-3007
Fax: (410) 358-1780
Toll Free Phone: (800) 583-1693
Toll Free Fax: (800) 358-1617
Address: 6105 Oakleaf Ave., Baltimore, MD 21215
Email: sales@vannsspices.com

Specialty Meats
Several online retailers will ship meats and poultry.

For natural beef, lamb, and pork:
Niman Ranch
www.nimanranch.com
Phone: (866) 808-0340
Fax: (510) 808-0339
Address: 1025 E. 12th St., Oakland, CA 94606
Email: info@nimanranch.com

For organic beef:
Davis Mountains Organic Beef
www.davismountainsorganicbeef.com
Phone: (877) 366-2333
Fax: (972) 265-0290
Address: 5601 Democracy Drive, Suite 190, Plano, TX 75024

For natural lamb and lamb sausages:
Jamison Farm
www.jamisonfarm.com
Toll Free: (800) 237-5262
Fax: (724) 837-2287
Address: 171 Jamison Lane, Latrobe, PA 15650
Email: john@jamisonfarm.com

Barley Malt Extract
Eden Foods sells barley malt extract made from U.S. organically grown barley, sprouted, kiln roasted, and slowly cooked into a thick, dark brown syrup—an ancient process using only the grain's own enzymes created in the sprouting process and the knowledge and care of artisan maltsters. It has a rich, mellow flavor that's half as sweet as refined sugar and ideal for barbecue sauces made with beer. Eden Foods also sells soy sauces and oils.

Eden Foods
www.edenfoods.com/store
Phone: (517) 456-7424
Fax: (517) 456-7025
Address: 701 Tecumseh Road, Clinton, MI 49236
Email: websales@edenfoods.com

199

The following list may help readers find specific brands in the beer styles mentioned in this book. This list was provided by Information Resources, Inc. and consists of bottled beers that have been sold in grocery stores, pharmacies, liquor stores and convenience stores in recent years. Many beers made in the United States are not listed here and many of the beers listed are sold only in limited geographic areas. Consult your local specialty beer retailer for assistance in finding the brands sold in your area.

American Bottled Beers by Style

Amber Ale
Abita Amber
Alaskan Amber
Amberjack Amber
Anderson Valley Boont Amber Ale
Anderson Vlly Blks Extr Spcl Btt
Angel Creek Amber Ale
Arcadia Lake Superior E S B
Ballast Point Copper Ale
Bbc Altbier
Belfast Bay Lobster Ale
Bells Amber Ale
Bells Big Porch Ale
Bells Third Coast
Boulder Amber Ale
Breckenridge Avalanche Ale
Brothers Honey Amber Ale
Butte Creek Organic Ale
Cascade Lakes Rooster Tail Ale
Cottrell Ale
Deadhorse
Dergys Amber Ale
Dicks Mountain Ale
Dock Street Amber
Eddie Mcstiffs Amber Ale
El Toro Poppy Jasper Ale
Empyrean Luna Sea Ale
Firestone Double Barrel Ale
Fish Tale Organic Amber Ale
Flying Dog Old Scratch Ale
Flying Monkey Amber Ale
Fordham Copperhead Ale
Full Sail Amber Ale
Garten Brau Wisconsin Amber

Great Divide Arapahoe Amber Ale
Greenshields Amber Ale
Gritty Mcduffs Best Bitter Ale
Hales Amber Ale
Half Dome Amber Ale
Harpoon Ale
Highland Gaelic Ale
Hood Canal Agate Pass
Hoppy Face Amber Ale
Idaho Amber Ale
Ithaca Amber Ale
Lagunitas Tocaloma Amber Ale
Lakefront Cattail Ale
Lakefront Riverwest Stein
Lang Creek Amber Ale
Left Hand Sawtooth Ale
Long Trail Ale
Long Trail Long Trail Ale
Lost Coast Alley Cat
Lost Coast Amber Ale
Mactarnahan's Amber Ale
Manitou Amber Ale
Mehana Roys Private Reserve
Middle Ages Beast Bitter Ale
Middle Ages Grail Ale
Mogollon Wapiti Amber Ale
New Amsterdam Ale
New Belgium Fat Tire Amber Ale
New Holland Sundog
New York Harbor Ale
Newport Storm Hurricane Ambr Ale
Nutfield Old Man Ale
Oak Creek Amber Ale
O'dells Levity Ale
Orchard Street Stock Ale
Otter Creek Copper Ale
Otto Brothers Teton Ale
Palmetto Amber
Port Townsend Amber Ale
Red Tail Ale
Rogue Ale
Rogue American Amber Ale

Rogue Youngers Special Bittr Ale
Samuel Adams Boston Ale
Scuttlebutt Amber Ale
Sierra Blanca Alien Amber Ale
Slo Brewng Co Grdn Ally Ambr Ale
Sonora Desert Amber Ale
Spanish Peaks Black Dog Ale
Speakeasy Prohibition Ale
Sprecher Special Amber
St Arnold Amber Ale
St Stans Amber Alt
St Stans Dark Alt
Stonecoast Sunday River Alt
Sun Valley White Cloud
Thirsty Dog Hoppus Maximus
Thomas Creek Amber Ale
Tommy Knocker Ornery Amber
Troegs Hopback Amber Ale
Uinta Redrock Amber Ale
Wasatch Amber Ale
Wasatch Superior Ale
Widmer Drop Top Amber Ale
Wild Fly Ale
Wild Goose Amber
Yards Extra Special Ale

Amber Lagers
Anchor Steam Beer
Bayern Amber Lager
Blue Ridge Amber Lager
Boulevard Bobs 47 Lager
Captial Wisconsin Amber
Carolina Lager
Karl Strauss Amber Lager
Michigan Sunset Amber Lager
Mojave Red Lager
New Amsterdam Amber Lager
Olde Hickory Ruby Lager
Page Iron Range Amber Lager
Portsmouth Lager
Raptor Red Lager
Rio Salado Monsoon

Samuel Adams Boston Lager
Saranac Adirondack Amber Lager
Schild Brau
Snake River Lager

Belgian-Style Ales
Allagash Double Ale
Allagash Grand Cru Ale
Allagash Special Reserve
Avery Karma Ale
Avery Salvation
Avery The Reverend
Dogfish Head Raison D Etre
Flying Fish Belgian Dubbel Ale
Hair Of The Dog Golden Rose Ale
Hennepin Belgian Ale
New Belgium Abbey Belgn Styl Ale
New Belgium La Folie Ale
New Belgium Transatlantique
    Kriek Ale
New Belgm Trippl Belgn Styl Ale
New Glarus Belgian Red
Ommegang Abbey Ale
Ommegang Three Philosophers
Pranqster Golden Ale
Rare Vos Ale
Rogue Monk Madness Ale
Stoudts Abbey Triple
Two Brothers Domaine Dupage
Victory Golden Monkey
Weyerbacher Merry Monks Ale
Weyerbacher Prophecy
Yards Saison Belgian Ale

Blonde Ales
Berkshire Gold Spike Ale
Big Sky Crystal Ale
Butte Creek Mt Shasta Ale
Carolina Blonde Ale
Coast Range California Blond Ale
Eddie Mcstiffs Cream Ale
Green Flsh Brewng Co Extr Pl Ale

Ice Harbor Columbia Kolsch Ale
Lake Superior Kayak Kolsch
Market Street Cream Ale
New Holland Full Circle
Red Brick Ale
Redhook Blonde Ale
Sea Dog Windjammer Blonde Ale
Shoal Draft
St Arnold Lawnmower Ale
Widmer Sweet Betty Blonde Ale
Yellow Rose Blonde Ox

Bock

Bayern Doppelbock Lager
Big Ass Bock
Capital Autumnal Fire
Capital Miabock
Celis Pale Bock
Evil Eye
Gordon Biersch Blonde Bock
Jaguar High Gravity Lager
Lakefront Big Easy
New Glarus Bock
Otter Creek Mud Bock
Samuel Adams Chocolate Bock
Samuel Adams Double Bock
Saxer Bock
Sierra Nevada Pale Bock
Sprecher Maibock
St Arnold Bock
Stoudts Honey Double Mai Bock
Sudwerk Doppel Bock
Summit Heimertingen Mai Bock
Tommy Knockr Butthd Dopplbck Lgr
Troegenator Double Bock

Brown Ale

Abita Turbodog
Acme Califronia Brown Ale
Arcadia Nutbrown Ale
Arrogant Bastard Ale
Avery Ellies Brown Ale

Balcones Fault Red Granite
Bells Best Brown Ale
Berkshire River Ale
Big Sky Moose Drool Brown Ale
Blackstone Nut Brown Ale
Brooklyn Brown Ale
Brooklyn Dark Ale
Capital Brown Ale
Carolina Nut Brown Ale
Cascade Laks Angs Macdgls & Drk
Columbus Nut Brown Ale
Cottonwood Low Down Brown Ale
Dicks Danger Ale
Dogfish Head Indian Brown Ale
Empyrean Third Stone Brown Ale
Golden Gate Original Ale
Goose Island Hexnut Ale
Great Lakes Cleveland Brown Ale
Green Flsh Brewng Co Nt Brwn Ale
Greenshields Nut Brown Ale
Gritty Mcduffs Best Brown Ale
Hebrew The Chosen Br Geness Ale
Ipswich Dark Ale
Ipswich Nut Brown Ale
Ithaca Nut Brown Ale
Left Hand Deep Cover Brown Ale
Legend Brown Ale
Long Trail Hit The Trail Ale
Lost Coast Downtown Brown Ale
Michigan Nut Brown Ale
Midnight Sun Kodiak Nut Brwn Ale
Montana Nut Brown Ale
Nightwatch Dark Ale
Nimbus Nut Brown Ale
Oak Creek Nut Brown Ale
Old Brown Dog
Page Burly Brown Ale
Petes Wicked Ale
Rogue Hazelnut Brown Nectar Ale
Samuel Adams Brown Ale
Santa Fe Nut Brown Ale
Sierra Blanca Nutbrown Ale

Skagit River Teelie Brown Ale
Sonora Topdown Brown Ale
Sprecher Pub Brown Ale
St Arnold Brown Ale
Sweet Georgia Brown
Three Floyds Pride & Jy Mld Ale
Tommy Knocker Maple
   Nut Brwn Ale
Tuscan Hogsback Brown Ale
Tw Fishers Festival Dark Ale
Uinta Bristlecone Brown Ale
Wachusett Country Nut Brown Ale
Wolavers Brown Ale
Work
Ybor Brown Ale
Yellow Rose Honch Grand Brwn Ale

Barley Wine

Anchor Old Foghorn Barleywin Ale
Avery Hog Heaven
Bells Hopslam Ale
Bells Third Coast Old Ale
Brooklyn Monster Ale
Dogfish Head Immort Ale
Dogfish Head Old Schl Barleywin
Full Sl Old Boardhd Barly Wn Ale
Marin Old Dipsea Barleywine Ale
Moylans Old Blarney Barleywine
Rogue Old Crustacean Ale
Sierra Nevad Bigft Barly Win Ale
Sierra Nevada Big Foot Ale
Talon Barley Wine Ale
Weyerbacher Blithering Idiot
Weyerbacher Insanity

Dark Lagers

Capital Dark
Harpoon Munich Dark
Lakefront Eastside Lager
New Belgium 1554 Black Ale
Rio Salado Thunderhead
Samuel Adams Black Lager

203

Saranac Black Forest
Sprecher Black Bavarian Ale

ESB (Extra Special Bitter)
Alaskan Esb
Avery 14er Esb
Crooked River Esb
Deschutes Bachelor Esb
Flying Fish Esb Ale
Laconner Esb
Lakefront Organic Esb Ale
Oasis Capstone Esb Ale
Redhook Esb
Stoudts Scarlet Lady Ale Esb
The Governator Ale

Fruit Beers
9th Street Market Lime Cactus
9th Strt Markt Bld Orang Grapefr
9th Strt Markt Pomegrant Rspbrry
Abita Purple Haze Raspberry Wht
Bells Cherry Stout
Belmont Brew Strawbrry Blond Ale
Bert Grants Mandarin Hefeweizen
Breckenridge Raspberry Porter
Buffalo Bills Pumpkin Ale
Butte Creek Christmas Cranberry Ale
Celis Raspberry
Columbus Apricot Ale
Dogfish Head Aprihop
Dogfish Head Au Courant
Dogfish Head Punkin Ale
Eddie Mcstiffs Raspberry Wheat
Elysian Night Owl Pumpkin Ale
Great Divide Wild Raspberry Ale
Hurricane Reef Raspberry Wht Ale
Lakefront Cherry Lager
Lakefront Pumpkin Lager
Long Trail Blackberry Wheat Ale
Longs Peak Raspberry Wheat
Lost Coast Raspberry Brown Ale
Magic Hat No 9 Ale

Marin Blueberry Ale
Marin Raspberry Trail Ale
New Glarus Apple Ale
New Glarus Raspberry Tart
Oxford Raspberry Wheat Ale
Petes Wicked Strawberry Blonde
Post Road Pumpkin Ale
Pyramid Apricot Ale
Rio Salado Typhoon
Samuel Adams Cherry Wheat
Saxer Lemon Lager
Schlafly Specl Releas Pumpkin Ale
Sea Dog Wild Blueberry Wheat Ale
Shipyard Pumpkin Ale
Slo Brewing Co Blueberry Ale
Smuttynose Pumpkin Ale
Spanish Pks Blc Dg Hny Rspbr Ale
Sweetwater Blueberry Ale
Tommy Knocker Tundrabeary Ale
Tw Fishers Huckleberry Ale
Ufo Raspberry Hefeweizen
Unita Punkin
Wachusett Blueberry Ale
Wasatch Pumpkin Ale
Wasatch Raspberry Wheat
Weyerbacher Imperial Pumpkin Ale
Weyerbacher Raspberry Imperial Stt
Widmer Widberry

Golden Ale
Abita Gold
Bards Tale Dragon Gold
Blue Ridge Golden Ale
Boulder Buffalo Gold Ale
Butte Creek Gold Ale
Buzzards Bay Golden Ale
Columbus Golden Ale
Crooked River Lighthouse Gold
Dergys Golden Classic Ale
El Toro Golden Ale
Empyrean Chalc Canyn Hny Gld Ale
Estes Park Gold Ale

Flying Dog Tire Biter Ale
Hoptown Golden Ale
Humboldt Gold Nectar Ale
Jersey Shore Gold
Karl Strauss Endless Summer Gold
Keoki Kauai Gold
Key West Sunset Ale
Kona Pacific Golden Ale
Laughing Dog Cream Ale
Middle Ages White Knght Lght Ale
Moylans Celts Ale
O' Fallon Gold
Orchard Street Golden Ale
Peregrine Golden Ale
Pike Golden Ale
Port Townsend Chets Golden Ale
Rogue Golden Ale
Skagit River Gold Ale
Ybor Gold Ale

Honey Beers
Big Sky Summer Honey Ale
Grays Honey Ale
Great Divide Bee Sting Honey Ale
Mactarnahan's Oregon Honey Beer
Mount St Helena Honey White Ale
Quake Honey Cream Ale
Rogue Honey Cream Ale
South Shore Honey Pils

IPA - India Pale Ale
Alaskan IPA
Anchor Liberty Ale
Anderson Valley IPA
Arcadia IPA
Avery India Pale Ale
Bear Creek Jacks India Pale Ale
Bear Republc Racr 5 Indi Pal Ale
Bear Republic Red Rocket Ale
Bells Two Hearted Ale
Berkshire India Pale Ale
Bert Grants India Pale Ale

Big Sky IPA
Breckenridge India Pale
Brooklyn East India Pale Ale
Butte Creek Organic Indi Pale Ale
Butte Creek Organic Revoltn X Impe
Cascade Lakes India Pale Ale
Cottonwood Endo India Pale Ale
Deschutes Inversion IPA
Dogfish Head 120 Minute IPA
Dogfish Head 60 Minute IPA
Dogfish Head 90 Minut Imperl IPA
Dogwood India Pale Ale
Eel River IPA
Fish Tale India Pale Ale
Founders Centennial IPA
Full Sail India Pale Ale
Goose Island IPA
Great Lakes Commodore Perry IPA
Green Flsh Brewng Co Wst Cst IPA
Greenshields India Pale Ale
Harpoon India Pale Ale
Hoptown India Pale Ale
Ipswich IPA
Jamaica Sunset India Pale Ale
Karl Strauss Stargazer IPA
Laconner IPA
Lagunitas India Pale Ale
Lagunitas Maximus India Pale Ale
Lake Placid 46er IPA
Laughing Dog India Pale Ale
Left Hand Twin Sisters Double IPA
Left Hand Warrior IPA
Legend Golden India Pale Ale
Long Trail India Pale Ale
Lost Coast India Pale Ale
Mactarnahan's IPA
Magic Hat Blind Faith
Marin IPA
Michigan High Seas India Pal Ale
Middle Ages Impaled Ale
Moylans IPA
New Holland Mad Hatter Ale

New Knoxville India Pale Ale
Pike India Pale Ale
Port Townsend IPA
Pyramid IPA
Quail Springs IPA
Redhook Ballard Bitter IPA
Redhook IPA
Sacramento India Pale Ale
Samuel Adams India Pale Ale
Saranac India Pale Ale
Scuttlebutt India Pale Ale
Sea Dog East India Pale Ale
Shipyard Fuggles IPA
Smuttynose IPA
Snake Dog IPA
Southern Tier IPA
Speakeasy Big Daddy IPA
Spilker Hopluia Ale
St Arnold Eilssa IPA
Stone India Pale Ale
Stone Ruination IPA
Stonecoast 420 IPA
Summit India Pale Ale
Sweetwater India Pale Ale
Tremont IPA
Trout River Hoppin Mad Ale
Tuppers Hop Pocket Ale
Two Brothers Heavy Handed IPA
Uinta India Pale Ale
Victory Hop Devil India Pale Al
Wachusett India Pale Ale
Weyerbacher Double Simcoe IPA
Weyerbacher Eleven Triple IPA
Weyerbacher Hops Infusion IPA
White Hawk IPA
Wild Goose India Pale Ale
Wolavers IPA
Yards India Pale Ale
Yellow Rose Cactus Queen Ale
Yellow Rose India Pale Ale

Marzen/Oktoberfest
Abita Fall Fest
Bayern Oktoberfest
Berkshire Octoberfest
Brooklyn Oktoberfest
Capital Brew Oktoberfest
Degroens Marzen
Dominion Octoberfest
Goose Island Oktoberfest
Gordon Biersch Marzen
Karl Strauss Oktoberfest
Lakefront Octoberfest
Left Hand Oktoberfest
Lewis & Clark
Olde Heurich Foggy Bottom Lager
Otter Creek Octoberfest
Schlafly Oktoberfest
Smuttynose Octoberfest
Sprecher Octoberfest
St Arnold Oktoberfest
Stoudts Marzen Fest
Sudwerk Marzen
Summit Oktoberfest
Thomas Hooker Octoberfest Lager
Thomas Kemper Oktoberfest Lager
Weeping Radish Fest

Pale Lagers Includes Helles, Dortmunder
Barrel House Duvenecks
    Dortmunder
Bells Lager
Bootie Lager
Brew City Lager
Brothers Classic Golden Lager
Capital Bavarian Lager
Capital Brew
Cooks
Crooked River Lager
Cugino
Dominion Lager
Durango

205

Fordham Lager
Founders Noble Lager
Full Sail Session Premium Lager
Golden Bear Lager
Golden Eagle
Great Lakes Dortmunder Gold Lagr
Great Lakes Eliot Ness Lager
Hu Dey
Hurricane Reef Lager
Kona Long Board Lager
Legend Lager
Lemp St Louis
Magic Hat Mother Lager
Mehana Hawaii Lager
Mehana Tsunami Lager
Mountain Creek Lager
Olde Buzzard Lager
Palmetto Charleston Lager
Petes Wicked Helles Lager
Red Brick Golden Lager
Rio Grande Outlaw Lager
Saranac Traditional Lager
Spanish Peaks Monterey Lager
Sprecher Pale Lager
Stoudts Golden Lager
Sudwerk Lager
Sun Lager
Three Stooges Lager
Tommy Knocker Glacier Lager
Wasatch Ist Amendment Lager
Wasatch Slickrock
Weeping Radish Hellis Gold Lager
Wingwalker Lager

Old And Strong Ales

Bells Sparkling Ale
Black Eye Ale
Dogfish Head Burton Baton
Eye Of The Hawk Ale
Founders Dirty Bastard
Gearys Hampshire Special Ale
Great Divide Hibernation Ale

Great Lakes Nosferatu
Hair Of The Dog Adam Ale
Hair Of The Dog Frd Ale
Lagunitas Copper Ale
Lake Placid Ubu Ale
Left Hand Chainsw Double
   Swtth Ale
Long Trail Double Bag Ale
Marin Anniversary Ale
Middle Ages Tripel Crown
North Coast Old Stock Ale
Rogue Brutal Bitter Ale
Rogue Dads Little Helper
Rogue Dead Guy Ale
St Arnold Divine Reserve Ale
Sweetwater Ale
Three Floyds Robert The Bruce
Weyerbacher Quad

Specialty Beers

Big Horn
Bison Gingerbread Ale
Boulder The Gabf 25th Year Beer
Boundary Water Wildrice Lager
Cave Creek Chili
Dogfish Head Midas Touch
Dogfish Head Pangaea
Dogfish Head Zwaanend Ale
Humboldt Hemp Ale
Lakefront Golden Maple Root Beer
Lakefront Grist
Lazy Magnolia Southern Pecan
Middle Ages 10th Anniversary Ale
Real Full Moon Pale Rye Ale
Rogue Chipolte Ale
Rogue Juniper Pale Ale
Rogue Morimoto Black Obi Sob Ale
Rogue Smoke Ale
Samuel Adams Utopias
Saranac Black And Tan
Southern Brewery Chocolate Ale
Thomas Creek Multi Grain Ale

Weyerbacher Decadence
Woodstock Froach Heather Ale

Pale Ale

Acme California Pale Ale
Alaskan Pale Ale
Anderson Valley Poleeko Pale Ale
Arcadia Anglers Ale
Balcones Fault Pale Malt
Ballast Point Yellowtail Pal Ale
Barrel House Cumberland Pale Ale
Bbc American Pale Ale
Bear Republic Extra Pale Ale
Bells Pale Ale
Berkshire Steel Rl Extr Pal Ale
Big Hole Headstrong Pale Ale
Big Sky Scapegoat Pale Ale
Bison Pale Ale
Blue Heron Pale Ale
Boulder Extra Pale Ale
Boulder Hazed & Infused
Boulder Singletrack Copper Ale
Boulevard Pale Ale
Brooklyn Pennant Pale Ale
Carmel Pale Ale
Carolina Pale Ale
Carrabassett Pale Ale
Casco Bay Pale Ale
Chamberlain Pale Ale
Coast Range Desperado Pale Ale
Columbus Pale Ale
Cooperstown Old Slugger Pale Ale
Deschutes Cascade Ale
Deschutes Mirror Pond Pale Ale
Diamond Bear Pale Ale
Dicks Danger Pale Ale
Dogfish Head Shelter Pale Ale
Dogwood Pale Ale
Dominion Ale
Dominion Pale Ale
Firestone Windsor Pale Ale
Fish Tale Wild Salmon Pale Ale

Flying Dog Classic Pale Ale
Flying Dog Doggie Style Ale
Flying Fish Extra Pale Ale
Founders Pale Ale
Full Sail Pale Ale
Full Sail Rip Curl
Gearys Pale Ale
Golden Leaf
Goose Island Honkers Ale
Great Divide Denver Pale Ale
Great Lakes Burning Rivr Pal Ale
Hair Of The Dog Ruth Ale
Hales Moss Bay Extra Ale
Hales Pale Ale
Half Dome Pale Ale
Harper Hll Dos Oks Oildal Pl Ale
Hebrew The Chosen Beer Messh Bld
Highland St Terees Pale Ale
Humboldt Pale Ale
Hurricane Reef Pale Ale
Ipswich Ale
Islander Pale Ale
Ithaca Pale Ale
Keoki Kauai Sunset
Kona Fire Rock Pale Ale
Lagunitas Dog Town Pale Ale
Lake Superior Special Ale
Lakefront Cream City Ale
Left Hnd Jackmns Americn Pal Ale
Leopold Bros Pale Ale
Lost Coast Pale Ale
Magic Hat Fat Angel
Manitou Old Missn Lighthous Ale
Mehana Mauna Kea Pale Ale
Michigan Mackinac Strts Pal Ale
Mobjack Pale Ale
Mogollon Pale Ale
Mount St Helena Pale Ale
Mt Tam Pale Ale
New Holland Paleooza Ale
New Knoxville Pale Ale
New River Pale Ale

Nimbus Palo Verde Pale Ale
North Coast Red Seal Ale
O'dells Cutthroat Pale Ale
Old Thumper Xsp Ale
Olde Buzzard Pale Ale
Olde Heurich Foggy Bottom Ale
Orchard Street Jingle Pale Ale
Orchard Street Pale Ale
Otter Creek Pale Ale
Otto Brothers Old Faithful Ale
Page Voyageur Ale
Palmetto Pale Ale
Pike Pale Ale
Pony Express Rattlesnake Pal Ale
Pyramid Pale Ale
Redhook Chinook Copper Ale
Reudrichs Red Seal Ale
Rio Blanco Pale Ale
Sacramento River Otter Ale
Samuel Adams Pale Ale
Santa Fe Pale Ale
Saranac Traditional Pale Ale
Schlafly Expedition Reserve
Schlafly Pale Ale
Scorpion Tale
Shipyard Export Ale
Shoalls Pale Ale
Sierra Blanca Pale Ale
Sierra Nevada Pale Ale
Skagit River Yellow Jacket Ale
Slo Brewing Co Brickhous Pal Ale
Snake River Pale Ale
Sonora Burning Bird Pale Ale
Southern Tr Phn & Mtts Extraordn
Spanish Pks Blc Dg Yllwst Pl Ale
Speakeasy Untouchable Pale Ale
Squatter Full Suspension Pal Ale
St Stans Whistle Stop Pale Ale
Starr Hill Pale Ale
Steelhead Pale Ale
Stone Levitation Ale
Stone Pale Ale

Stoudts American Pale Ale
Summit Extra Pale Ale
Sweetwater 420 Pale Ale
Thomas Hooker American Pale Ale
Three Floyds Extra Pale Ale
Tommy Knocker Pick Axe Pale Ale
Tremont Ale
Tuckerman Pale Ale
Tuscan Pale Ale
Tw Fishers Centennial Pale Ale
Uinta Cutthroat Pale Ale
Upland Pale Ale
Wachusett Country Ale
Wasatch Premium Ale
Widmer Hopjack Pale Ale
Williamsville Studley Pale Ale
Wingwalker Pale Ale
Wolavers Pale Ale

Pilsner

Bayern Pilsner Lager
Brooklyn Lager
Brooklyn Pilsner
Butte Creek Organic Pilsner
Capital 1900
Capital Special Pilsner
Casco Bay Pilsner
Degroens Pilsner
E J Phair Pilsner
Goose Island Pilsner
Gordon Biersch Pilsner
Greenshields Pilsner
Hurricane Reef Pilsner
La Tropical Pilsner
Laconner Pilsner
Lagunitas Pilsner
Lakefront Klisch Pilsner
Laughing Skull Pilsner
Left Hand Polestar Pilsner
Legend Pilsner
Market Street Pilsner
New Belgium Blue Paddle Pilsner

North Coast Scrimshaw Pilsner
Pyramid Coastline
Ray Hills American Pilsner
Rio Grande Desert Pils
Rogue Morimoto Imperial Pilsner
Samuel Adams Golden Pilsner
Saranac Golden Pilsner
Schlafly Pilsner
Sierra Blanca Pilsner
Sierra Nevada Summerfest
Sprecher Pilsner
Squatter Pilsner
Squatter St Provo Girl Pils
Sudwerk Pilsner
Summit Grand
Thomas Creek Pilsner
Troegs Sunshine Pils
Uinta Club Pilsner
Victory Prima Pils

Porter

Alaskan Smoked Porter
Anchor Porter
Anderson Vally Dp Endrs Drk Prtr
Avery New World Porter
Bbc Dark Star Porter
Bear Creek Porter
Bells Porter
Berkshire Dns Bns Coffe Hous Prt
Berkshire Draymans Porter
Berkshire Shabadoo Black And Tan
Bert Grants Perfect Porter
Blackhook Porter
Blue Ridge Porter
Boulder Porter
Boulevard Bully Porter
Butte Creek Organic Porter
Canal Street Porter
Cascade Lakes Monkey Face Porter
Crooked River Robust Porter
Dergys Porter
Deschutes Black Butte Porter

Dominion Black & Tan
Flying Fish Porter
Gearys London Porter
Great Divide Saint Brigids Portr
Great Laks Edmnd Fitzgerld Portr
Highland Oatmeal Porter Ale
Left Hand Black Jack Porter
Legend Chocolate Porter
Legend Porter
Mactarnahan's Blackwatch
   Crm Porter
New Amsterdam Black & Tan
O' Fallon Smoked Porter
O'dells Cutthroat Porter
Orchard Street Porter
Otter Creek Stovepipe Porter
Palmetto Porter
Port Townsend Porter
Rock Creek Black Raven Porter Ale
Rogue Mocha Porter
Samuel Adams Holiday Porter
Scuttlebutt Porter
Sea Dog Hazelnut Porter
Sierra Nevada Porter
Smuttynose Robust Porter
Southern Tier Porter
Stone Smoked Porter
Summit Great Northern Porter
Sweetwater Exodus Porter
Uinta Kings Peak Porter
Wasatch Polygamy Porter
Wild Goose Porter
Yellow Rose Vigilante

Red Ale

Barrel House Redlegg Ale
Blue Ridge Esb Red Ale
Boulevard Irish Ale
Butte Creek Rolands Red Ale
Casco Bay Riptide Ale
Casco Bay Riptide Red Ale
Crooked River Irish Red

Flagship Red Ale
Founders Red Ale
Goose Island Kilgubbin Red Ale
Grays Irish Ale
Great Lakes Conways Irish Ale
Green Flash Brewng Co Rby Rd Ale
Hoptown Paint The Town Red Ale
Humboldt Red Nectar Ale
Ice Harbor Runaway Ale
Jamaica Red Ale
Karl Strauss Red Trolley
Katahdin Red Ale
Lake Tahoe Crystal Bay Red Ale
Magic Hat Humble Patience
Mehana Volcano Red Ale
Midnight Sun Sockeye Red Ale
Mobjack Red Ale
Moylans Irish Red Ale
Nutfield Auburn Ale
Park City Tie Died Red
Pennichuck Eng 5 Ine Frhs Rd Ale
Petes Wicked Red Rush
Pioneer Black River Red Ale
Renegade Red Ale
Rogue St Rogue Red Ale
Sacramento Red Horse Ale
Southern Brewery Scarlet Ale
St Stans Red Sky
Stony Face Red Ale
Triple Hop Red Ale
Trout River Rainbow Red Ale
Wachusett Quinns Irish Ale

Scotch And Scottish Ale

Bert Grants Scottish Ale
Columbus 90 Shilling
Empyrean Burning Skye Ale
Flying Dog Road Dog Scottish Ale
Four Peaks Kilt Lifter Ale
Moylans Kiltlifter Scotch Ale
O'dells 90 Shillings Ale
Pike Kilt Lifter Scotch Ale

208

Port Townsend Scotch Ale
Sacramento Sac Squatch Sctch Ale
Schlafly Scotch Ale
Sleeping Gnt Bck Cntry Sctch Ale
Smuttynose Scotch Ale
Trout River Scottish Ale

Stout
Alaskan Oatmeal Stout
Anderson Vlly Brny Flts Otml Stt
Arcadia Starboard Stout
Avery Out Of Bounds Stout
Avery The Craz Imperial Stout
Bear Republic Big Bear Black Stt
Bells Expedition Stout
Bells Java Stout
Bells Kalamazoo Stout
Bells Rye Stout
Bells Special Souble Cream Stout
Big Sky Slow Elk Oatmeal Stout
Bison Chocolate Stout
Black Hawk Stout
Blue Fin Stout
Boulder Stout
Breckenridge Oatmeal Stout
Brooklyn Black Chocolate Stout
Cabezon Stout
Deschutes Obsidian Stout
Dicks Cream Stout
Dogfish Head Chicory Stout
Dogfish Head World Wide Stout
Dogwood Stout
Dominion Stout
El Toro Oatmeal Stout
Goose Island Oatmeal Stout
Great Lakes Blackout Stout
Gritty Mcduffs Black Fly Stout
Hoptown Old Yeltsin Stout
Ipswich Oatmeal Stout
Laconner Stout
Lakefront Fuel Cafe
Lakefront Snake Chaser Stout

Left Hand Imperial Stout
Left Hand Milk Stout
Lost Coast Stout
Magic Hat Heart Of Darkness
Millstream Oatmeal Stout
Mogollon Apache Trout Stout
New Holland Stout
North Coast Old No 38 Stout
Nutfield Stout
Old Rasputin Russian Imperl Stt
Olde Hickory Stick Stout
Pike Brand Pike Street Stout
Port Townsend Stout
Roffeys Lake Effect Stout
Rogue Chocolate Stout
Rogue Stout
Sacramento Russian Imperial Stt
Samuel Adams Cream Stout
San Quentin Breakout Stout
Saranac Stout
Schlafly Oatmeal Stout
Sierra Nevada Stout
Snake River Zonker Stout
Spilker Xpo Stout
Squatter Capt Bastards Oatml Stt
St Arnold Winter Stout
Steelhead Extra Stout
Victory Storm King Stout
Weyerbacher Old Heathen
Widmer Snow Plow Milk Stout
Wild Goose Oatmeal Stout
Wolavers Oatmeal Stout
Yards Love Stout
Yellow Rose Wildcatrs Refnd Stout
Yellowstone Valley Black Widow

Wheat Beers (Weizen, American Wheat)
Anchor Wheat
Anderson Valley High Rollers Wht
Barrel House Hckng Hlls
   Hefwzn Wh

Bells Four Ale
Bells Love Ale
Bells Oberon
Bells Wheat Eight Ale
Bells Wheat Six Ale
Bert Grants Hefeweizen
Boulder Sweaty Betty Blonde
Boulevard Lunar Ale
Boulevard Wheat
Breckenridge Mountain Wheat
Brooklyner Weisse
Butte Creek Wheat Ale
Capital Island Wheat Ale
Carmel Mission Hefeweizn Wht Ale
Dominion Summer Wheat Ale
Ebelweiss
Flying Dog In Heat Wheat
Founders Wheat Ale
Garten Brau Kloster Weizen
Goose Island 312 Urban Wheat Ale
Gordon Biersch Hefeweizen
Grand Teton Workhorse Wheat Ale
Great Divide Whitewater Wht Ale
Grizzly Wolff Wheat
Ithaca Apricot Wheat Ale
Laconner Wheat Ale
Lake Tahoe Hefeweizen
Left Hand Haystack Wheat Ale
Leopold Bros Hefeweizen
Lost Coast Great White
Magic Hat Circus Boy
Magic Hat Hocus Pocus
Marin Hefeweiss
Marin Star Brew Triple Wheat Ale
New Belgium Sunshine Wheat
Nor Wester Hefe Weizen
North Coast Blue Star Wheat
O'dells Easy Street Wheat Ale
Park City Baja Especial
Pyramid Hefeweizen Ale
Pyramid Wheaten Ale
Ramstein Blond Wheat

209

Ramstein Dark Wheat
Rio Salado Hurricane
Sacramento Hefeweizen
Samuel Adams Hefeweizen
Santa Fe Wheat Ale
Saranac Wildberry Wheat
Schlafly Hefeweizen
Shipyard Sirrus Summer Wheat Ale
Sierra Nevada Wheat Ale
Smuttynose Weizenheimer
Spanish Peaks Black Dog Whit Ale
Spilker Cortland Wheat
Sprecher Hefeweizen Ale
Squatter Hefeweizen
St Arnold Kristall Weizen
Sudwerk Hefeweizen
Summit Hefeweizen

Tabernash Weiss
Thomas Kemper Hefe Weizen
Thomas Kemper Weizenberry
Tommy Knocker Jck Whackr Wht Ale
Trout Slayer Ale
Tw Fishers Light Wheat
Ufo Hefeweizen
Uinta Hefeweizen
Upland Wheat Ale
Victory Sunrise Weissbier
Wasatch Hefeweizen
Wasatch Weizenbier
Widmer Hefeweizen
Wild West Hefenweizen
Ybor Calusa Wheat Tropical Ale
Yellow Rose Bubba Dog Wheat

Wit Beer
Allagash White
Avery White Rascal
Big Hole Mythical White Ale
Celis White
Great Lake Holy Moses White Ale
Lakefront White Beer
Mothership Wit
New Holland Zoomer Wit
Spanish Peaks Summer White Ale
Victory Whirlwind Witbier
Weyerbacher Blanche

Index

214

217

218

219

Pages with illustrations are in **boldface**.

221

222

223

225

226

228